The I AM

GOD

BY WOODROW KROLL

BACK TO THE BIBLE®

THE I AM GOD
published by Back to the Bible
©1998 by Woodrow Kroll
International Standard Book Number
0-8474-1471-X

Edited by Rachel Derowitsch
Cover design by Design Resource

For information:
BACK TO THE BIBLE
POST OFFICE BOX 82808
LINCOLN, NEBRASKA 68501

1 2 3 4 5 6 7 8—04 03 02 01 00 99 98

Printed in the USA

CONTENTS

FOREWORD

When Gustav Dore painted a picture of Christ, an admirer commented, "You must love him to paint him like that!" To which Dore replied, "I do love him . . . but if I loved him more, I could paint him better!"

In this book, Dr. Woodrow Kroll paints Christ as He is seldom painted: He is portrayed as the One who is more than qualified to match His power with our needs. Christ is honored as the "I AM," the One who becomes all that is necessary for us to walk with God. This book helps us to understand how our relationship with Him can be personal and intimate.

In our pluralistic age, it is fashionable to put Christ on the same shelf as other religious leaders. Increasingly, pressure is put upon the church to be more "inclusive" by narrowing the gap that exists between Christ and other options. We are told that the exclusivity of Christianity is bigotry, a kind of primitive narrow-mindedness that must be hidden, if not exterminated. This book unashamedly places Christ above other competing religions, showing Him to stand alone amid a blizzard of religious options.

Readers will be impressed with the claims of Christ, the promises that no other man has ever dared to make. In this book we see Christ's own words, in their context, applied to us. We are encouraged to learn that if Christ is all He claims to be, we can become all that God wants us to be.

Read this book and share it with your friends. You will be blessed and strengthened. It will help you love Him more so that you can "paint Him better."

—Erwin Lutzer

INTRODUCTION

Have you noticed how many people seem to be dissatisfied with their name? For whatever reason, they prefer another name to the one given to them by their parents.

We have devised many inventive ways to alter our names. For example, we can use our initials only instead of our name. That's what biblical scholar Frederick Fyvie Bruce did, whom we know as F. F. Bruce. Others use both the first name and the middle initial. We refer to the legendary film producer and director as Cecil B. De Mille, not Cecil Blount De Mille. Still others opt for a first initial and a middle name. Apparently American author F. Scott Fitzgerald didn't want us to know his first name was Francis. I can understand why John Ronald Reuel Tolkien preferred J. R. R. Tolkien.

Some people prefer a nickname to their given name. William Franklin Graham just sounds too formal for Billy Graham. Often people drop parts of their name for simplification, as did Oscar Fingal O'Flahertie Wills Wilde. But for others, you would never think of not using their full name. You've probably never heard of George Shaw, but I'll guess you've heard of George Bernard Shaw.

The ones that really puzzle me are those who go by a name that has nothing to do with their real name. Have you heard of Denton True Young? He's the guy the Cy Young Award is named after in baseball, but his name wasn't Cy.

Do you know God's name? Some people are surprised to learn that "God" is not God's name. The Hebrew *El* means "god" in the widest sense, both true and false. But that's more of an identifier than a name. The plural form *Elohim* is the most frequent designation for God in the Bible. It's used 2,500 times in the Old Testament. Although it is a plural, Elohim is considered a singular noun. But that, too, is not really His name. God's name is YHWH (or YHVH), which was considered too sacred to pronounce; so Adonai ("my Lord") was substituted in reading and its vowels were combined with the consonants YHWH to give the

English name Jehovah or Yahweh. Thus, in the Bible the personal name of God appears as LORD (all capital letters).

But the God of Abraham, Isaac and Jacob was not known by name to any of the patriarchs. He told Moses, "I am the LORD. I appeared to Abraham, to Isaac, and to Jacob, as God Almighty, but by My name LORD I was not known to them" (Ex. 6:2-3). God likes His name. The expression "I am the LORD" occurs 160 times in the Old Testament, 71 times in the Pentateuch alone.

Since the name LORD is derived from the verb "to be," God loved to call Himself, and be called, "I AM." When He appeared to Moses at the burning bush, God referred to Himself as, "I AM WHO I AM." (Ex. 3:14). God loves to be called by the name that best describes His essential nature—"I AM."

God loves His "I AM" name

So thrilled was God with the "I AM" name that He used it hundreds of times to demonstrate His relationship with those He loved. Sometimes He used it formally, as an absolute name (Gen. 15:7; Ex. 3:14; Isa. 42:8); other times He used it descriptively (Lev. 22:32; Num. 14:42; Isa. 43:25). Still other times He simply used the "I am" statement as a declarative (Gen. 15:1; Song. 2:1; Isa. 44:6). In all of these, however, we come away knowing more about the essence and person of God than we did before.

"I am the Almighty God" — Genesis 17:1

"I am the Lord who sanctifies you" — Leviticus 22:32

"I am the Rose of Sharon" — Song of Solomon 2:1

"I am the LORD your God, the Holy One of Israel"
— Isaiah 43:3

"I am the First and I am the Last" — Isaiah 44:6

"I am the God of Bethel" — Genesis 31:13

"I am the LORD, the God of all flesh" — Jeremiah 32:27

The modifiers may change to show the diversity of God's character and activity, but the constant is His "I am" statement. This book is about what that statement means to you and me.

What the "I Am" statements signify

When Jehovah refers to Himself as the "I AM" God, what does that mean? How should we interpret the LORD's fondness for referring to Himself as the "I AM"? What does He want to convey to us by making this His favorite expression for Himself?

Here's what God's "I AMs" are designed to express.

Self-existence. "I am" implies that God needs no one else to exist in order for Him to exist. If He had never created men and women, birds and animals, trees and flowers, stars and suns, He would still have existed. He is the "I AM" God.

Personality. Using the first person pronoun indicates that God is a person, not a force or an idea. God is personal, a being with the full range of personal attributes. He is the "I AM" God.

Life. God is; that means He is alive. He is a divine Life Form. We were created in His image and draw our spiritual life from Him. "Yet pealed the bells more loud and deep, 'God is not dead, nor doth He sleep,'" wrote Henry Wadsworth Longfellow. He is the "I AM" God.

Immutability. God is the same yesterday, today and forever. His existence and essence do not change. "For I am the LORD, I do not change" (Mal. 3:6). The "I AM" always will be. He is the "I AM" God.

Reality. "I am" means that God is real. He is; He is not a figment of the imagination. In fact, He is the ultimate reality. All other forms of reality find meaning only in Him. He is the "I AM" God.

Necessity. We must come to grips only with what is real, not what is imaginary. Since the "I AM" is reality, He is also a necessity. We can go through life ignoring everyone else, but we cannot ignore Him. He is the "I AM" God.

Alternative expressions of God's identity

We identify God by what He does and what He says. Each "I am" statement about God helps us to know more of His person and essence. But Jehovah also used alternative methods to identify His personal existence. One such method was the "I am He" expression. While this is not identical with the "I am" statements, it accomplishes the same thing.

Here are some examples of Jehovah's "I am He" expressions. All of them indicate that He is the "I AM" God.

When God told Moses that He would be a refuge for Israel, the "I AM" God said, "Now see that I, even I, am He, and there is no God besides Me" (Deut. 32:39).

Here's an "I am He" statement of comfort to all who are sliding down the far side of the hill. "Even to your old age, I am He, and even to gray hairs I will carry you" (Isa. 46:4).

And how about this? "I, even I, am He who comforts you. Who are you that you should be afraid of a man who will die?" (Isa. 51:12).

Without question, the Jews knew the expression "I am He" was equivalent to saying "I am the 'I AM' God." When Jehovah said, "I am He," He was describing something about Himself that always brought benefit to His people. Every "I am" statement of the Bible is designed to open the way for our benefit.

Jesus as the "I AM" God

Jesus used "I am" statements exactly the way Jehovah did. And, equally important, He used them to show His linkage, even His equality, with the "I AM" God of the Old Testament. The pages that follow are about the "I am" statements of the New Testament, specifically the "I am" statements of Jesus found in the Gospel of John.

Like God the Father's, Jesus' "I am" statements demonstrate His self-existence, personality, life, immutability, reality and necessity. Jesus is not just an historical figure; He is real today. His reality demands that you interact with Him. You cannot ignore Him. You must come to grips with Him and His "I am" claims.

And like God the Father, Jesus used the "I am" statements in a variety of ways. Sometimes He used them formally and absolutely; sometimes descriptively or declaratively. In order to gain the widest perspective of Jesus' ability to supply everything we need, we will explore more than the absolute "I am" statements of Jesus.

The absolute "I am" statements use the Greek words *ego eimi* with a subject and predicate nominative. That means when Jesus said, "I am the Way," He was equating "I" with "Way." There are seven such statements in the Gospel of John in which Jesus uses *ego eimi* absolutely. They are, in order of appearance, "I am the bread of life" (6:35; cf. 41, 48, 51); "I am the light of the world" (8:12, cf. 9:5); "I am the door (or gate of the sheep)" (10:7, 9); "I am the good shepherd" (10:11, 14); "I am the resurrection and the life" (11:25); "I am the way, the truth, and the life" (14:6); and "I am the true vine" (15:1, 5).

The other "I am" statements Jesus made identify additional ways in which He is fully sufficient to meet our deepest needs. While they are not written in the absolute, they are absolutely true.

Jesus as the "I am He" God

But there's more. As Jehovah used the "I am He" expression to say that He was the "I AM" God, Jesus did the same. Once Jesus confounded the Jewish religious leaders (that happened a lot) by saying, "If you do not believe that I am He, you will die in your sins" (John 8:24). Just four verses later He said, "When you lift up the Son of Man, then you will know that I am He, and that I do nothing of Myself; but as My Father taught Me, I speak these things" (v. 28).

Speaking to His disciples, when He predicted that one of them would betray Him, Jesus said, "Now I tell you before it comes, that when it does come to pass, you may believe that I am He" (John 13:19).

And here's the most astounding example of all. When Judas led a detachment from the chief priests and Pharisees to arrest Jesus, the Savior asked, "Whom are you seeking?" They said, "Jesus of Nazareth," to which He replied, "I am He." They were so bewildered that they drew back and fell to the ground. Strange behavior. Why were they dumfounded? Better still, why when Jesus repeated, "I am He," did they fall to the ground?

The Jews knew that Jehovah used the expression "I am He" to describe Himself as the "I AM" God. When Jesus used the same expression, it wasn't just to say, "I am Jesus of Nazareth." It was to say, "I am He, the 'I AM' God." That was enough to make the officers of the chief priests and Pharisees cringe and cower.

Jesus is all you need

Whatever Israel needed, Jehovah supplied. He is the "I AM" God. But Jesus, too, is the "I AM" God. Perhaps the "I am" statements explored in this book will enhance our understanding that Jesus is all we really need. We find our full and complete sufficiency in Jesus Christ.

J. B. Phillips, a 20th century London pastor and paraphraser of the Bible, described in his book *Ring of Truth* what happened to him when he discovered Jesus was all he needed. While translating the New Testament, Phillips discovered something remarkable about the "I AM" God.

Phillips wrote,

> What happened to me as I progressed, was that the figure of Jesus emerged more and more clearly, and in a way unexpectedly. Of course, I had a deep respect, indeed a great reverence for the conventional Jesus Christ whom the Church worshipped. But I was not at all prepared for the unconventional man revealed in these terse Gospels: this was no puppet-hero built out of the imaginations of adoring followers. This man Jesus, so briefly described, rang true, sometimes alarmingly true. I began to see why the religious Establishment of those days wanted to get rid of him at all costs. He was sudden death to pride, pomposity and pretense. [1]

I pray you will discover the same while reading about Jesus in this book.

To encounter the "I AM" God is to encounter life, reality, necessity and more. The "I am" statements of Jesus do not just describe variations of His unique ability or personality; they are statements of what He can do for you. They are snapshots of the sufficiency of God. They are eternal proofs that Jesus is all you need.

Discover Him as J. B. Phillips did. Find in Him all that rings true. Discover the "I AM" God, who is death to pride and pretense. Find out what the "I AM" God can do for you. Your sufficiency is in Christ. Read on to discover why Jesus is all you need.

"I am the "I AM" God; let Me be there for you!"

CHAPTER 1

THE "I AM" GOD

Jesus said to them, "Most assuredly, I say to you, before Abraham was, I AM."
JOHN 8:58

It was almost four decades ago, but seems like only yesterday. Her name was Abigail Cresswell, Miss Abigail Cresswell. Everyone at Lincoln High School had what can best be described as a love/hate relationship with Miss Cresswell. She was the senior English teacher, which accounts for the hate relationship. She was stern-looking (the female counterpart to Ichabod Crane), and she had a demanding, no-nonsense approach to English. She wore her hair in a tight bun. Her long skirts were accented by frilly blouses, buttoned to the chin. She was right out of the 19th century, the perfect stereotype of an old-maid school teacher.

But there was something extraordinary about Miss Abigail Cresswell. This is the love part of her students' relationship with her. She was fair, honest and appreciative of good work. Miss Cresswell's most cherished students were those in her college English class. Surely these students were destined for great things—legislators, CEOs, teachers. Miss Cresswell would see to it. She wouldn't let us get away with anything.

Grammar was her specialty. She could spot a split infinitive, the disagreement between subject and verb or a dangling participle a mile away. She was tough as nails, and we loved her for it. That's why every time I read what Jesus said to the Jewish leaders in John 8:58, I receive a phantom visit from Abigail Cresswell. Surely the consummate grammarian, Miss Abigail Cresswell, would cringe at the words, "Before Abraham was, I AM." But there was no denying it; that's what Jesus said.

The idea of using the simple past tense of a linking verb with the present tense is just preposterous, unless something deeper is going on here.

For Jesus to say "I AM" juxtaposed with "Abraham was" would have been unthinkable to Miss Cresswell. What makes it acceptable, however, is that something deeper is going on here.

Jehovah: The "I AM" God

It is significant that the Lord Jesus used the same expression of Himself as did Jehovah when He confronted Moses at the burning bush on Mount Horeb. It was here that Jehovah commissioned Moses for service. God told him, "I have surely seen the oppression of My people who are in Egypt, and have heard their cry because of their taskmasters, for I know their sorrows. . . . Come now, therefore, and I will send you to Pharaoh that you may bring My people, the children of Israel, out of Egypt" (Ex. 3:7, 10).

Israel was about to learn something truly astonishing: God had not abandoned them during their 430 years of Egyptian bondage. He was not cowering beneath the great and mighty Egyptian Empire. God was keenly aware of Israel's plight. He winced as every lash from the taskmaster's whip lacerated their backs. He felt the pain of each aching muscle as the Jewish slaves struggled to build Pharaoh's cities, Pithom and Raamses. No, Jehovah was not unaware of their misery.

Moreover, He heard Israel's cry of distress. Divine ears were attune to every "Why God?" and "How long?" Each whimper, each scream, each wail reached His ears. Most importantly, He knew their sorrows. The stress of life lived in oppression was not missed by God. His spirit vibrated with their spirits. He knew well how abominable their lives were, and what's more, He cared. Now it was time for Jehovah to act.

What was true for ancient Israel is also true for you and me. God is never unaware of our pain. He understands our loneliness and feels our desperation. Furthermore, He is not unsympathetic with our needs. We are His creation, His children, His loved ones. His heart resonates with our heart. And that's not all. God has a plan for our rescue from pain, loneliness and desperation. He formulated that plan long before He created the world. But His plan has a timetable, and it's His timetable. Moses was a part of God's plan to rescue Israel, but only in God's time. God always performs what He promises, always on His schedule. "He has made everything beautiful in its time" (Eccl. 3:11).

But since Moses was to be the great deliverer of Israel, he had to be convinced that it was indeed God who was calling him, commissioning him and enabling him. Moses had to be persuaded that God would accompany him when he confronted the great Pharaoh of Egypt. God was keenly aware of Moses' need, so when He appeared to Moses in the burning bush, Jehovah clearly identified Himself, saying, "I am the God of your father—the God of Abraham, the God of Isaac, and the God of Jacob" (Ex. 3:6).

Was that enough? No. Still unconvinced, Moses needed more. He's like a lot of us. We'll believe there are billions of stars in the galaxies we can't see, but when we see a sign that says, "Wet Paint," we need further proof. Often when God calls us to do something extraordinary, our first response is to say, "It can't be done!" or at least, "It can't be done by me." But it can be done by you, because whomever God calls for service He always enables as well. It was true for Moses; it's true for us.

Once we're over that, our next response usually is Moses' reply: "It can't be God who is telling me to do this." But it was God; it was unmistakably God. Moses' question still rings in our ears: "Indeed, when I come to the children of Israel and say to them, 'The God of your fathers has sent me to you,' and they say to me, 'What is His name?' what shall I say to them?'" (v.13).

Jehovah's answer was not only stunning, but set the stage for all future revelations of Himself. God said, "I AM WHO I AM" (v. 14). Who commissioned Moses to shepherd the Israelites out of Egyptian enslavement? Jehovah said to Moses, "Say to the children of Israel, I AM has sent me to you."

As if to reinforce the importance of this "I am" statement, in the next verse Jehovah affirmed, "This is My name forever, and this is My memorial to all generations" (v. 15). There will never be a generation, never a century, never a split second of time when God's name is not "I AM WHO I AM." That was as much the divine name when Jehovah revealed Himself to Moses as it was when Jesus revealed Himself to the Jews in the first century. And things have not changed. That is God's name in the 21st century and beyond. His eternality is imbedded in His name— "I AM WHO I AM."

What's in a name?

What did God actually say when He revealed Himself as the "I AM" God? The Hebrew word comes from the verb *hawah*, meaning "to be"; but since it has a consonantal prefix, "Y," it becomes *Yehawah* or *Yahweh* or, in English, Jehovah. The jury is still out on which is the preferred pronunciation and spelling. Most scholars today prefer Yahweh; most people understand Jehovah. The point is still the same. God's name, His personal name, means "to be" and may be rendered by any tense of that verb. "I shall be what I shall be, and what I have been." The ancient Jews understood it to mean, "I am He who was, I am He who is now, and I am He who is to come." When you refer to the timeless God, tense doesn't matter.

God's personal name—"The Eternal One"—was considered too holy to be spoken by human lips, so when the Jews read the Scriptures audibly they substituted either "Elohim" or "Adonai" in place of "Yahweh." They would never speak the sacred name. Even now many Jews write the word "God" as "G-d," reflecting a continuing awe for the holiness of His person.

This attitude is something we Christians could take to heart, even if we don't carry it that far. We use God's name so lightly today, almost as a vocalized pause or as a filler in a sentence. When we do this, it is in express disregard for the third of the Ten Commandments (Ex. 20:7), which forbids us to use the Lord's name vainly, without purpose.

Jehovah revealed Himself to Moses as the "I AM" God, the eternal one, the God who is above time. "I AM WHO I AM" covered it all. No god could precede Him; no god could follow Him; no god could compare with Him.

Jesus: The "I AM" God

It was this deep respect for the name of God which so upset the Jews of Jesus' day. He used the same "I AM" with regard to Himself. How dare He? They thought He was demon-possessed. He claimed to have been sent by God (John 8:42). He said God was His Father and that the Pharisees were not from God but rather from their own father, the devil (v. 44). That must have hurt. It was not the way to win friends and influence people, but it was the truth. When Jesus claimed to be honored by God, His Father (v. 54), these Jews were really set off on a tirade.

But the real clincher was when Jesus said, "Before Abraham was, I AM'" (v. 58). That was unforgivable. No one messed with Father Abraham. No one placed himself alongside Abraham or was allowed to be compared favorably with the great prophet. But it gets worse. When Jesus said, "Before Abraham was, I AM," He wasn't just comparing

Himself to Father Abraham; He was claiming preexistence to Abraham. Jesus said that before Abraham was just a twinkle in Terah's eye, the man from Nazareth was already alive.

Preposterous!

How could this be?

It couldn't be, unless Jesus was somehow God, and that was the problem. To claim that He preexisted Abraham was to claim eternal existence, and that claim could be made only by God. If Jesus preexisted Father Abraham, Jesus had to be God. That didn't set very well with the Pharisees of Jesus' day. It still doesn't with the Mormons, Jehovah's Witnesses and other cults who do not believe Jesus is the great I AM.

Nevertheless, Jesus appropriated to Himself the same expression as did Jehovah in the Old Testament. In essence, Jesus said, "You know the God you revere so much you won't even say His name? The God who is the I AM God? The God who is eternal, ever-existent? Well, I am that God. I am the one whom the Father sent to give to you the express picture of who God is. I am the I AM God."

All He claimed to be

Do you think the Jews understood what that meant? Many people don't. Those who say Jesus never claimed to be God miss this passage altogether. Those who say Jesus was a good man, a good teacher, a moral person, but not God, must have been absent when this chapter was read. But the Jews of Jesus' day knew exactly what Jesus was saying, and what He meant. To say, "I am the I AM God" was to claim equality with Jehovah, and the Jewish leaders interpreted it exactly that way. The proof is in their reaction. "Then they took up stones to throw at Him" (v. 59).

Why stone Jesus for what He said if He wasn't claiming equality with God the Father? They knew He was making Himself equal with God. He used the same name as God. To these Pharisees that was brazen blasphemy. The legal penalty for blasphemy was clear: "Whoever blasphemes the name of the LORD shall surely be put to death, and all the congregation shall certainly stone him" (Lev. 24:16). Jesus had to be stoned; He claimed equality with God when He said, "Before Abraham was, I AM." The people weren't merely suspicious of His intent; they were convinced of it. Stones had to fly!

Long before Bethlehem

But was Jesus' intent really to make Himself God? Or was it just to shake up these religious bigots? I don't think it was either of these. Jesus didn't make Himself to be God. He already was God. And He certainly had deeper and more ethical intentions than just to shake up the false religious leaders. This is all about time and eternity. Jesus' intent was to show those who had gathered around Him that, while they had no problem adoring Father Abraham (who was a captive of time), they were having a great problem adoring Jesus (who predated time and invaded it, but was not held captive to it).

Why was it so hard to believe that Jesus was eternal? Was it because they knew Him as the carpenter's son of Nazareth? Was it because the stories of His birth in a Bethlehem stable just didn't fit One who preexisted time? Was it because they were so blinded by hatred and unbelief that they just wouldn't hear of Jesus being the I AM God? Was their unbelief too entrenched even to consider the possibility that Jesus was the eternal, preexistent God? Was it all of these or a combination of these?

For that matter, why can't many people today believe that Jesus is the I AM God? Is it because of their unbiblical views of His origin? Is it because they believe He was an angel and therefore a prisoner of time? Is it because they want to protect the timelessness of God? Can they not merge in their minds the Bethlehem birth and the eternality of Jesus? Is their scientific bent so strong they cannot admit any possibility they can't scientifically justify? Why do men and women have such difficulty in believing that Jesus is the "I AM" God?

Your "I AM" God

Do you have trouble seeing Jesus as the "I AM" God? Even though that's what He claimed, do you say in your heart, "It can't be. Jesus cannot preexist time. He cannot be the same as the I AM WHO I AM, who appeared to Moses. He cannot have been before Abraham."

But why not? What does the Bible say? John's Gospel begins with this astounding admission: "In the beginning was the Word, and the Word was with God, and the Word was God. He was in the beginning with God. . . . And the Word became flesh and dwelt among us, and we beheld His glory, the glory as of the only begotten of the Father, full of grace and truth" (John 1:1-2, 14).

There can be no question but that the "Word" of John 1 is the Lord Jesus Christ. Any honest, unbiased reader of the Bible has to admit this, especially when it says the Word was made flesh and dwelt among us. Isn't that what the Christmas event was all about?

> Veiled in flesh the Godhead see; Hail th' incarnate Deity,
> Pleased as man with men to dwell, Jesus, our Emmanuel!
> Hark, the herald angels sing, "Glory to the newborn King."
>
> — Charles Wesley

But Jesus' claim to be the "I AM" God is not recorded in the Gospel of John only. The Revelation, the foremost book of apocalyptic literature, also portrays Jesus as the "I AM" God. Revelation is the crowning unveiling of Jesus Christ, revealing who He is. John was told to "write the things which you have seen, and the things which are, and the things which will take place after this" (Rev. 1:19). The charge to record past, present and future when unveiling the Person of Jesus Christ relates directly to the "I AM WHO I AM" God. Remember, the Jews themselves interpreted this as meaning, "I am He who was, I am He who is now, and I am He who is to come."

The Book of Revelation has a wonderful way of revealing Jesus as the "I AM" God. Instead of "Before Abraham was, I AM," Jesus becomes even more graphic in the final book of the Bible: "I am the Alpha and the Omega."

The Alpha and Omega

What could Jesus have meant when He said, "I am the Alpha and the Omega, the First and the Last" (Rev. 1:11)? The possibilities are not limitless, but the meaning is clear. Jesus is the first letter of the Greek alphabet—*alpha*—and He is the last letter of the Greek alphabet—*omega*. He is there at the beginning and He will be there at the end.

Can this be said of other religious leaders? Can it be said of Buddha? What about Mohammed? Or how about David Koresh (Branch Davidians) or Marshall Applewhite (Heaven's Gate)? Not at all. The "I AM" God is really God, not just a prophet from God, and certainly not a false prophet from God.

The four living creatures of Revelation did not cease day and night to proclaim, "Holy, holy, holy, Lord God Almighty, Who was and is and is to come!" (Rev. 4:8). It is evident from the context that they are worshiping Jesus as God. He is worshiped as Creator (Rev. 4:11; cf. Gen. 1:1; John 1:1-3, 14; Col. 1:15-17; Heb. 1:1-3). He is the Lion of the tribe of Judah, the Root of David (Rev. 5:5). He is the One who redeemed us to God by His blood "out of every tribe and tongue and people and nation" and has made us "kings and priests to our God" (vv. 9-10). Can this possibly refer to anyone but Jesus Christ? Not a chance.

How could these living creatures be so confused as to call Jesus of Nazareth the Lord God Almighty? How could they say He is the One "who was and is and is to come"? How would that be possible, or do they understand something the cultists do not understand? Do they have knowledge my Jewish friends have chosen to reject?

When the 24 elders gather around God's throne and worship God, they say, "We give You thanks, O Lord God Almighty, the One who is and who was and who is to come" (Rev. 11:17). Same words, but this time they seem to be directing them to God the Father. Don't let that confuse you. God is everlasting, eternally existent in three Persons—Father, Son and Spirit. What is said of one Person of the Godhead can be said of the others as well. At one time God the Father is called the "I AM" God; at another time it's God the Son.

How can this be if Jesus is not God? It can't be. The interchangeability of names like "Lord God Almighty" and attributes like immutability prove that while we are not always talking about the same Person, we are talking about the same God—the Almighty, immutable "I AM" God. The Bible says that Jesus is just as much the "I AM" God as Jehovah is.

Liar, lunatic or eternal God

Before Abraham was, the "I AM" God was, and for Jesus to say such a thing can mean only one of two things: either He is a liar and a lunatic, or He is, in fact, the eternal God. The choice is yours; the truth is His.

In their book *No Greater Savior*, Richard Lee and Ed Hindson observe, "If the story of Jesus is a lie, it is the greatest hoax ever perpetrated on the human race. But if it is the truth, then we must take Him seriously. To fail to do so could cost us everything. Each of us must stop at some point and consider the question: Who is Jesus Christ? Was He a deceiver? Was He deceived? Or was He divine?" [1]

In his phenomenal work *Mere Christianity,* C. S. Lewis wrote:

> A man who was merely a man and said the sort of things Jesus said would not be a great moral teacher. He would either be a lunatic, on a level with the man who says he is a poached egg, or else he would be the Devil of Hell. You must make your choice. Either this man was, and is, the Son of God, or else a madman or something worse. You can shut Him up for a fool; you can spit at Him and kill Him as a demon; or, you can fall at his feet and call Him Lord and God. But let us not come up with any patronizing nonsense about His being a great human teacher. He has not left that open to us. He did not intend to.[2]

Will you recognize Jesus for who He claims to be—the "I AM" God? Or will you be duped by Satan's lie about Jesus—that He is a man, an angel, a good teacher, but certainly not God? Satan is the master truth twister. His lies about the "I AM" God pervade our time and space, but God's truth pervades eternity and heaven. Make your choice carefully. How you view Jesus Christ impacts your eternal destiny.

What does the "I AM" God mean to you?

So if Jesus is the eternal, preexistent, before Abraham was "I AM" God, what does this mean to you? How does His eternality impact your life? How does it change the way you view Him? How does it change the way you live?

Whenever those of us who are trapped in time encounter One who is eternal, our lives should be profoundly changed by Him. Jesus is such a One. He is the "I AM" God. How does that impact your life?

The "I AM" God distinguishes Himself from all others

Most people do not see any differences between religions. "They're all working for the same thing, peace and harmony and union with God." But this couldn't be farther from the truth. All religions are not created equal, because all founders of religion were not created equal.

Mohammed (c. 570-632), the Arab founder of Islam, was a wealthy merchant. At age 40 he had a vision in a cave near Mecca. Subsequent visions and teachings are recorded in the Koran, the holy scripture of Islam. His new religion alienated the leaders of Mecca. In 622, to escape an assassination attempt, he fled to what would become known as Medina. Muslims date their calendar from this flight, called the Hegira. Mohammed ruled Medina ruthlessly as a theocratic state. In 630 he conquered Mecca and established Islam as the religion of Arabia.

No one had heard of Mohammed before his vision. His birth was not predicted, anticipated or prophesied. He just happened on the scene and founded a religion, one which not only has designs on world conquest but also has some pretty fanatical methods to make sure that its followers do.

There is no correlation between Jesus and Mohammed when it comes to eternality. Jesus claimed to be God; Mohammed did not. Muslims see Mohammed as the last and most perfect messenger of God, following Adam, Abraham, Moses and Jesus. Mohammed got in line; Jesus existed before the line was formed. Jesus' birth was prophesied (Isa. 7:14; 9:6; Mic. 5:2); it was anticipated by every young Jewish virgin who prayed that she would be chosen to bear the Messiah. While the Muslim world dates history from Mohammed's Hegira, Christians and much of the non-Christian world date history from the night when it can be said, "the hopes and fears of all the years are met in thee tonight"—the birth of Jesus.

Buddha was another founder of a great religion. Actually, this is just a title given to Siddhartha Gautama (c. 563-483 B.C.). Buddha, in Sanskrit, means "the enlightened one." Siddhartha was born into a noble family of the Himalayan foothills, but at the age of 29 he left his family to become a wandering ascetic. Alone and untaught, Buddha meditated and fasted for six years. It was at this point that he claimed divine enlightenment while sitting under the holy tree Bodh Gaya. That was the beginning of Buddhism. Siddhartha spent the rest of his days traveling northern India preaching his message of enlightenment.

Buddha and Mohammed aren't that different, really. Both were seekers after something new, some enlightenment not shared by others. Both claim to have had visions that initiated their religion (a common theme that runs throughout false religions and cults). But they are extremely different from Jesus Christ.

Jesus did not found a religion; He established a relationship for us with the eternal God. A religion grew up around Him and His teachings; but unlike the others, Jesus did not have a vision of beginning a new religion. Before there was a Jew, before there was a Muslim, before new religion. Before there was a Jew, before there was a Muslim, before there was a Christian, before there was a Buddhist, or a Hindu, or a Taoist, or a spiritist, or a nature worshiper, before anyone there was God—the Eternal One. The "I AM" God came to this earth to atone for the sins of men and women and to open the door to heaven for us. The Christian religion grew as a result of His coming, but it wasn't the reason for His coming.

Jesus distinguishes Himself from other religious leaders by preexisting them all and by distancing Himself from them in His character, His essence and His being. They are men and women; He is the thoroughly sufficient, eternal "I AM" God.

The "I AM" God is not taken by surprise

Lots of things surprise us. We are surprised at birthday parties, surprised by the things our children say (especially when they are younger), surprised when we win the employee of the month award. But surprise, by definition, means to be taken unawares. Surprises are enjoyable when what takes us unawares brings good to us, but what if we are surprised by something bad? What about the surprise that comes when you learn you have cancer or that your wife is leaving you or that you made a huge mistake on your income tax return and the IRS is coming to see you? These are not the kinds of surprises anyone enjoys getting. Yet they happen.

I don't suppose anyone would be more surprised at the pervasive spread of Islam during the last century than Mohammed. What chance did a religion which sprang from the deserts of Arabia have taking root in Hyde Park in London or Central Park in New York? Surprise! What were the prospects of a religion of northern India, which began more than 2,500 years ago, seeing a resurgence in the closing years of the 20th century? Little or none, but who could have guessed the Beatles would embrace the tenets of Eastern religion and have so many followers? Surprise!

While these things may surprise us, Jesus was not unaware of them. Nothing takes Him by surprise. While others are the prisoners of time, born in it and bound by it, Jesus is the invader of time. While He transcends time, one night in a little place called Bethlehem He invaded time and became a man. The theological word is *incarnation*; it simply means that Jesus took on flesh and was born of the seed of David. It was all done according to a divine timetable. "But when the fullness of the time had come, God sent forth His Son, born of a woman, born under the law, to redeem those who were under the law" (Gal. 4:4-5).

Jesus is the timeless "I AM" God who existed before time began and will exist long after time is swallowed up by eternity. Since Jesus supersedes time, He has perfect knowledge of all things in time and is never surprised. Therefore, He doesn't have to adapt His eternal plans to the surprises of this life. There are no surprises with Him. He is the "I AM" God. You never need worry whether or not He is sufficient to handle the surprises in your life. They are only surprises to you.

The "I AM" God is in complete control

My home in Lincoln, Nebraska, is just 3.3 miles from the international headquarters of Back to the Bible. I can drive to work in about five minutes, unless I am stopped by a train. There is a railroad crossing about a mile from our office; it's a pretty busy set of tracks. Here in the Midwest coal is hauled east, goods are hauled west, and grain is hauled in all directions. Many of these products are transported by rail. There is a 120-car limit to the number of cars a train can pull, but when I get stopped by a train, there's no reason to count the cars. It will be 120 almost every time.

I often sit there at the crossbars thinking about what it would be like living in one of those boxcars or grain cars. Especially one of the middle ones. You don't have any idea where you're going; you barely know where you've been. You are just a car, attached to other cars, going wherever the tracks run and the engine takes you. If you could only free yourself from the surrounding cars, fly up high and get a bird's-eye view, you could see the end from the beginning. Then you would understand more.

Life is like that. We can only see what's happening within the confines of our little boxcar. We don't have the perspective of eternity to see where the train is going or where time is taking us. It's hard to see how anything good can come from a spouse addicted to alcohol or other drugs. It's hard to understand why Christian ministries always seem to be strapped for cash. It's hard to appreciate why certain people come into our lives, people who don't seem to contribute anything positive to us. If only we had a way to see the end from the beginning, then we could make sense of a lot of things. We would understand why that person was brought across our path. We would know what would become of our drug-addict spouse, our rebellious teenager or our aging parents.

But we don't have such a perspective. That's because we are riding in the center boxcar and cannot see the end from the beginning. We are stuck in the car of the present, attached to other cars called our past and our future, not knowing for sure where things are headed. That's why having a relationship with the "I AM" God is so important to us. Jesus said, "Before Abraham was, I AM," meaning He was on the tracks before our train even got moving. The Alpha was there when our train pulled out, and the Omega will be at the station when we get to our destination.

Jesus knows the end from the beginning. That's why He can comfort us when we mourn; He can help us choose the right future and correctly reflect on our past. We don't have to worry about the things that happen to us in the present, because the "I AM" God has our past, present and future covered.

Trust the "I AM" God to know what's best for your future. Trust Him to do what's best for you in the present. Trust Him to make the best of your past. Only Jesus Christ is totally sufficient to meet your needs, past, present or future. He is sufficient because the "I AM" God is not bound by time; He is Lord of eternity.

What does it mean to you that Jesus is eternally existent? It means you have not placed your faith in a man, but in the sufficiency of the "I AM" God. It means your life is in the hands of One who invades time but also supersedes it. It means you have placed yourself, your fortunes and your future in hands now scared with nails, but eternally outstretched to care for you. It means Jesus is always there for you, day and night, past or present, good times or bad. Who but Jesus is sufficient to care for you with no boundaries of time? Who, indeed, but the "I AM" God.

"I am the Light of the World; let Me illumine you!"

CHAPTER 2

I Am

THE LIGHT
OF THE WORLD

Then Jesus spoke to them again, saying, "I am the light of the world. He who follows Me shall not walk in darkness, but have the light of life."

JOHN 8:12

Look around you. Put your theological glasses on, the ones you received as a child in Sunday school. What do you see? Much of the world today is enslaved by false religions. Everywhere people are pursuing belief systems that promise eternal bliss. But that bliss has a catch. If you're to enjoy it, you must adhere solely and completely to the ideology of this teacher or that prophet. If you don't, you can't be at one with yourself or attune to the cosmos.

A great deal of the world lives in the darkness of ignorance—worshiping their ancestors, unseen spirits, the earth, the sun, the moon, trees, animals, etc. Even where the light of the Gospel has glistened in the darkness, some have perverted it. They have redefined the Gospel with their own meaning and have added their own books or teachings to "explain" the Bible. Warren Wiersbe said, "Where there is light there will always be bugs." That's the way it is in religion today.

When Anthony Hoekema authored his book on the cults in 1963, he entitled it *The Four Major Cults.*[1] There were more, of course, but they were not numerous enough or significant enough to warrant inclusion in the book. But when J. Gordon Melton edited the current *Encyclopedic Handbook of Cults in America,*[2] he included entries on no less than 700 cults. And of the 1,600 denominations currently listed in the *Encyclopedia of American Religions,*[3] 44 percent of them are non-Christian.

31

The darkness is still thick, even after centuries of light.

It wasn't any different in Jesus' day. Jesus spoke the words recorded in John 8:12 at one of the darkest times of His ministry. He was in the court of the Temple at Jerusalem. It was the Feast of Tabernacles and the court was jammed with hundreds of people. The ubiquitous Pharisees had just caught a woman in the act of adultery. These hypercritical hypocrites wanted to trap Jesus into saying something that contradicted the Law. This may be their chance. They brought the adulterous woman and threw her at Jesus' feet.

More Light than the Law

Moses' law taught that anyone taken in adultery should be stoned to death. "The man who commits adultery with another man's wife, he who commits adultery with his neighbor's wife, the adulterer and the adulteress, shall surely be put to death" (Lev. 20:10). It's odd that they brought only the woman to Jesus and not the man. He deserved to be stoned as well. Where was he?

The Pharisees knew the Levitical law. What's more, they knew Jesus did as well. How would He handle this situation? The Pharisees thought if they could get Jesus to disobey Moses' law, they could disprove His claims of messiahship before the eyes of the people who had flocked around Him. On the other hand, if He imposed the penalty of the law and had her stoned, they could say He was unmerciful, unmoved by the woman's cries for help. It was an ethical Catch 22. The situation was hopeless for Jesus. Either way the Pharisees would win, or so they thought.

Jesus' response was profound in its simplicity: "He who is without sin among you, let him throw a stone at her first" (John 8:7). At this the Pharisees stared at each other and began to squirm. This was supposed to be their victory, not Jesus'. Soon they slipped away in every direction, scurrying back into their spiritual darkness.

The Savior told the woman to go her way and sin no more, and then said to those still hanging around, "I am the light of the world" (v. 12). Insincerely they had asked Jesus for insight in handling a tough situation, but instead the Pharisees heard the last thing they wanted to hear—the light of Jesus would enlighten the whole world, not just this little ethical dilemma.

William Barclay commented,

> When Jesus made his claim to be the Light of the World the scribes and Pharisees reacted with hostility. That claim would sound even more astonishing to them than to us. To them it would sound like a claim—as indeed it was—to be the Messiah, and, even more, to do the work that only God could do. The word *light* was specially associated in Jewish thought and language with God. "The Lord is my light" (Psalm 27:1). "The Lord will be your everlasting light" (Isaiah 60:19). "By his light I walked through darkness" (Job 29:3). "When I sit in darkness the Lord will be a light to me" (Micah 7:8). The Rabbis declared that the name of the Messiah was Light. When Jesus claimed to be the Light of the World, he was making a claim to be both Messiah and God.[4]

This was much bigger than one adulterous woman. In fact, it was much bigger than the Pharisees. Jesus is the Light of the World. Only Jesus is sufficient to light the dark crevices of your life, reveal all that hinders your relationship with God, and make things right. What the Law couldn't do, Jesus can. We don't need more Law; we need more Light. We need Jesus, the Light of the World.

More Light than the eye

The second time Jesus claimed to be the Light of the World He was ministering to a man who was physically challenged, not spiritually challenged (John 9). Blind from birth, the wretched man sat at the entrance to the temple. The Twelve accompanying Jesus saw the man and immediately asked if his blindness was his fault or that of his parents. If you saw a blind man sitting next to you in church, would you automatically assume his blindness was due to his sin? Would you think his parents were to blame? Such a question would not occur to you or me today, but it was prevalent in Jewish thinking of the day. The people of God assumed that all calamities, all infirmities, were the result of sin. Since this man was blind, they reasoned, somebody had to have sinned.

This same thinking was reflected in the attitude of Job's three friends. They just couldn't get it through their thick heads that Job was innocent before God. How could he be? Look at all the horrible things that happened to him. There had to be hidden sin somewhere. But there wasn't. Job was blameless and upright (Job 1:1).

It is true that sometimes there is a connection between sickness, disease or calamity and sin. In her book *Fetal Alcohol Syndrome*, Amy Nevitt reports that more than 8,000 babies a year are born in the United States with this illness.[5] FAS is caused by women drinking alcohol during their pregnancy. These are cases where clearly the parent is to blame for the child's infirmity. Yet often we are also our own worst enemies. Death by drug overdose and HIV infection because of promiscuity, obesity because of overeating and hypertension from self-inflicted stress are all examples of how we can be to blame for our own illnesses or infirmities. But we should never assume that a person born blind or deaf has displeased God in some way. God is the creator both of mouths that are eloquent and mouths that are mute, and He created both for His glory (Ex. 4:11).

In answering His disciples' question about the unfortunate blind man, Jesus again declared, "I am the light of the world" (John 9:5). The Light of the World was about to give the light of eyesight to a man who had never seen a rose of Sharon, or the face of a child, or even the faces of his parents. This means that Jesus is the Light of the World to all the world—to those who are ethically and morally sightless and to those who are unable to see physically. He is sufficient to provide light to all who need to believe the gospel.

What the Light of the World means

Why did Jesus portray Himself as the Light of the World? How are we to understand this great "I am" statement? To answer these questions we need only consider the function of light. What does light do? What happens when light is directed onto a darkened object? Answer these questions and you have answered why Jesus said, "I am the light of the world."

Light is essential to life

Have you ever taken a healthy plant out of your window and put it in the back of a closet? Don't try it with one that you love. The plant will shrivel up and die. Light is essential to life.

If there were no sun to produce light, there would be no life on the earth. The ground would be unable to yield its increase. There would be no mangos on the tree, bananas on the stock or grapes on the vine. There would be no ripe tomatoes to toss into your salad. There would be no luscious lettuce or green peppers. In fact, without the light of the sun, there would be no salad. Vegetable life is almost totally dependent on light. That's why the best growing areas of the world are the sub-tropic and tropic areas—the areas that get the greatest amount of sunlight.

Without the process of photosynthesis, we would be deprived of much that we call essential in this life. The dictionary defines photosynthesis (just in case it's been a long time since Biology 101 for you) as "the synthesis of chemical compounds with the aid of radiant energy and especially light." It may be an oversimplification, but not much, to say, "No light, no life." Without light from the sun, soon we would all starve to death, and plant life as we know it would cease to exist on earth.

There is a popular commercial on television for Windex, a commercial window cleaning spray. The ad shows a mother and a daughter standing at double French doors leading to the bright outdoors. The mother has a spray bottle of Windex and the daughter has the dreaded "other" brand. Both spray, both rub the glass, both wipe it clean. But as proof that the mother's spray worked better, after the mother and daughter have gone, the camera pulls back to reveal a hanging plant, anchored to the ceiling about the middle of the double doors. Soon the plant rifles out a stalk that attaches itself to the wall near the Windex-clean door and the plant pulls itself precariously toward that side of the double door. The point? When you clean with Windex, the window is so much cleaner that even plants will make an effort to get to that window to receive more light.

Light is the key. No light, no life. As light is essential to physical life, Christ is no less essential to spiritual life. Only Jesus has the power to forgive our sins. Only He died to atone for them. Only He can shine the light of life into our hearts. Only He is sufficient to bring the light of God to the darkness of our lives. "For with You is the fountain of life; in Your light we see light" (Ps. 36:9). When Jesus brings light, He brings life.

Light illuminates the earth

Have you ever wondered about the other planets? Why does Mars exist? If the space probes tell us anything, they tell us there are no little green men on Mars. In fact there are no black men, brown men, white men or any men on Mars. As far as we can tell, Mars is uninhabited. So why does it exist? What about Jupiter and Saturn and the others? Better

35

still, have you ever wondered why the sun exists? Nobody can live there. There's no ice cream there. You can't even get a tan there. So why does the sun exist?

Sounds a bit ludicrous, doesn't it, asking why the sun exists? Anybody in their right mind will answer, "The sun is there to give light and heat to our universe," and that's true. God's purpose for the sun is to give light to the earth and warmth to make life possible here. Move to Venus, the second planet from our sun, and you wouldn't enjoy your stay. It's only 67.2 million miles from the sun; too close, too hot. You'd fry. Move to Mars, the fourth planet from our sun, and you wouldn't enjoy your stay either. It's 141.5 million miles from the sun; too far, too cold. You'd freeze. It's only this third rock from the sun that's suitable for human life forms as we know them.

God designed the sun to give light and heat for those souls living on this planet. Without the sun, there'd be no light. Without the sun, we'd grope around in darkness. We'd need artificial light and heat for everything.

On Saturday night, October 25, 1997, it began to snow here in Lincoln, Nebraska. By morning's light 13.5 inches of snow could be measured at the Lincoln airport; I had more than 20 inches in my backyard. The heavy, wet snow snapped limbs from trees as if they were pretzels. Small trees where pasted to the ground by the wet snow. It was the worst snow devastation I have ever seen. It looked like a tornado had blown through our city. Initial estimates by the mayor of Lincoln were that 25,000 trees in city parks and city streets alone were a total loss (not to count the thousands of trees in people's yards). Power was out all over the area. Some people were left in the dark for a week.

It's when you're sitting in the dark, shivering because there is no heat in your house, that you come to appreciate what is blatantly evident—without the sun there is no natural light or heat on the earth. The sun illumines the earth. That's why God created the sun. Genesis 1:14-16 says, "Then God said, 'Let there be lights in the firmament of the heavens . . . to give light on the earth . . . . Then God made two great lights: the greater light to rule the day, and the lesser light to rule the night."

Jesus is like that. He is the Light of the World in the spiritual sense. He covers the world. He brings light and heat to improve the quality of our life. Without this spiritual light, the earth would be a dark, cold hell.

It is only because of the light of the Gospel that the world can rise out of the darkness and coldness of sin and enjoy fellowship in the warmth of God's light. Who could do these things except the "I AM" God? Only Jesus is sufficient to light up your life and give you the warmth that you soul craves.

Zacharias, the father of John the Baptist, recognized this. He prophesied, "Blessed is the Lord God of Israel, for He has visited and redeemed His people, and has raised up a horn of salvation for us in the house of His servant David . . . to give knowledge of salvation to His people by the remission of their sins, through the tender mercy of our God, with which the Dayspring from on high has visited us; to give light to those who sit in darkness and the shadow of death, to guide our feet into the way of peace" (Luke 1:68-69, 77-79).

The horn from David's household is Jesus Christ. He brings light to the world. The Dayspring from on high who has visited us is the babe in the manger, the Savior on the cross, the Lord ascended on high. Jesus, the Sun of Righteousness (Mal. 4:2), illumines the world spiritually just as the sun in our solar system illumines the world physically.

> The whole world was lost in the darkness of sin;
> The Light of the world is Jesus;
> Like sunshine at noonday His glory shone in,
> The Light of the world is Jesus.
> Come to the Light, 'tis shining for thee;
> Sweetly the Light has dawned upon me;
> Once I was blind, but now I can see;
> The Light of the world is Jesus.
>
> — Philip P. Bliss

If your world is a bit dark these days, you need some light. Only Jesus Christ is sufficient to shine the kind of light into your life that can dispel that darkness. Only Jesus is sufficient to light up your life. Let Him illumine your world today. Let Him light up your life by trusting what He did for you at Calvary to pay the penalty for your sins. Only Jesus is sufficient to pay that penalty. Only Jesus can bring you from darkness into the glorious light of the Gospel.

Paul called the Gospel "the power of God, who has saved us and called us with a holy calling, not according to our works, but according to His own purpose and grace which was given to us in Christ Jesus before time began, but has now been revealed by the appearing of our Savior Jesus Christ, who has abolished death and brought life and immortality to light through the gospel" (2 Tim. 1:8-10). Christ Jesus brought light to our world when He appeared as our Savior. I know He brought light to the darkness of my life. If He is your Savior, He has brought light to your life as well.

Light divides the darkness

There is another aspect to what the sun does that depicts what Jesus does as well. The sun divides the darkness from the light. Before God created the light, there was nothing but darkness. The sun was designed to give light and heat and to divide the periods of the day into light and darkness, as well as the seasons of the year into cooler and warmer. The sun divides the darkness every day. Unless you live in Alaska, at the tip of Chile or some other extremely northerly or southerly place, the sun divides each day into day and night (even in the extreme places to a lesser extent).

But the function of the sun is not only to provide the right amount of light and heat, equally divided to the Northern and Southern hemispheres; it is also designed by the Creator to demonstrate physically what the Lord Jesus does spiritually. Jesus Christ divides the light from the darkness in this world. He is doing that at this very moment. When the Son of Righteousness shines on us and we trust Him as Savior, the darkness of sin is divided from the light of God and is clearly distinguishable. There's no question about where Jesus is. Where Jesus is, there is light; where He is not, there is darkness. Jesus is the great divider of men (Matt. 10:34-42). He is the stumbling stone (1 Pet. 2:8). He is the rock of offense (Rom. 9:33). He shows us what the truth is and in the process shines His eternal light on the darkness that hides the truth. We know what the darkness is when we see the light.

This division that Jesus brings between light and darkness has an impact on how we Christians live our lives. Paul counsels the Corinthian believers with a barrage of biting questions: "For what fellowship has righteousness with lawlessness? And what communion has light with darkness? And what accord has Christ with Belial? Or what part has a believer with an unbeliever?" (2 Cor. 6:14-15).

Did you notice the context of these verses? Paul said them in the context of telling the Corinthian Christians not to yoke themselves with unbelievers. Why? Because believers live in the light, but unbelievers live in the darkness of sin. The light makes the difference.

People who do not appreciate who Christ is or what He has done for them still live in darkness. When we clearly see what it's like to live in the light, why would we ever want to link ourselves with a chain to the darkness? Jesus said, "I am the light of the world. He who follows Me shall not walk in darkness, but have the light of life" (John 8:12).

In light of this (no pun intended), where do your allegiances lie? Are you still tethered to the things that are characterized by darkness, or are you walking in the light? Are there times of the day or night when your mind slips back into the darkness of sin, or are you allowing the Spirit of God to remove that darkness? How much of your day is spent walking in darkness? You can't walk with the Lord and walk in darkness at the same time. Wherever Jesus walks, the Light shines.

Light dispels the darkness

There is one final lesson we can learn from the sun that relates directly to what Jesus does for us as the Light of the World. The light from the sun dispels the darkness. When we are in darkness, we welcome the sunrise because it dispels the night and enables us to make our days more productive.

Picture the hills to the east of your home, or the mountains or the sea. Whatever is there, picture it. Then picture the whole sky black with inky darkness. It's been that way for hours when suddenly a lighter shade of darkness appears, then a bit lighter, and a bit lighter until the sky is filled with brilliant reds and yellows and oranges. It's sunrise; the sun has dispelled the darkness. A new day has dawned.

That's exactly what it is like when the Light of the World comes into our life. We were blindly groping around in the darkness of sin when Jesus came, convicted us of that sin and offered the free gift of salvation. When we repented of our sins and received His free gift of salvation, the darkness was dispelled by the light. If Jesus were not sufficient to dispel the darkness in our lives, we would live eternally in inky blackness. If we look elsewhere for light, we find all other sources insufficient to bring eternal change to our dark world. Jesus alone is sufficient to be the Light of the World.

What happens when light dispels the darkness? Many things. With darkness comes ignorance. Jesus the Light gives us insight. Psalm 18:28

says, "For You will light my lamp; the LORD my God will enlighten my darkness." When we trust Jesus as Savior, suddenly the ignorance of sin is gone and the knowledge of salvation floods our minds. For this light, God gives us Jesus, His Living Word. But we need ongoing light, a continual dispelling of ignorance, and for that God gives us His written Word. "The entrance of Your words gives light" (Ps. 119:130). The light of the Living Word brings to our minds the facts of the Gospel, and with the aid of the Holy Spirit we believe them. We trust the sufficiency of Christ's atonement for our sins. Jesus becomes our Savior. Then the light of the written Word continues to illumine our minds and dispel our ignorance about God and His plan for our lives. Thank God for the Bible. It lights our path and shines as a lamp to our feet.

But with darkness also comes fear. Are you afraid of the dark? Many people are, whether they admit it or not. I remember the first time I stayed at one of the speaker's cabins at the Billy Graham Training Center at the Cove in Asheville, North Carolina. I had finished my teaching for the day, and I was sitting at my computer writing late into the night when my eyes got heavy. It was time to go to bed. But my cabin was one mile up a gravel mountain road. My wife, Linda, wasn't with me on this occasion; I was all alone. There wasn't a light to be seen anywhere in the thick North Carolina pines. I switched off the light, fell into bed and lay there a few minutes in the ghastly darkness. It was eerie. I couldn't see a thing. It was the blackest black, the darkest dark, I had ever experienced. So I did what any red-blooded American male would do. I jumped out of bed, stumbled into the next room and turned on a tiny light. I couldn't take it; it was just too dark. Fear comes with darkness.

But when Jesus brings His light into our lives, He dispels our fears. Psalm 27:1 reminds us, "The LORD is my light and my salvation; whom shall I fear? The LORD is the strength of my life; of whom shall I be afraid?" The presence of light dispels the darkness, and when the darkness is gone, fear is gone. Who is sufficient to dispel the fear from our lives? Only the Light of the World. When we have Jesus as our light, we have no cause to fear.

Does that mean we will never be afraid again? Of course not. Sometimes we'll encounter circumstances that cause us to be afraid, but when we remember who is in the darkness with us we can draw on the strength of His light. That's why the psalmist could say confidently, "Yea, though I walk through the valley of the shadow of death, I will fear no evil; for You are with me" (Ps. 23:4). It's the presence of the Savior that takes away our fears because He takes away our darkness.

With darkness often comes sin, and that's reason enough to invite the Light of the World to illuminate our lives. You can't bring conviction of my sin to me, and I'm not sufficient to bring conviction to you. We share the stain of sin and have little hope of convicting each other. But Jesus is the perfect Lamb of God who takes away the sin of the world (John 1:29). He is sufficient. When He shines the light of His countenance on our lives, sin becomes an embarrassment.

Jesus said, "And this is the condemnation, that the light has come into the world, and men loved darkness rather than light, because their deeds were evil. For everyone practicing evil hates the light and does not come to the light, lest his deeds should be exposed. But he who does the truth comes to the light, that his deeds may be clearly seen, that they have been done in God" (John 3:19-21).

It's a sobering thought. The more sin we allow in our lives, the less we welcome the Light of the World. The more distant we live from the Savior, the less of the light of His presence we enjoy.

What does the Light of the World mean to you?

The great cosmic conflict is the battle between light and darkness. Darkness pervades the world, but Jesus is the Light of the World. When darkness is invaded by the light, the darkness cannot continue to exist. So when you and I are invaded by the Light, darkness must go. What does the presence of the Light mean to your life? Allow me to suggest several things. See if you agree.

When the Light comes, the darkness must go

Every life touched by the Light of the World is changed. Not only are we born again when Jesus comes into our life, but the hidden things of darkness must go. Darkness and light cannot coexist. That means when we shine the light of Christ on the activities of our life, the loves of our life, the spending habits of our life, many of them will scurry to dark corners like cockroaches when the light is turned on in the night. They should not be in our lives and we know it.

We are faced with a dilemma: some things love the darkness, and we are now touched by the Light. Since light dispels darkness, either the Light will feel out of place in our darkened life, or the darkness will be uncomfortable in the presence of the blinding Light. When Jesus is King of our life, sin must give up its throne. We have to make a choice, and we have to make some adjustments.

The adjustments may come quickly in some cases and more slowly in others, but come they must. When the rock is lifted, some bugs must immediately flee to darker quarters. When the Light comes into our lives, some forms of sin must immediately be sent packing. Paul talked about them in Colossians 3:5-6: "Therefore put to death your members which are on the earth: fornication, uncleanness, passion, evil desire, and covetousness, which is idolatry. Because of these things the wrath of God is coming upon the sons of disobedience." To "put to death" means to murder, to intentionally kill. When the Light enters our life, some sins must be squashed like a bug running from the Light.

Other things will take more time. Paul also talked about them in Colossians 3:8. "But now you must also put off all these: anger, wrath, malice, blasphemy, filthy language out of your mouth." These dark things die too, but they are starved to death. We simply don't feed them and they wither away. Jesus can help. He is sufficient to starve those things in your life that must die. Ask Him what does not please Him in your life. Allow His light to shine on those things and squash them like a bug. If they hide before you can squash them, don't leave anything lying around in your life that would feed them. Starve them to death. If you find your sufficiency in Christ Jesus, the bugs in your life that are spiritual pests will find little to live on.

When the Light comes in, the darkness goes out. You can't have it both ways. John says it this way: "Little children, let no one deceive you. He who practices righteousness is righteous, just as He [God] is righteous. He who sins is of the devil, for the devil has sinned from the beginning. For this purpose the Son of God was manifested, that He might destroy the works of the devil" (1 John 3:7-8). The devil rules in darkness, but Jesus came to bring light and destroy the works of the devil in your life.

Turn the Light on in your life. Send Satan and his insects scurrying for cover.

Wherever the Light leads us, we must follow

Hiking in the woods in the middle of the night can be, well, interesting. You hear all kinds of strange noises. You think you see things that just aren't there. You watch shadows move with the skill of raven ghosts. You imagine all kinds of interesting scenarios about your untimely demise. But the most challenging thing about hiking in the woods in the middle of the night is finding the path that leads to safety. If you're going to follow the path, you've got to have a light.

When Jesus comes into our lives as the Light of the World, He proves Himself sufficient to provide the light we need to stay on the path that leads to God. He does this several ways. First, we have the Holy Spirit as our inner guide. He helps us identify the next step, the next move that takes us closer to God. He is our teacher, our guide (John 14:26).

We also have the Bible. "Your word is a lamp to my feet and a light to my path" (Ps. 119:105). What a wonderful picture of how the Light affects our life. Instead of walking bewildered through a maze of ethical and moral dilemmas, without a clue of right from wrong, we have God's Word to shine a light on our path. When we read the Bible and take it seriously, we are never left to guess which path is His path. It is lighted clearly for us. We may still have trouble with obedience, but we will have no difficulty with insight.

That's not true of those who do not trust the sufficiency of the Light of the World. They stumble through life, from crisis to crisis, wondering what's the right thing to do, who's the right person to trust. They do not have the insight of God's Word. In fact, the Bible says they are hopelessly unable to walk in the Light because "the natural man does not receive the things of the Spirit of God, for they are foolishness to him; nor can he know them, because they are spiritually discerned" (1 Cor. 2:14).

These people aren't stupid. Their IQ isn't the problem. Their spiritual darkness is. Some who do not have Jesus as the Light in their lives are brilliant people, but blinded by their sin, in a spiritual stupor and groping in the darkness for any little scrap of insight for living.

So what does this mean for those who have the Light? Just this. When the Light of the World shines on a path for us, He wants us to follow. We can take only one step at a time, just as far as the light shines, but the "I AM" God shines the light only where He wants us to follow Him. Where He lights a path before us, we must take a step of faith, even if it means boldly going where no one has ever gone before. Where He leads me I must follow. When He says to you, "This is the way, walk in it" (Isa. 30:21), you have no other option. To walk elsewhere is to walk in the dark woods. To walk in God's way is to walk with the path well lighted by His Word. The choice is yours, but choose carefully. The paths divide quickly and the destinations are very distinct.

When we're touched by the Light, we must share Him with others

To walk in the Light does not mean we walk alone. To follow the Light, Jesus Christ, means we trust and obey Him. It means we believe in His sufficiency to save us from the darkness of our own sin. And once we are born again, out of a heart of gratitude we keep His commands. One of those commands is to let our light shine so that others may see the true Light in us.

Immediately after pronouncing the beatitudes on those who would obey God, Jesus continued to teach His disciples, saying, "You are the light of the world. A city that is set on a hill cannot be hidden. Nor do they light a lamp and put it under a basket, but on a lampstand, and it gives light to all who are in the house. Let your light so shine before men, that they may see your good works and glorify your Father in heaven" (Matt. 5:14-16).

Did you catch the switch here? Time and again Jesus said that He was the Light of the World. In fact, once He even said, "As long as I am in the world, I am the light of the world" (John 9:5). But what happened when Jesus was taken out of the world? What happened to the light when He ascended to the right hand of His Father on high?

You and I are what happened. The flame ignited by the Lord Jesus as the Light of the World was fanned by the Spirit of God on the day of Pentecost. Jesus ascended to the Father, but all who were touched by the Light are called to touch others with the Light. That's why Jesus said, "You are the light of the world." We are now His lights, the only lights the world will see that can light the way to heaven and the true Light.

How bright is your light? Would your neighbors be surprised to learn that you are bearing the torch of Christianity? Would your boss or your work team be shocked to find you can exist in their dark world without shining any light into it? Have you hidden your light under the basket of professionalism or fear or embarrassment? How bright is your light?

Take a moment to think about this. What would be your future if the person who passed the Light on to you allowed it to flicker to the same degree you are allowing your light to flicker right now? Are you a light-bearer or a light-buryer?

Jesus said, "I am the light of the world." He was the true Light, the real thing, the one John the Baptist came to bear witness to. Jesus is the Light who came into the world, but the darkness did not comprehend it (John 1:5). "He came to His own, and His own did not receive Him," and that's bad news. But there's good news too. "But as many as received Him, to them He gave the right to become children of God, even to those who believe in His name" (John 1:11-12).

Have you read about people who have that special malady called "Seasonal Affective Disorder"? Those who have SAD are so sensitive to a lack of light that even the shorter daylight hours that normally accompany winter cause them to experience clinical depression. Well, those who have never trusted the Light of the World have a much more severe malady. Are you ready to be used of God to help people who are spiritually SAD find sufficiency in the Light?

If you've been touched by the Light of the World, reflect it. Show His light to family and friends. Let them see that Jesus Christ is sufficient for all things in your life. Be a beacon of light. Shine in the dark place where you live or work. Shine brightly. You may be the only light your neighbors will ever have to light their way to God.

You don't have to make a lot of noise to shine for Jesus. D. L. Moody once said, "We are told to let our light shine, and if it does, we won't need to tell anybody it does. Lighthouses don't fire cannons to call attention to their shining—they just shine."

Wouldn't it be a shame if your light was dimmed or diffused by sin? You can make a difference in this dark world. You don't need to light a candle; you just need to let your light shine.

"I am the Bread of Life; let Me sustain you!"

CHAPTER 3

I Am

THE BREAD OF LIFE

And Jesus said to them, "I am the bread of life. He who comes to Me shall never hunger, and he who believes in Me shall never thirst."
JOHN 6:35

Bread. There's nothing in this world like bread. Take a warm piece of homemade bread from the oven (or today, out of the breadmaker), spread some real butter on it (not "Someday I'll Be Butter Too!" or "It Kinda Tastes Like Butter") and eat it before it cools. Now that's a meal. Is there any better aroma in the world than the sweet smell that arises from baking bread? It's wonderful.

I lived in France during one of my semesters of seminary and fell in love with genuine French bread the first moment I ate it. I soon learned those Frenchman don't have long, thin loaves of French bread sticking out of their basket like antennae just to balance their bicycle. Bread is a main course. The Portuguese make a sweet bread that is out of this world. It's hard to beat a good slice of Jewish rye bread. And German Pumpernickel? Well, don't even get me started. Bread is like people; it comes in all shapes, all sizes, all colors and all nationalities.

But if you ask me, there is no better bread in all the world than the bread baked in the Holy Land. I have broken bread with a Bedouin family (one sheik, two wives and a parcel of children) in the wastelands of the Sinai, far from civilization. With a customary smile and a friendly greeting, the man invited us to sit in his tent. While he brewed coffee that most closely resembled what work crews use to blacktop roads, the women whipped up some bread. They put the lid to a barrel over an open fire, began to mix up some flour and water, and in just two minutes I was eating a nomad's delicacy. It was a little like eating thin-crust pizza without the toppings.

Then there is Arab pita bread. A little restaurant on Manger Square in Bethlehem serves the best pita bread in the world, bar none. This Arab pita is not like the pathetic pita we get here in the United States. This bread is not the size of a CD but rather the size of a Frisbee. It is thick, chewy and always served steaming hot right out of the oven. It's the closest thing to heavenly manna I know.

Manna for free

Bread is the essential staple of life. It's one of the basic needs of mankind. With bread and water, it is possible to live indefinitely. Is there any food we take for granted more than our daily bread? The only time we miss it is when we don't have it. Israel knew about that.

God's people had been liberated from more than four centuries of cruel bondage in Egypt. Jehovah had taken them out of their taskmaster's country with a high hand (Ex. 14:8; Num. 33:3). But they had barely arrived at the Red Sea, the last, great barrier to their freedom, when the armies of Pharaoh closed in behind them. God parted the waters so the people could cross on dry ground; the Egyptians, meanwhile, were all drowned when the waters came crashing together again. It's a classic story recorded in Exodus 12-15.

Israel was relieved. Egypt was behind them forever. With renewed enthusiasm and heads held high, they set their sights on the Promised Land. But soon there was a problem. The leeks and garlic and cucumbers and all the good stuff they were used to in Egypt were now off the menu permanently. What would they eat? They had none of Egypt's delicacies, and they really had grown fond of that leek and garlic soup. What's worse, they didn't even have life's one staple—bread. What would they do? The prone-to-complain Israelites did what they did best—they complained. "Oh, that we had died by the hand of the LORD in the land of Egypt, when we sat by the pots of meat and when we ate bread to the full!" (Ex. 16:3).

God heard Israel's complaint (which, of course, is just one of the downsides to complaining—God always hears). He said to Moses, "I will rain bread from heaven for you" (v. 4). Not a bad deal. Free bread. No mixing. No kneading. No baking. Just free bread falling from the sky. But it wasn't like the pita from Bethlehem. The Bible describes this manna as "a small round substance, as fine as frost on the ground" (v. 14). Instead of the size of a Frisbee, it was the size of coriander seed. Instead of being served hot and fresh on every Jewish table, it was served round and hard on the Sinai desert.

Smaller than a bread box

Have you ever wondered what this manna was like? Has the biblical description made an impression on your mind of just what this manna looked like and how unbelievably difficult it was to gather it? Picture this. Manna is described as small, round, semi-white and much like a coriander seed. The coriander plant is from the carrot family and produces a grayish seed the size of a small peppercorn. It's used both to flavor foods and as medicine. But the key here is the color and the size. It was very small and whitish-gray in color.

Now, get the picture. Except for the Sabbath, the Israelites were to gather enough of this "bread" to last them just one day. If more than a day's supply was collected it would rot and begin to smell. Talk about your daily bread! They couldn't sock some away in their portable pantry; they had to collect it every morning. And it wasn't served to them; they had to go out and find it. Think about that. This was more challenging than it might sound.

The manna was very small, about the size of the head of a pin. It was spread over the Sinai sands. It was roughly the same color as the sand. Can you imagine what a chore it was to sift the manna from the sand? They had to make certain they were eating manna and not a "sand"wich. They had to gather enough to feed the whole family, but not a bit more. Manna may have been free, but it wasn't easy!

Better than manna

In time, the Jews forgot how difficult it was to retrieve manna in the wilderness, but they never forgot that it came from God. In fact, they took pride that God gave the manna to them and to no one else. The Israelites knew they were special. They were the "manna" people.

In John 6, the people of Capernaum were curious about Jesus' obvious miracle-working powers. After all, He had just fed 5,000 with five barley loaves and two small fish (vv. 1-13). But the people wanted more—not more lunch, but more signs of Jesus' powers. They asked, "What sign will You perform then, that we may see it and believe You?" (v. 30). To support the legitimacy of their craving for a sign, they pointed to the manna in the wilderness. They said, "Our fathers ate the manna in the desert; as it is written, 'He gave them bread from heaven to eat'" (v. 31). And then it happened.

Jesus announced something shocking. He said, "Moses did not give you the bread from heaven, but My Father gives you the true bread from heaven" (v. 32). While the Jews were still bragging on the provision of manna centuries before, Jesus focused their attention on the present and God's heavenly provision for them now. He continued, "For the bread of God is He who comes down from heaven and gives life to the world" (v. 33). The bread of God is not an "it"; such bread is a "He," a person. When the Jews clamored, "Lord, give us this bread always," they could not have anticipated His reply: "I am the bread of life. He who comes to Me shall never hunger" (v. 35).

To the Jews that was a braggadocios bombshell. They muttered against Jesus because He said, "I am the bread which came down from heaven" (v. 41). How dare He? "Is not this Jesus, the son of Joseph, whose father and mother we know? How is it then that He says, 'I have come down from heaven?'" (v. 42). And then Jesus really torched their tunics when He said, "I am the bread of life. Your fathers ate the manna in the wilderness, and are dead. This is the bread which comes down from heaven, that one may eat of it and not die. I am the living bread which came down from heaven. If anyone eats of this bread, he will live forever" (vv. 48-51).

This is the consummate put-down in the Bible. The Jews bragged how God had sustained their forefathers by sending manna from heaven. Jesus pointed out the obvious: their fathers were all dead. But He offered something revolutionary and unique. He offered Himself as the Bread of Life, the true bread from heaven, God's real bread. And He stunned the speechless religious leaders with this promise: "If anyone eats of this bread (meaning if anyone takes Him as the Bread of Life), he will live forever (v. 51).

The "I AM" God couldn't have made the contrast more striking. Alexander Maclaren noted, "The bread which we eat sustains life; the Bread which He gives originates it. The bread which we eat is assimilated to our bodily frame; the Bread which He gives assimilates our spiritual nature to His. And so it comes to be the only food that stills a hungry heart, the only food that satisfies."[1]

Jesus confronted them with a decision. Eat the manna after laboriously gathering it from the sands of Sinai and die anyway, or taste the Bread of Life as God's free and untethered gift and live forever. The choice is yours.

Jesus said, "I am the bread of life." He is sufficient to satisfy your spiritual hunger. If there is a huge emptiness in your life, if you are hungry for something that will fill your life with meaning, Jesus is the Bread of Life. He can take away all your spiritual growls and give you the most satisfying bread you have ever tasted—Himself. He is sufficient to feed you with eternal life. He alone is sufficient.

Of all the "I am" statements in the Bible, why this one? Why does the "I AM" God liken Himself to bread? What is it about bread that exhibits the qualities that Jesus manifests in providing salvation for us? Think about these things.

Bread is the basic substance of life

When Jesus prayed, "Give us this day our daily bread" (Matt. 6:11), He wasn't just singling bread out for special attention, as opposed to a salad or a center cut of beef or a pizza. He was using bread as the staff of life. "Give us this day our most basic physical needs." Bread is basic. It is essential, foundational, not just for building a sandwich but also for building a life.

When Adam and Eve sinned against God and were cursed, one element in the punishment for Adam's sin was God's promise that "in the sweat of your face you shall eat bread" (Gen. 3:19). For humankind, life would continue each day, but only by the sweat of labor and not by the abundance of Eden. When the seven lean years came to Egypt, Genesis 47:13 records, "Now there was no bread in all the land; for the famine was very severe." This did not mean there was a simple bread shortage; there was a terrible famine in which the basic foods of life were missing.

More and more you see homeless people standing at the corners of the street. Often they are holding signs that read: "Will work for food." In Bible days the signs would have said: "Will work for bread." Bread was the most fundamental of all foods. If you didn't have bread, you didn't eat. Lamenting the weakness of Israel, Hannah prayed, "The bows of the mighty men are broken . . . those who were full have hired themselves out for bread" (1 Sam. 2:4-5).

Why did Jesus say, "I am the bread of life?" Because there is nothing more basic to life than bread. Without bread we starve physically. Without Jesus Christ we starve spiritually. No one else can satisfy the needs of a spiritually hungry soul; only Jesus. He knew that and the "I AM" God wanted us to know it when He said, "I am the bread of life."

If you're going to live today, really live, Jesus must fill up your life like bread fills up your stomach. As bread is the necessary substance of this life, Jesus is the necessary substance of your eternal life. "Whoever eats My flesh and drinks My blood has eternal life" (John 6:54). All Jesus meant by this is that whoever places their faith in Jesus' death at Calvary and asks Him to cover their sins with the sacrifice of His blood, that person has eternal life. Whoever chooses another diet for their salvation will find only hopeless starvation. Jesus alone is sufficient to be the Bread of Life for us. His atonement alone will cover our sins and free us from the guilt and penalty of those sins. Only Jesus is the Bread of Life.

Bread is for hungry people

I mentioned earlier that I was a student in France three decades ago. When I arrived in Europe to attend the University of Strasbourg, I had prepaid my tuition, my room in the university dormitory and my meals at a student dining hall. Because I had no extra cash with which to buy things for my family back home, my first week at the university I sold half my meal tickets to other students. That gave me spending money, but it also deprived me of a lot of meals. No matter. After the first few meals at the student dining hall, I wasn't sure it was food anyway.

At that point, lunch (and sometimes dinner) became a luxury. So I really loaded up at breakfast. All there was to eat was bread, butter, jam and café au lait. Why do I say that's all there was? That was a banquet to a starving student! I loved the French café au lait, and the bread was fresh each morning from the local bakery. I would eat bread until it was coming out of my ears.

An empty stomach craves bread; a full stomach loathes it. It is when we are hungry that we need bread, not when we are full. So it is with sinners. It's when we hunger for real forgiveness and salvation and not just religion or some sort of sensual satisfaction that we most appreciate

Jesus as the Bread of Life. Bread is for hungry people. Jesus is for hungry people. Self-satisfied sinners will never hunger and thirst after righteousness.

When the Prodigal Son ran away from home, he found himself in a foreign land feeding pigs. I think God must have a sense of humor. What could be a more degrading job for a young Jewish boy than feeding the pigs? But when he realized what an idiot he had been, the prodigal said to himself, "How many of my father's hired servants have bread enough and to spare, and I perish with hunger!" (Luke 15:17). Ultimately what drove him back to his father was his stomach. When he was hungry enough, he swallowed his pride and came home again.

That's the way it is with us. When we are full of ourselves, our work, our bank accounts or our pleasures, we are never hungry enough to come back to our Heavenly Father. It is only when we are famished, when we are starving spiritually, that we see our need for the Bread of Life. Men and women do not come to Christ until they want the Savior more than anything else.

If you are hungry today and don't know what's gnawing away at your soul, remember the words of Scripture: " Hungry and thirsty, their soul fainted in them. Then they cried out to the LORD in their trouble . . . . Oh, that men would give thanks to the LORD for His goodness . . . for He satisfies the longing soul, and fills the hungry soul with goodness" (Ps. 107:5-6, 8-9). Hungry? Jesus is the Bread of Life. Discover that He is sufficient to give you life eternal. Only Jesus can satisfy your hungry soul.

Bread is the universal cure for hunger

Mention tortellini and you think of Italian cuisine. Talk about Cajun food and you think of New Orleans. Somebody brings up the subject of Peking duck and your mind turns to Chinese food. What pops into your head when I say bratwurst? German food. How about baklava? Tacos? Scones? Falafel? Shish Kebab? Let's make it easier. What countries come to mind when I say Hungarian goulash? Irish stew? Polish sausage? You get the point.

Some places in the world are noted for that special dish or desert or sandwich. But what if I mention bread? What country do you think of then? While some countries prefer rice or maize or other grains as their staple, bread is the most universal principal fare. You can find bread served before your meal, with your meal or as your meal, just about anywhere you travel in the world.

That's what makes the metaphor of Jesus, the Bread of Life so inviting. He is universal in His appeal. He is not the Savior of Europeans but not Latinos; He is not the Savior of men but not women; He is not the Savior of whites but not blacks; He is the Savior of the world. Bread feeds the world, regardless of ethnicity or skin color. Only Jesus is sufficient to feed the world, all the world.

John the Baptist pointed to Jesus and exclaimed, "Behold! The Lamb of God who takes away the sin of the world!" (John 1:29). The apostle John affirmed, "And we have seen and testify that the Father has sent the Son as Savior of the world" (1 John 4:14). After the woman at the well trusted Jesus as her personal Savior she testified to her fellow citizens. When they came out to meet Him, they declared, "This is indeed the Christ, the Savior of the world" (John 4:42).

What makes Jesus the Bread of Life? Because He alone is the universal answer to a spiritually hungry world. Jesus is the Savior for Asians, Europeans, Latinos, Africans, Australians, Americans, Canadians, Tahitians, everyone. Jesus' own words are, "The bread of God is He who comes down from heaven and gives life to the world" (John 6:33). No one is sufficient to give life to the world but the Bread of Life.

Joy to the world! The Lord is come;
Let earth receive her King;
Let every heart prepare Him room,
And heaven and nature sing.

— Isaac Watts

There is one final element about Jesus as the Bread of Life we should think about. His sufficiency to feed a world starving in spiritual hunger is well attested in the Bible. But having bread and eating it are two different things. Jesus provides Himself as the Bread of Life, but to be filled we must consume the Bread.

Bread is beneficial only if eaten

Have you noticed that bread is not a particularly handsome food? Now think about it. When the presentation is made and your food is neatly arranged on your plate, is bread the focus of that presentation?

I have eaten the tastiest fish on the island of Bora Bora, smothered in a vanilla sauce worthy to die for. It was not only a treat to the taste buds, it was almost too pretty to eat. Have you seen what a French chef can do with pastries? Never mind eating them; they are a work of art to the eyes. But not bread. The primary function of bread is not to garnish a meal. It's just not an especially beautiful thing.

Jesus is the Bread of Life. He is the one essential of eternal life. He is the grain of wheat that had to fall into the ground and die before it could bear fruit (John 12:24). It's not a pretty picture. Isaiah prophesied of Jesus the Messiah, "He shall grow up before Him as a tender plant, and as a root out of dry ground. He has no form or comeliness; and when we see Him, there is no beauty that we should desire Him" (Isa. 53:2).

Jesus was not born to become *Time* magazine's "Man of the Year." He did not come to be a movie star, a high-priced musician or a World Wrestling Federation showman. Jesus did not come to astound the intellectual world (although He did). Jesus did not come to amaze the common world (although He did that too). Jesus came to earth for one reason. He came to die.

The "I AM" God came as a grain of wheat to die and be raised from the dead to pay the price for your sins and mine. Jesus came as the Bread of Life to give us life. His words still ring in our ears: "For the bread of God is He who comes down from heaven and gives life to the world" (John 6:33). "I am the bread of life. He who comes to Me shall never hunger" (v. 35). "I am the bread which came down from heaven" (v. 41). "He who believes in Me has everlasting life" (v. 47). "I am the bread of life" (v. 48). "This is the bread which comes down from heaven, that one may eat of it and not die" (v. 50). "I am the living bread which came down from heaven. If anyone eats of this bread, he will live for ever" (v. 51). "This is the bread which came down from heaven . . . . He who eats this bread will live for ever" (v. 58).

In John 6, Jesus again and again refers to Himself as the bread that came down from heaven, the bread that gives eternal life. But just as we must eat of white bread or rye or sourdough bread if we are to benefit from it, so also we must partake of the Bread of Life if we are to benefit from His death. Bread is made for eating, not for analyzing, looking at or wondering about.

Don't go away hungry

If you want to have your spiritual hunger filled, Jesus is the answer. But if you want eternal life from the Bread of Life, you must grab hold of this bread and make it a part of you. You must trust Jesus Christ as your personal Savior, your very own Savior. Others have eaten of this life-giving bread and have been filled. Their spiritual hunger is gone. They have been satisfied with the sufficiency of Christ. Follow them to the bakery. Do what they did. If you want spiritual life, everlasting life, eternal life in heaven, you must eat. Come by faith and receive this Bread of Life, and all the spiritual and nutritional benefits of the bread will all be yours.

Jesus was born in Bethlehem (which means the "house of bread"). He died on Calvary's cross in Jerusalem. But as the Savior of the world, He comes to your table and offers Himself to you as the Bread of Life. You don't have to remain hungry. "Oh, taste and see that the LORD is good; blessed is the man who trusts in Him!" (Ps. 34:8).

What does the Bread of life mean to you?

If you have trusted Jesus as your Savior, think of all the wonderful benefits of having the Bread of Life as your very own. He sits at the table of your life and invites you to "Come and dine." Think of what it means that the bread which brings eternal life has blessed your life.

The Bread of Life gives you a personal relationship

Imagine the thrill of going to the grocery store. I know, for men this represents unalloyed joy. But just think of walking down the canyons of those aisles stacked high with good things to eat. You pass through the cereal section and see 101 demonstrations of ways you can package grain. You whisk your way through the frozen foods and eyeball everything from frozen pizza to frozen peas. You turn the corner and pass through the green grocer's domain. There you see fresh broccoli, lettuce, turnips and scallions. Snuggled next to them are grapes, cantaloupes, bananas, oranges and apples. It's all pretty exciting, isn't it? But it's all quite impersonal. One banana looks pretty much like the rest. One turnip is difficult to distinguish from another.

Then, imagine you round the bend and head for the home stretch. You pass through the bread isle and see racks and racks of breads. There's Wonder Bread and Keystone. You see Strohmans, Roman Meal and

58

Earth Grains. There's Pillsbury, Pepperidge Farms, Sunbeam and something oddly named Beefstak Bread. Not to mention Kroger, Food Lion, Winn Dixie, Giant, IGA, Safeway or my personal favorite, Piggily Wiggily. Every loaf of bread has a name proudly identifying its baker.

Would it shock you if you came across a loaf of bread with your name printed on it instead of the bakery's name? Would it please you? What if the next time I went to the store, instead of seeing a loaf of Wonder Bread I saw a loaf of Woodrow Bread? Would I be shocked? You bet. Would I be surprised? Sure. But would I be pleased? Probably. Would I be happy if my bread were personally baked for me and my name was placed on it? I think I would.

That's the way it is with Jesus the Bread of Life. He isn't just a loaf of bread for the world; He's my bread. My name is written down on His delivery list (Rev. 20:12). The Bread of Life has made a personal connection with me. He said, "I am the Bread of Life." He used the first person pronoun. You can't get more personal than that.

Jesus is my bread; He is my life. He has blessed my life with eternity. I have found in Him all the sufficiency I need for life. And if you are born again, you have found that same personal sufficiency. Your name was on the wrapper just like mine was. The Bread of Life gives you a personal relationship with Him. He is your Bread of Life.

The Bread of Life provides the only bread worth having

As you know, there are many of types of breads from which to choose. In fact, when you order toast in a restaurant, it's surprising if you aren't offered a selection of bread for toasting. There's sourdough, white, whole wheat, a variety of other grains, pumpernickel and the rye family (German rye, Jewish rye, dark rye, light rye, marble rye). But when it comes to the Bread of Life, there is only one. Jesus and Jesus alone is the Bread of Life. He is not one of many varieties that lead to heaven and eternal life. He is the exclusive variety. That makes Him the only bread worth having.

He said, "I (myself) am the bread of life." Jesus is not a sandwich, a bread tray or a selection. He and He alone is the Bread of Life. Sandwiches have many ingredients besides bread, especially if it is a good hoagie. Bread trays have dozens of selections for us to choose from. But that's not the way it is with eternal life. Jesus said, "I (alone) am *the* bread of life" (italics mine).

When I trusted Jesus as my Savior, I wasn't looking for an alternative to my life. I was looking for a Savior, and Jesus is the only Savior this world will ever have. All God's salvation eggs are in one basket. While this world has many religions, it has only one Savior. He alone is the Bread of Life. Only Jesus is sufficient to be bread worth having.

The Bread of Life gives you significant quality of life

We hear a lot these days about quality of life, especially in the right-to-die debate. People are concerned that those who are elderly or infirm have a particular quality to their lives. But the issue is just as real for the right-to-live question. Long before you must face death, you have to face life. It can be just as scary. What's more, you face death only once; you face life every day.

With Jesus as your personal Bread of Life, you receive a specific quality of life. When Jesus said, "I am the bread of life," He was literally saying, "I am the bread of *the* life." Greek scholars would call this a qualitative genitive, referring not just to any kind of life but to spiritual life, to eternal life, to life worth living now and worth having forever. Jesus is sufficient to give daily bread that makes the life of the Christian more precious and blessed than any other. But He is also sufficient to give us a significant quality of life in the hereafter.

"Beloved, now we are children of God; and it has not yet been revealed what we shall be, but we know that when He is revealed, we shall be like Him, for we shall see Him as He is" (1 John 3:2). Sweet bread now and sweet bread forever. That's what the Bread of Life means.

The Bread of Life is entirely satisfying

Every time I read the account of Jesus as the Bread of Life in John 6, one verse just keeps coming back to encourage me. It may be the most unusual verse in the whole chapter. It's verse 35: "And Jesus said to them, 'I am the bread of life. He who comes to Me shall never hunger, and he who believes in Me shall never thirst.'"

Don't you find that a bit odd? It's easy to see how the Bread of Life can knock the edge off your hunger, but quench your thirst? When you are thirsty, I mean really thirsty—perhaps after you have mowed the lawn or cooked over a hot stove for a big meal—have you ever said to someone, "Oh, please, I'm so thirsty. Would you get me a piece of bread?" Never said that? I'm not surprised. Get me a tall, cold glass of water maybe, but not a warm piece of fresh bread.

How can it be said that the Bread of Life both satisfies our hunger and quenches our thirst? Remember, bread is the essential need of life. Jesus Christ as the bread of your life meets all your basic spiritual needs. He completely satisfies, even in those areas you wouldn't expect.

Jesus wants us to come to Him and to believe in Him as Savior. You can't do one without the other. That's why the "I AM" God equates the two actions. For the Bread of Life, believing and coming to Him are inextricably linked together. You cannot believe that Jesus is the Bread of Life without coming to Him for salvation. Faith sprouts feet when we see Jesus as the totally satisfying Bread of Life. Come and believe.

Bread. There's nothing in this world like bread. Take a warm piece of homemade bread from the oven, spread some real butter on it, and eat it before it cools. Now that's a meal. The Bread of Life. There's no one in this world like Him. Find your sufficiency in the only One who can spiritually feed the starving masses. The world needs bread; world hunger is a growing problem. But the greater problem is the world's spiritual hunger. Only the Bread of Life is sufficient to cure that problem. Isn't it time we all shared bread a little more?

D. T. Niles once said, "Evangelism is just one beggar telling another beggar where to find bread." If you have tasted the goodness of the Bread of Life, share what you have received. God has a way of blessing us bountifully when we share the Bread of Life. Look around you. See that brother-in-law, that neighbor, that person on the other side of your cubicle? Do they look like they are starving spiritually? Give them some of your bread. Give them daily bread. Give them the Bread of Life.

"I am the Good Shepherd; let Me lead you!"

CHAPTER 4

THE GOOD SHEPHERD

"I am the good shepherd. The good shepherd gives His life for the sheep."
JOHN 10:11

If I say the word "salesman," what comes to your mind? Someone who calls you constantly just to "check" on you, and sell you something if he can? If I say "construction worker" you think of someone with a hard hat, a tool belt and a T-shirt, right? But what if I say "shepherd"? You likely get a mental picture of someone smelly, unkempt, shabbily dressed, with a stick in his hand and a herd of sheep in tow. Actually, this stereotypical image of a shepherd is not only biblical; even today it is quite accurate in the Middle East.

For those of us who live in the United States, this "I AM" passage from John 10—I am the Good Shepherd—may be a bit foreign. While there are sheep ranchers in some western states, there aren't many in Illinois, Massachusetts, Florida, Pennsylvania—in fact, in most of the United States. Americans know very little about the life of a shepherd. On the other hand, if you live in Great Britain, Ireland, New Zealand or Australia, you may know a little more about sheep and their shepherds. A recent issue of *National Geographic* pictured ranchers in Australia herding 12,000 sheep on a 42,000-acre station with a Cessna airplane. If you live in Mongolia or Mexico you probably are even more sheepwise. But there's no more appropriate place to learn about a shepherd and his sheep than in the Middle East.

The profession of sheep herding is still a popular one in Israel, Jordan, Syria, Lebanon, Egypt and most Middle Eastern countries. In these pastoral and semi-nomadic societies, sheep are like investments—as certificates of deposit, mutual funds and precious metals are to people in Europe or North America. They are their stock in trade. For most Bedouin, sheep make the economy run. They are the most reliable, most prevalent commodity bought and sold in many countries in the Middle East. Sheep are to the shepherds of Israel what cattle are to the gauchos of Argentina or stocks and bonds to the Wall Street broker. They are their assets, their product, their concern day and night.

Shepherds are important in the Bible. The Scriptures often make use of the shepherd/sheep analogy. Think of Psalm 23, the favorite psalm of many Christians and Jews. "The LORD is my shepherd; I shall not want. He makes me to lie down in green pastures; He leads me beside the still waters. . . . Your rod and Your staff, they comfort me. . . . You anoint my head with oil; . . . Surely goodness and mercy shall follow me all the days of my life." Little wonder this psalm is a favorite. Its subject is the tender care the "I AM" God gives to us, His sheep. We all can identify with that.

One of the most sensitive portraits of the Messiah in the Bible is found in Isaiah 53. It features the shepherd motif, but in a very different mode. Isaiah speaks of the Man of Sorrows bearing our grief and carrying our sorrows, being wounded for our transgressions and bruised for our iniquities. Then Isaiah 53:6 relates why this was necessary in language every shepherd would understand: "All we like sheep have gone astray; we have turned, every one, to his own way; and the LORD has laid on Him the iniquity of us all."

The shepherd/sheep theme is an integral part of the New Testament as well. Everybody likes a good story, and Jesus was among the best storytellers ever. One of His most popular parables was the story of ninety-nine sheep whose compassionate shepherd went into the wilderness to find the one lonely lost sheep. Jesus said, "What man of you, having a hundred sheep, if he loses one of them, does not leave the ninety-nine in the wilderness, and go after the one which is lost until he finds it? And when he has found it, he lays it on his shoulders, rejoicing" (Luke 15:4-5). Think of all the lessons we can learn from the shepherd in this story.

But just as there are rugged gauchos and gentle gauchos, wealthy Wall Street brokers and broke brokers, there are also good shepherds and bad shepherds. Much of the reason the "I AM" God chose to call Himself the Good Shepherd was to show Israel there really was a difference in shepherds. They had been abused by bad shepherds for generations, but all that was about to change. God had now given them His Son, a gentle shepherd, sensitive and loving—One who truly cares for His sheep.

Jesus announced to these body battered and spirit-broken people, "I am the good shepherd." That had to be good news for them, and it is certainly good news for us.

The condemnation of inattentive shepherds

John 10 is the last public address of Jesus that John records. It's quite fitting, therefore, that Jesus used the figure of the Good Shepherd to distinguish His ministry from the many indolent and indifferent shepherds who had preceded Him. To appreciate what Jesus had to say, we must read John 10 in light of the Old Testament. Most of the spiritual shepherds of God's flock had been derelict in their duty toward Israel. They were ruthless, godless and clueless about the real needs of their people.

God raised up prophet after prophet in Old Testament days to castigate the shepherds who had failed in their duty to love and protect the sheep. If we can get inside the heads of these prophets for a moment, we can better understand why Jesus' statement "I am the good shepherd" should have given so much hope to Israel. Let's sample a few of the prophets' words.

Jeremiah's tearful words

Jeremiah was the major prophet during the decline and fall of the southern kingdom of Judah. Bible commentator Herbert Lockyer Sr. noted, "Jeremiah is often called 'the weeping prophet' because he wept openly about the sins of his nation (Jer. 9:1). He was also depressed at times about the futility of his message. As the years passed and his words of judgment went unheeded, he lamented his unfortunate state: 'O LORD, You induced me, and I was persuaded; You are stronger than I, and have prevailed. I am in derision daily; everyone mocks me' (Jer. 20:7)."[1]

Jeremiah 23:1-2 records, "'Woe to the shepherds who destroy and scatter the sheep of My pasture!' says the LORD. Therefore thus says the LORD God of Israel against the shepherds who feed My people: 'You have scattered My flock, driven them away, and not attended to them. Behold, I will attend to you for the evil of your doings,' says the LORD."

Few heeded Jeremiah's message; nevertheless, he was faithful in delivering it. Judah's shepherds failed to tend to their sheep—the people of Israel—and the people had wandered far from God and become scattered.

Isaiah's scathing words

Isaiah's ministry extended from about 740 B.C. until 701 B.C. In his 40 years of preaching and prophesying, he alternated between a message of doom and a message of hope. Unfortunately, his efforts did not effect a significant change in the people of Judah. They continued to rush headlong toward a date with destiny and a Babylonian king named Nebuchadnezzar.

Isaiah's record of God's warning to greedy shepherds was particularly scathing. He said, "His watchmen are blind, they are all ignorant; they are all dumb dogs, they cannot bark; sleeping, lying down, loving to slumber. Yes, they are greedy dogs which never have enough. And they are shepherds who cannot understand; they all look to their own way, everyone for his own gain" (Isa. 56:10-11).

Those are harsh words, but justified. Isaiah likens Judah's leaders, the shepherds of the flock of Israel, as lazy dogs who love to sleep and greedy dogs who never have enough. It was a love of pleasure and greed that destroyed the moral fiber of ancient Israel. Is there a lesson here for us today?

The recurring theme of these Old Testament blasts from the breath of God is that His shepherds—the prophets and priests—had become lazy, greedy and uncaring toward the sheep. They were in the shepherd business for what they could get out of it, not what they could give to it. They didn't care for the sheep; they cared only for themselves.

That's why Jesus presents Himself as the Good Shepherd. He is a clear alternative to the past. He offers Himself in great contrast to those shepherds who are in it for the money. As the Good Shepherd, Jesus is sufficient to lead our lives to the sheepfold for shelter and safety. The Good Shepherd is sufficient to lead us to crystal-clear water to drink and verdant meadows to eat. The Good Shepherd is sufficient for life's basic wants and needs, but more than anything else, the Good Shepherd loves us. We can find in Him the sufficiency of God's love that we find nowhere else. Israel had never seen a shepherd like the Good Shepherd; neither have we.

The contrast between the Good Shepherd and Israel's shepherds

This is not to say that all of Israel's shepherds were bad. Some were of the variety that Jesus praises. For example, Moses was a shepherd in

Midian when God appeared to him at the burning bush (Ex. 3:1-10). His used all the shepherding skills he had gained with Jethro's flocks to keep the wandering Israelites from straying away from God.

David was the classic shepherd figure of the Old Testament. Early in his life he was associated with sheep. In fact, David was so closely identified as a shepherd with his sheep that when Samuel came to anoint one of Jesse's sons to be king, David was left among the sheep. He wasn't deemed worthy of consideration (1 Sam. 16:1-13). But it's only man who is taken with the beauty on the outside; God is more interested in the beauty of what's on the inside (1 Sam. 16:7; 1 Pet. 3:3-4). The shepherd of Bethlehem became the shepherd of Israel.

Other notable shepherds come to mind as well. Abraham had sheep and cattle aplenty when he came out of Egypt (Gen. 13:1-5). Isaac did his stint with the sheep too (Gen. 26:13-14). So did Jacob—working 21 years just to get Rachel and his own flock (Gen. 29). And Amos was called as a faithful herdsmen of Tekoa to be a faithful prophet of God (Amos 1:1). Yes, there were faithful shepherds of Israel in the Old Testament, but they seem to be exceptions to the rule.

It was the failure of Israel's shepherds to fulfill their responsibility that called forth the prophecy that God would raise up a Good Shepherd in due time. God told Ezekiel, "Son of man, prophesy against the shepherds of Israel, prophesy and say to them, . . . 'Woe to the shepherds of Israel who feed themselves! Should not the shepherds feed the flocks?. . . Therefore I will save My flock . . . . I will establish one shepherd over them, and he shall feed them—My servant David. He shall feed them and be their shepherd" (Ezek. 34:2, 22-23). God's vision looked far beyond David and the Old Testament. He looked into the New Testament to John 10 and the Good Shepherd.

Insufficient shepherds

The shepherds of Jesus' day weren't much better than these undependable shepherds of ancient Israel. Some weren't even legitimate shepherds; they were just sheep stealers. They didn't enter the sheepfold by the door, but rather climbed over the stones piled together to create shelter for the sheep (John 10:1). Jesus called them common thieves and robbers. These are the kind of shepherds that start a little Bible study group so they can recruit adherents to their favorite belief and separate them from the life of the church.

Other shepherds were strangers to the sheep (John 10:5). They didn't belong there. These weren't their sheep. They would come to the sheepfold and even enter through the door. But when they called the sheep, nothing happened. The sheep didn't know their voice. They called, but they could not lead the sheep out to pasture. Strange shepherds were no better for the sheep than illegitimate shepherds. They are like those who deluge your mailbox with mail requesting funds for their ministry but have never invested anything in your life.

Then there were the hirelings. They weren't strangers and they weren't shepherds. They were hired hands, day laborers. They had no loyalty to the shepherd and no interest in the sheep. They were hired day by day like the workers in Jesus' parable of the laborers in the vineyard who were all paid the same (Matt. 20:1-16). They are like telemarketers who are hired to solicit funds from you but know nothing of you or the ministry they are calling for. Simply put, they are in it for the money.

Things haven't changed all that much in some places. In an article in *Moody*, Doug Erlandson hit the nail squarely on the head. He said, "'You deserve a break today.' 'Have it your way.' 'Reach for all the gusto you can.' What do these phrases have in common? The obvious answer: They're lines from familiar commercials. The not-so-obvious answer: They emphasize benefits for you, the consumer. . . . Marketers know that to sell a product, you must answer the consumer's primary question: What's in it for me?"[2]

When those who serve the Lord become more interested in serving themselves, in creating their own empire, in carving out a nice living, a nice house and a nice salary for themselves, when they show no compassion or care for their sheep, when their primary concern is "What's in it for me?" they have become like the shepherds God the Father blasted in the Old Testament and God the Son blasted in the New Testament. William E. Gladstone, former prime minister of Great Britain and a committed Christian, once said, "Selfishness is the greatest curse of the human race." Nowhere is that curse more evident than in self-centered shepherds of God's flock.

The sufficient Shepherd

In contrast with the pseudo-shepherds and the stranger-shepherds, the "I AM" God claimed, "I am the good shepherd." The word translated good (Gr. *kalos*) is often used to mean "worthy," "excellent," "beautiful" and more, depending on the context. It's the word used in John 2:10 when, after Jesus turned the water into wine at the wedding celebration in Cana of Galilee, the master of the feast accused the bridegroom of keeping the good (*kalos*) wine until last. Clearly the word is used to compare the inferior wine with the good wine.

Jesus is called the *Good* Shepherd as a contrast with the inferior shepherds who preceded Him and those who now are just in it for the money. Jesus is the preeminent choice as shepherd, transcending all who came before and all who would come after.

The contrast between these other shepherds and the Good Shepherd couldn't be more striking. But that contrast will become even more evident as we focus on the type of care Jesus gives to His own sheep. Only the "I AM" God is sufficient to be called the "Good Shepherd" because only Jesus can provide you with the care you need in this spirit-crushing, body-bruising, sheep-stealing world. Let's investigate the kind of care you can expect from the Good Shepherd.

The care of the Good Shepherd for others

In the Old Testament God was often called the Shepherd of His people. "The Lord is my shepherd" (Ps. 23:1). "Give ear, O Shepherd of Israel" (Ps. 80:1). "The words of scholars are like well-driven nails, given by one Shepherd" (Eccl. 12:11). "He will feed His flock like a shepherd; He will gather the lambs with His arm" (Isa. 40:11). It is not unprecedented, then, for God the Son to be called the Shepherd of His people in the New Testament.

What does the care of the "I AM" God for His sheep tell us about the sufficiency of Jesus Christ? Consider these things.

The Good Shepherd knows His sheep

"I am the good shepherd; and I know My sheep" (John 10:14). What does He mean that He "knows" His sheep? Jesus is God. God is omniscient; He knows everything, right? Of course He is aware of His sheep. But to know means so much more than to be aware of. To the Greeks the word meant to know facts. To the Jews, it meant much more.

When the "I AM" God says He knows His sheep, He is talking about His intimate relationship with them and His ownership and watchful care over them. The Good Shepherd has a personal interest in all of His sheep.

Alexander Maclaren explains:

> That is a knowledge like the knowledge of the shepherd, a bond of close intimacy. But He does not know them by reason of looking at them and thinking about them. It is something far more blessed than that. He knows me because He loves me; He knows me because He has sympathy with me, and I know Him, if I know Him at all, by my love, and I know Him by my sympathy, and I know Him by my communion. A loveless heart does not know the Shepherd, and unless the Shepherd's heart was all love He would not know His sheep.[3]

When Jesus told the parable of the ninety and nine, He was really patterning the good shepherd after Himself, the Good Shepherd. Think of it. The shepherd cared both for the masses and for the individual, for the ninety-nine sheep and for the one that was lost. He placed the ninety-nine in a place of safety and went out into the wilderness to retrieve the one that was lost. He cared not for himself, for his comfort or for his safety. He cared only for the needs of the lost sheep.

And when the lost sheep was found, the shepherd tenderly picked it up, placed it on his shoulders and carried it home to safety. But that's not the end of the story. There's that little item of rejoicing. He was so happy that his care for the lost sheep had paid off that he called his friends together and invited them to rejoice with him (Luke 15:6). As Mark Twain commented, "Grief can take care of itself, but to get the full value of joy, we must have somebody to divide it with."

Is this any different from what the Good Shepherd does with us, His sheep? We had gone astray in the brambles and high weeds of the world. It was a wilderness and we were lost, dead lost. But He loved us, He placed His other sheep in a safe place, and He came out to find us. "The Son of Man has come to seek and to save that which was lost" (Luke 19:10). And when He found us we were pathetic. We were so far from God we couldn't find our way back even if we wanted to. But He loved us; oh, how He loved us. He loved us with an everlasting love (Jer. 31:3).

He picked us up, cleaned us up and lifted us up on His shoulders. Now He is carrying us to the safety of His home in heaven. And why did the "I AM" God do all this for you and me? He did it because He knows us intimately, He cares for us deeply, He loves us personally, and because, unlike all those who have gone before Him, He is the Good Shepherd.

The Good Shepherd calls His sheep

Another contrast between the Good Shepherd and other shepherds is the way He treats His sheep. The "I AM" God who said, "I am the good shepherd," continued, "My sheep hear My voice, and I know them, and they follow me" (John 10:27). While thieves and robbers enter by climbing over the wall (v. 1), the doorkeeper opens the door of the sheepfold to the genuine shepherd "and the sheep hear his voice; and he calls his own sheep by name and leads them out" (v. 3).

Shepherds often banded together for safety. They found themselves far from villages, easy prey for robbers, and a long way from help when a wolf or a hyena came calling. Besides, the life of a shepherd was not a very exciting one. They often stayed together to combat the boredom of the Judean wilderness. They would put their sheep together in the sheepfolds at night. In the morning, each shepherd would enter the sheepfold and call his sheep, and they would follow their leader out. Shepherds knew their sheep well, even giving them names. The sheep were so familiar with the shepherd's voice, they would leave the sheepfold only when they heard their master's voice. Other shepherds could call and call, but with no response from any sheep but his own.

A good shepherd always treated his sheep with kindness and respect. His sheep were important to him and there was a special bond between them. I have seen that bond.

We were shooting the footage for the first of our Back to the Bible videos, *Sandals in the Sand*. One day we were filming in the hill country between Bethlehem and Tekoa. One of the scenes was at a cave that resembled the birthplace of the baby Jesus. We had a shepherd there with his sheep. We had to shoot the scene a number of times and to my amazement, the sheep made no attempt to wander away. Then I discovered why.

The Bedouin shepherd kept his sheep at his side (and mine) by making an almost inaudible clicking sound with his mouth. It was the kind of thing you and I would do to call a dog. The noise he made with his mouth didn't sound all that unique to me, but the sheep certainly thought it was unique.

At one point we needed the sheep to go into the cave. I tried my hand at getting them in. They didn't know me from Lil' Bo Peep and they wouldn't budge. Then I got an idea. I went into the cave, made the same clicking sound with my mouth and waited for the sheep to stampede into the cave. They paid no attention. As hard as I tried, they wouldn't respond to my voice.

The old shepherd smiled knowingly, came into the cave with me, made the clicking call to his sheep, and *en masse* they sauntered into the cave. "My sheep hear My voice, and I know them, and they follow Me."

When the Good Shepherd calls His sheep—people like you and me—it proves that He loves us, He cares about us, He wants to be with us. That's exactly what it means when Jesus calls us to salvation. "For God so loved the world that He gave His only begotten Son, that whoever believes in Him should not perish, but have everlasting life. For God did not send His Son into the world to condemn the world, but that the world through Him might be saved" (John 3:16-17). When we hear the voice of our Good Shepherd, we answer His call.

The Good Shepherd dies for His sheep

"I am the good shepherd. The good shepherd gives His life for the sheep" (John 10:11). Is it really likely that a shepherd, a man, a human being, would actually give his life for a sheep? Is the bond between shepherd and sheep that strong? Maybe not, but consider this.

When Jesus described the shepherd in the parable of the ninety and nine, the shepherd put the majority of the sheep in a safe place and went into the wilderness to find the lost sheep. While we naturally concentrate on the lost sheep in the dangers of the wilderness, we dare not forget that this shepherd could have stayed in the safe place with the majority, but he went into harm's way to look for the minority. Just how dangerous could it have been? Well, why do you think they call it the wilderness?

Sheep have a habit of eating grass in the craziest places. If there is a safe, grassy meadow far from the edge of a cliff, you won't find sheep there. They'll be on the edge, right where the danger is. And somehow sheep are masters of the art of nibbling themselves lost.

Once when I was riding on horseback down into the rose-red city of Petra in Jordan, I saw something I will never forget. I pulled up on my horse, stopped to make sure my eyes were really seeing what I thought they were seeing, and even took a couple of pictures. I saw a man lowering himself on a rope from a cliff at least two hundred feet above me.

About thirty feet below the summit there was a tiny ledge. On that ledge was a single, helpless sheep. The man was risking his life to retrieve one endangered sheep. Who said a man wouldn't enter harm's way to rescue a lost sheep?

But what Jesus did was infinitely more valuable. While the Jordanian shepherd risked his life, Jesus gave up His life. He voluntarily took our sin upon Himself, voluntarily suffered the hideous torture of the cross, and voluntarily died in our place. He didn't come risking His life on a rescue mission; He came to give His life on that mission. When He left heaven, He knew He would die before He returned. And now we know too. "Knowing that you were not redeemed with corruptible things, like silver or gold . . . but with the precious blood of Christ, as of a lamb without blemish and without spot" (1 Peter 1:18-19).

The ultimate sacrifice of Christ's life was His death. "For when we were still without strength, in due time Christ died for the ungodly. For scarcely for a righteous man will one die; yet perhaps for a good man someone would even dare to die. But God demonstrates His own love toward us, in that while we were still sinners, Christ died for us" (Rom. 5:6-8).

Was Jesus different as the Good Shepherd from all those who went before Him? Absolutely. None of them would die for their sheep. They were in it only for the money. Jesus was in it for the love. His death was sufficient to redeem us. Only Jesus gave His life for your sins. Only in Him will you find the sufficiency of the Good Shepherd.

The Good Shepherd secures His sheep

The "I AM" God is eternally capable of keeping His sheep safe. This is His promise: "My sheep hear My voice, and I know them, and they follow Me. And I give them eternal life, and they shall never perish; neither shall anyone snatch them out of my hand" (John 10:27-28).

It was the death of our Good Shepherd that gave us eternal life, but it is His eternality that guarantees it. He is the "I AM" God, preexistent and eternal. It is because the Sovereign Savior is not bound by time that He can guarantee our eternal life. Just as He chose us in Him before the foundation of the world (Eph. 1:4) and redeemed us through His blood, forgiving our sins (v. 7), He also gave us an eternal inheritance (v. 11) and the Holy Spirit as a divine guarantee of that inheritance (v. 14). That's sufficiency. That's security.

What the Good Shepherd said in John 10:28 is a strong affirmation of our security. The original language says, "They will indeed not ever perish." The Greek can't say it much stronger than that. As His sheep, our security is not found in ourselves (who in his right mind would entrust security to a sheep?). Our security is found in the ability of the Good Shepherd to defend and preserve His flock. We are in the strong hand of the Sovereign Savior, the eternal "I AM" God. Not only can we not slip from His hand, but we cannot be snatched from His hand either.

The care of the Good Shepherd for His sheep is a thing of beauty. The Good Shepherd knows His sheep, knows them lovingly and intimately. He calls His sheep, calls them softly and tenderly. He died for His sheep, died for them purposefully and sacrificially. He secures His sheep, secures them strongly and eternally. In the "I AM" God, you'll find everything you need for this life and the next. He is sufficient for all things.

What does the Good Shepherd mean to you?

When the sheep hear the voice of their shepherd, magical things happen. Watch a flock of sheep and their shepherd for even a short time and you can witness that magic. The same happens when the Good Shepherd's sheep hear His voice. Some people are more independent than sheep and they don't always respond to the Good Shepherd in the same way that simple sheep respond to their shepherd.

When you hear the Good Shepherd's voice, what are some ways you should respond? How will you show the Good Shepherd that you find in Him your complete sufficiency? Here's how.

Sheep reciprocate the shepherd's love

We dare not miss the reciprocal quality of the relationship between the Good Shepherd and His sheep. Jesus said, "I am the good shepherd; and I know My sheep, and am known by My own" (v. 14). Notice that second "and." It makes all the difference in a relationship. It takes two to have a relationship. One can love, but it takes two in love to reciprocate a relationship.

My wife, Linda, and I were married in 1965. We dated for almost five years before we were married. She was beautiful, the type of girl everybody enjoyed being around. And I, well, the words "ugly duckling" come to mind. I spotted her in our church youth group and knew she was the one for me. But my love alone for her would never have carried our relationship all these years. She had to reciprocate my love; she had to love me too. Praise God, one day she began to feel drawn to me. Our love grew and flourished. When we said, "Till death do us part," we both meant it. The rest is history.

God's love was somewhat different. He loved us unconditionally. He loved us initially. He loved us wholly. And yet we were the ugly duck-lings. We didn't have to win His love; He loved us first. There was every reason for us to love Him, but why would He love us? Yet He did, and we responded to His love. "In this is love, not that we loved God, but that He loved us and sent His Son to be the propitiation for our sins" (1 John 4:10).

We love the Good Shepherd because the Good Shepherd loves us. We know the Good Shepherd because the Good Shepherd knows us. Sheep love their shepherd because their shepherd loves them. It seems to me that loving the sheep is the hard part, not loving the shepherd. If you have found your sufficiency in the Good Shepherd, tell Him you love Him. I don't think He ever tires of hearing it. Better still, show Him. I know He never tires of seeing it.

Sheep relish to hear the shepherd's voice

There are certain advantages to being the Bible teacher for an inter-national media ministry. For one, my voice is recognizable to some peo-ple all over the world. Often I have folks come up to me and say, "I did-n't recognize your face, but I couldn't mistake that voice." Once a woman rushed up to me after a meeting, shook my hand vociferously and said, "It's so good to put a voice and a face together." Then she said, "You have a great voice!" I assume that was a compliment.

About six months after my first granddaughter, Whitney, was born, my daughter Tracy called me from her home in New York State. I an-swered the phone in my study and heard Tracy sobbing. I tried to calm her down; I repeatedly asked, "Tracy, what's the matter?" All I could get out of her was, "Whitney, Whitney." I was terrified. What had happened to Whitney? Why was my daughter having such a difficult time getting it out?

Finally, after Tracy calmed down, she said, "You live so far from us. I'm afraid Whitney is going to grow up and not even know her grandfather's voice." In a typical fatherly response that demonstrated more good sense than compassion, I said, "Tracy, turn on the radio."

My grandchildren don't often get to see their "Papa," but they delight in hearing his voice, even if it's only on the telephone, or in my case on radio or other media. Grandchildren are a lot like sheep. Sheep relish in hearing the voice of their shepherd. That comes from experiencing his love and finding everything they need in him.

How about you? Do you relish hearing the voice of the Good Shepherd? Do you find what He said, written in His Word, a source of enjoyment? Or has it been awhile since you heard His voice? Have you nibbled away from Him and failed to enjoy His presence? Sheep enjoy hearing their master's voice, but when they nibble too far from the shepherd, they find him unbearable and unenjoyable. How about you?

Sheep respond to the shepherd's call

As I learned when my Bedouin friend "clicked" his sheep into that cave with me, sheep not only reciprocate love to their shepherd and relish in hearing his voice, but they also respond to that voice. We sheep of God's fold have some things to learn from the sheep of the Bedouin's fold.

We respond to the Good Shepherd's call to salvation when we feel the prompting of the Holy Spirit and respond in faith. But that's only the beginning of a lifelong relationship with the Good Shepherd. We also respond to His call for intimacy. He wants us to enter the fold with Him, to enjoy the warmth of His presence. It must break the Good Shepherd's heart when we prefer to skip the fold rather than be faithful in attending church.

But there's even more than that. The Good Shepherd gave His life for His sheep, and He calls us to demonstrate that same kind of willingness in behalf of others. "I am the good shepherd . . . and I lay down My life for the sheep. . . . Greater love has no one than this, than to lay down one's life for his friends. You are My friends if you do whatever I command you" (John 10:14-15; 15:13-14).

Perhaps the Good Shepherd will not ask you to lay down your life; perhaps He will. What He does expect is that every sheep of His fold will respond to His call to serve Him in the way the "I AM" God deems appropriate. What does that mean for you?

Find meaning in life by enjoying the fact the Good Shepherd knows you by name. Find joy in life by walking in close proximity to the Good Shepherd. Find intimacy in life by delighting in the presence of the Good Shepherd in the shelter and safety of His sheepfold. Find purpose in life by serving the Good Shepherd when He calls your name.

If you find your sufficiency in the Good Shepherd, the idea of being called a sheep will become infinitely more attractive. After all, there's something incredibly comforting in knowing you are a lamb loved by the Good Shepherd.

> Fear not, O little flock upon the storm-swept hill;
> The Shepherd knows thy path, He guides thy footsteps still.
> His nail-pierced hand will keep and hold thee safe and fast;
> Fear not, O little flock, He'll bring thee home at last.
>
> — Adelaide A. Pollard

"I am the Door; let Me open for you!"

CHAPTER 5

THE DOOR

"I am the door. If anyone enters by Me, he will be saved, and will go in and out and find pasture."
JOHN 10:9

I have always been amazed at how profound the Lord Jesus was in His simplicity. He didn't talk about things that were farfetched or fanciful. His speech was plain, down-to-earth, understandable.

The Master wasn't talking for the sake of the intellectual or the scholar, but for the ordinary person. He talked about common things that everyone knew. And yet He employed these common things to impart profound eternal and spiritual truths. Nowhere is this better illustrated than in His statement "I am the door."

Everybody knows what a door is. Doors come in so many varieties. There are front doors, back doors, side doors, closet doors, barn doors, church doors, screen doors, storm doors and more. Some doors are large, like the ones on the Vehicle Assembly Building at Cape Canaveral, Florida (460 feet high). Some are small, like the ones to your economy rental car. Some are plain; others, highly decorated. There are French doors, Dutch doors and double doors.

Doors have even given rise to a whole vocation. Who hasn't heard of a door-to-door salesman? And doors have lent their name to a host of door-related items; e.g., door jambs, doorknobs, doorkeepers, door prizes, door stops and doorbells. If you get bored, go next door and chat with your neighbor. Or, if that doesn't work, you can even go hiking in the great outdoors. The possibilities are endless.

Regardless of what we call them, the function of doors is limited. Sure, you can hang things on them, like Christmas wreaths or "Welcome to our Home" signs, but that's decorative, not functional. As far as I can determine, the function of a door is fourfold. A door is designed to permit entry, to permit exit, or to prohibit entry or prohibit exit. That's it. That's all doors do. They let people in and out or they keep people from going in and out.

"Come in, the door's open."

"Close the door behind you."

"As your president, I will have an open-door policy."

"Can't you see my door's closed? Leave me alone!"

Often we talk about going through the door. "The easiest way to get out of here is just to go through that door marked 'Exit'; it'll lead you out." Actually, we mean to say *doorway* when we say door. We don't really go through the door. The only person I know who did that was the Lord Jesus (John 20:19). When the door is open, we go through the doorway. When it is closed we don't.

When the "I AM" God said, "I am the door," everybody knew what He meant. But when He continued, "If anyone enters by Me, he will be saved," that needed further clarification. Let's think about the four functions of a door. Maybe they will give us some insight into the sufficiency of Jesus to be the Door for us.

A door permits entry

Keep Jesus' words in context as you think about them. He described Himself as the Good Shepherd, the one who gave His life for the sheep. As He did, He interrupted that thought to say, "I am the door of the sheep" (John 10:7). By that He meant, "When the sheep enter the sheepfold, I am the one through whom they enter," or more appropriately, "I am the one who permits their entry." Jesus is the Door.

To be the door *of* the sheep means being the door for the sheep. If the sheep are to have access to the sheepfold, they have to come in by way of the door. Jesus is the Door for the sheep to enter the fold.

Since most of us are not shepherds, perhaps this is a good time to describe the sheepfold. It will help us to understand why it's important that Jesus is the Door.

In villages and towns, where numerous flocks were brought together, large communal sheepfolds were built. William Barclay observed that these provided a place "where all the village flocks were sheltered when they returned home at night. These folds were protected by a strong door of which only the guardian of the door held the key."[1] Jesus was referring to this type of sheepfold in John 10:2-3.

But out in the field, individual sheepfolds were built by the shepherds to insure the safety of their sheep. Since there was an abundance of stones in Israel (and still is), shepherds would choose small, round rocks—smaller than a soccer ball—and pile them on top of one another, building a crude defense. Sometimes the pens were rectangular and large enough to accommodate hundreds of sheep. Often, however, they were much smaller, circular and capable of handling only a couple of dozen sheep. You can still see such sheepfolds in the fields of Israel today. In fact, there's one in the Kidron Valley, just northeast of the city wall of Old Jerusalem.

The rock walls of the sheepfold were not high, just high enough to keep the sheep in and animals out. Thieves and robbers, however, conceivably could climb the walls and steal some sheep. Often the shepherds would place thorns on top the walls to prevent theft.

Sheepfolds were built in various sizes and shapes, but all folds had one thing in common. They had only one door. If sheep were to get into the fold, there was only one way to do it. They had to go through the doorway.

The sheepfold represents safety, shelter, strength, survival, security, sufficiency. It represents the church for us sheep while still on earth and glory for us sheep when we all get to heaven. What an incredible lesson Jesus taught us. Regardless of the sheep, the variety, the size, the amount, there was only one way to get into the fold—through Jesus. He is the only Door. In fact, the way He said, "I am the door," is emphatic in the original language. We could translate it, "I *alone* am the door of the sheep." There is no other.

Do you remember singing this little song in Sunday school when you were a kid? "One door and only one, and yet its sides are two. Inside and outside on which side are you? One door and only one and yet its sides are two. I'm on the inside, on which side are you?"

As an adult, do you appreciate the truth of that children's chorus? Jesus is the Door to heaven. He is the Door to eternal life. He is the only Door to God. But there are two sides to that Door. If you've trusted Jesus as Savior and used His sacrifice at Calvary to gain access through the single Door to heaven, you are on the inside. But if you have decided you don't need a Savior or you don't want to submit yourself to the Savior, you are on the outside, out in the cold, out in the world, out in the dark.

One door . . . and only one! "If anyone enters by Me," Jesus said, "he will be saved" (John 10:9). I know which side of the Door I'm on; on which side are you?

A door permits exit

But the "I AM" God intended much more when He said He is the Door. He also meant that once we have entered through Him, the Door to salvation, He is also the Door to our sustenance.

Jesus admits entrance to us for the shelter and safety of the sheepfold. He is not only the head of the Church; He is the Door to the church. But once we have entered the Body, His Church, by the Door of salvation, it is not the will of Jesus that we isolate ourselves from the world outside. The sheep did not spend their life in the sheepfold; they spent most of it in the field. They came to the fold at night or in times of danger.

It's easy to understand why the sheep would like it in the sheepfold. The outside world was filled with threats, challenges and death. Inside they were safe. Outside were lions, wolves, jackals, wild dogs, panthers, leopards, bears and hyenas. The Holy Land teems with wildlife, even today. In traveling around Israel, I have often seen foxes, ibex and wolves. For sheep, the safest place was in the fold. When they left the fold, they left the place of security.

The Bible frequently refers to those who threaten our Christian lives in terms of wild animals. "Beware of dogs, beware of evil workers" (Phil. 3:2). "Beware of false prophets, who come to you in sheep's clothing, but inwardly they are ravenous wolves" (Matt. 7:15). "Be sober, be vigilant; because your adversary the devil walks about like a roaring lion, seeking whom he may devour" (1 Pet. 5:8). It's easy to see why Christians today would want to stay in the comfort and safety of the church rather than venture out into the hazards and intimidations of the world.

But the same Door who gave us access to the security of the Church gives us access to the opportunities of the world. It is not in the smallness of the church that we find our pasture land but in the expansiveness of the world. Jesus, the Door, gives us a way to exit the sheepfold to get to the primary pasture lands, which are so necessary to our development.

Sheep need to run and grow, stretch their legs and graze. They need the wide-open spaces to do that. Their growth is not in the pen but on the hillsides of Judea. They develop their muscles by interaction with the harsh environment of the outside, not by inactivity in the protected environment inside the sheepfold. Climbing the rocky, dangerous overhangs of the Judean wilderness is good for the sheep.

The same is true for us Christians. We can't spend all our time in the fellowship of the local church. As sheep have to leave the sheepfold to grow, so do we. Growth comes with exercise, with stretching our legs, arms and minds. Growth comes with challenge, with difficulty, with making what we have heard from others in the church our very own in the world.

When you test what you believe against what you experience in the world, you know whether or not the truths you hold are valuable, believable and workable. Your friends and family will do as much to help you grow as your pastor and Bible study leader will. As they challenge your beliefs, as they test your patience, they stretch you, strengthen you and help you to mature spiritually.

But that's not all. There is another reason why the Door gives His sheep exit to the world. Jesus said, "Behold, I send you out as sheep in the midst of wolves. Therefore be wise as serpents and harmless as doves" (Matt. 10:16).

Jesus had a marvelously sympathetic heart. He saw people as living unhappily and precariously on a windswept hillside, foraging for food, lost, hopeless and alone. By nature these people are wolves, eager to gobble up His sheep. But these people also need the Savior, and the way to get people close to the Savior is to get them close to His sheep. So Jesus sends us out into the wolf-filled world and tells us to be as crafty as serpents, but as innocent as little doves.

Someone has estimated that it's 750,000 miles long, reaches around the earth 30 times and grows 20 miles longer each day. Do you know what it is? The line of people who are without Christ. We go out of the fold because the world needs us. It needs a Savior, and the Good Shepherd, the Door of the sheep, is the only Savior this world will ever have. That makes the Door's ability to give us entrance and give us exit all the more important.

Christians don't live exclusively in the world, nor do we live exclusively within the church. We come to church in order to worship the Lord, praise His name, get our spiritual batteries charged, learn the Word and, in general, get prepared to have the Door swing the other way and send us out into the world. He wouldn't send us out among the wolves if they didn't need a Savior or if there was any other way to accomplish His will.

When Jesus said, "I am the door of the sheep" (John 10:7), He meant both "I am the door to the sheep" (to enter the safety and security of the sheepfold) and "I am the door *for* the sheep" (to enter the world of hurting and needy people). The Door swings both ways. Are you going in and out to find pasture? Are you using the outward swing as well as the inward swing? If not, the Door is only partially beneficial to you—and of little benefit to the world.

Quakers are known for their "Quiet Meeting." This is a time when everyone sits quietly until the Spirit moves someone to speak. When a man who was not a Quaker visited his first "Quiet Meeting," he sat still for what seemed an interminably long time. Then the visitor whispered to his Quaker friend, "When does the service start?" His neighbor replied, "The service begins just after the meeting ends."

We can't stay inside the church and enjoy the fellowship if our hearts are breaking for a lost world. Jesus' heart was broken; that's why He came to earth. When our heart beats with His, it will be broken for those outside the fold. Our service begins as soon as the church meeting ends.

While a door permitting entry and exit is important, there's a whole other function to a door that is equally important. A door also prohibits entry and exit. That can be a pretty comforting thought as well. Have you seen who's outside of your door lately?

A door prohibits entry

You hear a knock at the door or the doorbell rings. You dutifully go to the door, peep through that little peephole and see a face peeping back at you. Do you recognize it? You know that face. Do you let him in? It's the Welcome Wagon, Pastor Smith, the Publisher's Clearing House crew, an insurance salesman, your son-in-law. Yes or no? Do you let him in? One thing's for sure; if you don't open the door, you don't let anyone in.

Doors are as useful to bar entry as the are to admit entry. Remember, we don't go through the door; we go through the doorway. If the door is closed, we don't even do that.

Jesus is the Door of the sheep. When those outside of the Door are a threat to the welfare of the sheep, they must go through Jesus before they can enter the fold. I find that delightfully encouraging, don't you?

Before cancer can get to you, it must go through Jesus and be admitted. Before financial disaster can get to you, it must go through Jesus and be allowed to enter. Before health and wealth can enter your life, they must pass through the Jesus Door. He can allow them to enter or He can keep them out.

Does that mean that whatever comes into my life has to pass the approval of Jesus Christ? It certainly does. When the noted preacher Samuel Chadwick was a boy, he often went to the local blacksmith shop to watch the smithy work. Chadwick remembered how the blacksmith would take a huge piece of iron and place it in the fire with tongs. Then he would work the bellows to make it white-hot. After removing the iron from the fire and laying it upon the anvil, the blacksmith would take a small hammer and begin to tap on the iron. No sooner would the smithy tap the iron with the small hammer than a big man on the other side of the anvil would come crashing down hard with a large sledge hammer, hitting the iron exactly in the same spot the blacksmith had just tapped. Young Chadwick inquisitively commented, "You don't do much good with that little hammer, do you?" The gentile blacksmith laughed and replied, "No, my boy, I don't. But I show that big fellow where to hit."

Nobody hits you unless the "I AM" God gives permission. Nothing comes into your life unless the divine Blacksmith says it's okay. Everything and everybody who enters the sheepfold must go through the one door. If they don't, they are but a thief and a robber and are not legitimate influences in your life. Everything Jesus allows into your life, whether you see it as good or bad, He has admitted to mold and shape your life according to His divine plan.

Is it possible that Jesus doesn't want you to be wealthy? Very possible. Jesus wants you to be complete, mature, filled with joy and happy in Him. Who says wealth will make you happy? (I know, you'd like to try.) Some of the wealthiest people in the world are the unhappiest people.

God will allow only what He wants you to have to pass through the Door.

Jesus restricts entrance to our lives in other ways as well. He keeps condemnation that results from sin from entering our lives. "There is therefore now no condemnation to those who are in Christ Jesus" (Rom. 8:1). If someone knocks at your door and says, "Hey, you! You're going to stand before the judicial bar of God one day and be eternally damned because of your sins," don't bother to defend yourself. Jesus Himself will say, "Hit the road, Jack. I died for the person behind that Door. No guilt or condemnation can be laid on them because they are cleansed by my blood, justified and declared righteous before My Heavenly Father." It's nice having that kind of Door screening those on our front porch and forbidding entry to all He chooses.

Don't worry about temptation either. Oh, it will knock at your door, but it doesn't have to get inside. "No temptation has overtaken you except such as is common to man; but God is faithful, who will not allow you to be tempted beyond what you are able, but with the temptation will also make the way of escape, that you may be able to bear it" (1 Cor. 10:13). Let the Door slam in the face of temptation.

And what about false teachers and those new devious doctrines? They'll come to your door too! But don't worry. "Whoever transgresses and does not abide in the doctrine of Christ does not have God. He who abides in the doctrine of Christ has both the Father and the Son. If anyone comes to you and does not bring this doctrine, do not receive him into your house nor greet him; for he who greets him shares in his evil deeds" (2 John 9-11).

It's really quite easy to determine if someone is peddling a false doctrine when they come to your door. If they propose a doctrine of God that does not include Jesus as equal with the Father and the Holy Spirit, there's no question. They do not have God.

It doesn't matter how pleasant they are, how well dressed or well mannered they are. It doesn't make any difference what they call themselves or what they want to give you. When they approach your door, ask them if they believe Jesus Christ is God as much as Jehovah is God, and if they hesitate a millisecond before responding, they do not have God. The door remains closed. Jesus is the Door and He best knows when to close the door to our sheepfold.

When Jesus shuts Himself to prohibit someone's entrance into your life, whether a friend, someone you're falling in love with or an energetic, slick TV preacher, don't try to pry that door open. That's when it's important to remember that one of the major functions of a door is to keep people out. Who better to determine who gets in and who stays out than the Door? "I am the door of the sheep."

Linda and I climbed aboard the minibus and began the journey out from Beijing. The twisting road took us to one of the great manmade structures on earth. Stretching 1,800 miles over deserts, plains and mountains, the Great Wall of China was built to keep out barbarians. Standing on that imposing wall, we had to wonder why it failed, but it did. No manmade innovation can keep out the barbarians. Only Jesus is sufficient to do that.

A door prohibits exit

When I was a boy growing up in western Pennsylvania, I remember not so fondly having to feed the chickens. We raised about 60,000 chickens a year, and I remember a string of nights when there was trouble in the chicken house. The chickens were restless, uneasy, making a lot of noise. We knew some animal was menacing them, but we didn't know what, so we put a monitor in the hen house to listen in on the alarmed chickens.

It wasn't very stimulating conversation, but one night there was a big ruckus. My father was not at home and he felt I was too young to use the shotgun, so I decided to go after the critter with a bow and arrow. Only one problem. My bow wasn't strung. Ingenious young lad that I was (but not too bright), I cut a length of cord from the Venetian blind in the living room window (my mother still remembers, and won't let me forget), strung my bow and went stalking for the intruder. I saw him slinking along the top of the chicken house, and with one arrow I brought down one of the biggest raccoons I have ever seen.

Satan is like a big raccoon. I even wonder if he doesn't look a little like a bandit. It is Satan's great quest to be able to steal some sheep from the Lord's sheepfold. He tries every way he can. He uses lies, deceit, trickery, chicanery, subtle attacks, even frontal attacks. He tries, but he doesn't succeed. The reason? The Door. When the sheep are in the fold and the Door is closed, the devil doesn't have the power to pry it open.

Did you notice in this story that the chapter begins with Jesus saying, "Most assuredly, I say to you, he who does not enter the sheepfold by the door, but climbs up some other way, the same is a thief and a robber" (John 10:1)? Is it possible for someone to get into the sheepfold without coming through the door? Not legitimately, but there are always those who try to climb over the top because they know the Door will not give them entrance.

Take note of what Jesus called such people: a thief and a robber. Anyone who would climb over the rock wall of the sheepfold to get to the sheep is nothing but a common criminal. But while Jesus said they climb over the wall to get to the sheep, did you notice what He didn't say? He didn't say they were able to steal any sheep. It's the attempt that makes a thief a thief, not his success. There are lots of prisoners sitting in a cell today for *attempted* robbery.

No sheep were ever stolen from Jesus' fold. How do I know this? Verses 7 and 8 say, "Most assuredly, I say to you, I am the door of the sheep. All who ever came before Me are thieves and robbers, *but the sheep did not hear them*" (italics mine). These weren't deaf sheep; they just couldn't be led out of the sheepfold by the voice of a robber. Why? The Door wouldn't let them out! The Lord Jesus prevents us from recognizing the voice of any shepherd but Him, our own Good Shepherd.

If remaining in the security of the sheepfold were up to me, I'd be worried about my chances of success. But it's not up to me. What keeps me in is not my own ingenuity, my own intelligence or my own will. What keeps me in the fold is the fact that the Door is closed. I'm in the sheepfold and I can't get out.

One of the strongest affirmations for the security of the believer is given by Jesus in this passage. "My sheep hear My voice, and I know them, and they follow Me. And I give them eternal life, and they shall never perish; neither shall anyone snatch them out of My hand. My Father, who has given them to Me, is greater than all; and no one is able to snatch them out of My Father's hand" (John 10:27-29).

The sheep in the sheepfold belong to the Good Shepherd. He not only tends them while they are out in the world grazing, protecting them and leading them back to the safety of the sheepfold, but He is the Door who keeps them securely inside the fold. The Heavenly Father gave the Shepherd His sheep—that's you and I and everyone who is born again. We have followed the Good Shepherd in faith. In return, He has given us eternal life. Absolutely no one can crash through the Door and steal the Shepherd's sheep. Not Satan. Not the cults. No one. Sheep can stray, but they cannot be stolen.

What's more, the Heavenly Father also lends a hand. No one can take the Christian out of the Savior's hand. But His Father, who is greater than all, also places His hand around the Savior's hand. Now you have two-fisted security. And where are you? In the tight grip of the Savior's hand, which is in the tight grip of the Father's hand.

No one can take you out of Jesus' fold. No one. God is greater than everyone and every thing. AIDS can't take salvation from you. Failure can't do it. Satan can't snatch you out of the Father's hand. Cancer can't let you slip through His fingers. You're there, tightly held both by the eternal "I AM" Father and the eternal "I AM" Son.

One of the greatest functions of any door is to keep what's out out, and to keep what's in in. Do you see why it's so relevant in your life that Jesus said, "I am the door of the sheep"?

What does the Door mean to you?

The applications to your life and mine are evident. All that you expect a door to do, Jesus does for you. He lets you into the fold—His church now and heaven later. He lets you out to do His work in the world. He keeps the door closed to all the quacks and charlatans of this world. But He also keeps the door closed so that those on the inside are not lost to those on the outside. But specifically, what does Jesus as the Door mean to you? Think about these things.

Jesus is the only true Door to God. When you gain access through Him, you have gained legitimate access to God.

We have passwords on our computers to keep others from accessing our files. They are somewhat like a secret door. The password to heaven, to forgiveness for your sins, to a fulfilling life with God is J-E-S-U-S. He is the only legitimate door and when you trust Him, you gain entrance to the heart of God.

With all the doors that lead to nowhere (or worse) in this life, isn't it grand to have gained access to God through the legitimate Door? It gives you a sense of belonging, a sense of satisfaction, a sense of security.

Loved with everlasting love, led by grace that love to know;
Spirit, breathing from above, Thou hast taught me it is so!
Oh, this full and perfect peace! Oh, this transport all divine!
In a love which cannot cease, I am His, and He is mine.

— George W. Robinson

Because you have discovered Jesus to be the only true Door to God, you don't have to worry about what's behind all the other doors.

Remember the game show *Let's Make a Deal?* Can't you hear Monty Hall say, "Let's see what's behind door number three"? That's okay for a game show, but life shouldn't be like that. Would you trust your eternal destiny to chance? Once you have trusted Jesus, you don't have to take whatever is behind all those other doors.

What might be behind the other doors? Anything and everything that is not behind the Door. Behind one door may be pleasure, hedonism, money and sex. But if it doesn't lead to God and heaven, it's the wrong choice. Behind another door may be a dark hallway that is the fast track to eternal hell, separation from God forever. That's not the door for you. Only Jesus is the Door to God. Only He is sufficient to give you access to heaven. Only Jesus provides the security and safety you need to live a life of confidence and peace. Aren't you glad you have the information from God's Word to make the right choice? That's what having Jesus as the Door means to the Christian—living happily with the right choice.

Knowing that Jesus is the true Door gives you confidence to expose every false door.

Just think of all the lovely, highly decorated doors that lead to nowhere, certainly not to heaven. There's the door of good deeds. Many have knocked at that door without success. Good deeds may lead to a feeling of fulfillment and satisfaction, but they don't lead to sufficiency in Christ. And there's the door of moral character. It's commendable, but it's not salvation. There are lots of people trapped in cults who have fine moral character, but they don't have passage by the Door.

What about the door of sincerity? Sincerely hoping you will get to heaven will never get you there. Lots of people are sincere, but they are sincerely wrong because they have chosen the wrong door. You need a Savior; you need the right Door. And then there's keeping the Ten Commandments. How many folks have scraped their knuckles knocking on that door, but they are still on the outside? The Ten Commandments represent God's moral code, but they do not present God's grace in opening the Door to salvation. The door of church membership has thwarted its share of people who wanted to get into the fold. But joining a church is not at all like being born again. One places you in an organization; the other relates you to a living organism—the Body of Christ.

No, we must keep coming back to that little chorus you learned as a child in Sunday school. "One door and only one, and yet its sides are two. I'm on the inside, on which side are you?"

There is only one door to forgiveness by God. There is only one door to eternal life in heaven. There is only one door to the security of the Good Shepherd's fold. There is only one person sufficient to be that Door. He is Jesus. Trust His Word.

The "I AM God" said, "I am the door of the sheep." If you haven't come by that Door, you haven't come to God. But if you have, all that the door means to the sheep in the fold, Jesus the Door means to you. What a reassuring thought!

"*I am the Son of God; let Me inspire you!*"

CHAPTER 6

THE SON OF GOD

"If He called them gods, to whom the word of God came (and the Scripture cannot be broken), do you say of Him whom the Father sanctified and sent into the world, 'You are blaspheming,' because I said, 'I am the Son of God'?"
JOHN 10:35-36

Without question, the "I am" statement of this chapter created the most controversy of them all, especially among the Pharisees. The religious leaders of Israel were always antagonistic toward Jesus. Frankly, He was a huge problem for them. He was articulate, gentle, kind, compassionate, humble and hard working. True, He did hail from Nazareth ("Can anything good come out of Nazareth?"), considered a backwater town in the wild and untamed north country of Galilee. But there was just something about Him, something intangible but real. He seemed so genuine, so good. In fact, He was too good to be true.

In addition to His integrity and character, there were all those miracles. Who ever heard of multiplying five barley loaves and two small fish into a outdoor meal for 5,000 people? It was unthinkable, and yet multitudes claimed to have been there, to have been a part of the world's largest fish fry. And there were the other miracles—the healings, the blind given sight, the lame walking normally again. How could the religious leaders explain all that away? Indeed, Jesus was a problem for them.

And most damaging for the Pharisees were the reports of people being raised from the dead. Now that can't happen. Maybe these Galileans were just sticking together, but that widow from Nain was telling everyone that Jesus raised her son from the dead (Luke 7:14-15). She must have been crazy, so they thought. Maybe a simple village woman could be discounted, but there was also Jairus. He claimed Jesus brought to life his 12-year-old daughter. He was a little more difficult to dismiss summarily because he was the ruler of a synagogue. Surely Jairus was a credible witness.

A festive occasion for a confrontation

These religious leaders had confronted Jesus many times before. Two months prior to this they challenged Him in the temple at the Feast of Tabernacles (John 7:2). That was October. Now it was December. Winter had come. The rains had begun to fall. It was cold and wet as Jesus made His way to the temple. To avoid the rain He walked under the colonnaded portico on the temple's east side. It was popularly known as Solomon's porch.

While the air was cold and damp, it was nevertheless a festive time. This was the eighth day and the Feast of Dedication was coming to an end. This feast is still celebrated in modern Judaism. Jews call it the Feast of Lights, better known, perhaps, as Hanukkah. Hanukkah commemorates the reconsecration of the temple by Judas Maccabeus in 165 B.C. The temple had been captured and desecrated in 168 B.C. by Antiochus IV, often called Antiochus Epiphanes. To show his disdain for the Jews, Antiochus sacrificed a pig on the altar of God. Nothing could have been more reprehensible to the people of Israel. But when Judas Maccabeus recaptured the temple and reconsecrated it, it was three years to the day after it had been defiled by Antiochus. That date was the twenty-fifth of Kislev—December 25, 165 B.C.

It should have been a delightful occasion in Jerusalem because this was the newest and one of the most joyous feasts of the Jewish calendar. The Jews were in no mood for fun and games, however. The festive air soon turned sour.

Hostile religious leaders challenge the "I AM" God

A slow walk under the colonnade during a cold winter's rain was abruptly interrupted. The religious leaders hated Jesus so much, they were so jealous of His popularity, that they accosted Him in the temple area. John 10:24 says, "Then the Jews surrounded Him and said to Him, 'How long do You keep us in doubt? If You are the Christ, tell us plainly.'"

This was no casual chat. The word John chose to describe how the religious leaders surrounded Jesus (Gr. *kukloo*) means "to close in around" or "to encircle." It's the same word Jesus used when speaking about the end of the age in Luke 21:20: "But when you see Jerusalem surrounded (*kukloo*) by armies, then know that its desolation is near." It's hardly a friendly term. The Pharisees weren't about to let Jesus wriggle out of their sight until they got an answer.

"Don't keep us in suspense," they said. "If you are the Messiah, tell us plainly." What's the problem? Had Jesus not already given them enough proof? Had He not done things that the Jews expected only from their Messiah? A quick check of history says He did.

Read my lips

John 5 records a long monologue where Jesus answered the Jews about making a claim of equality with God by forgiving sin. He told them the Son of God does only what His Father does, and He does it in the same way. As the Father raises the dead and gives them life, the Son does the same. As the Father has eternal life in Himself, so He has granted the Son to have eternal life in Himself. Wait a minute! Did Jesus say that He was equally eternal as the Father? Did He not tell these religious leaders plainly that as the Father was forever God, so the Son of God was forever God? Those are pretty direct claims and awfully hard to misunderstand.

In John 6:29 Jesus said, "This is the work of God, that you believe in Him whom He sent." Now it's obvious He is talking about Himself as the One sent from God. Follow me on this. If it is God's work that these Jews believe in Jesus, what does it mean if they don't believe in Jesus? If it is God's work that the Son was sent from the Father, what does it mean if the Jews don't believe Jesus was sent from the Father? It means that they are not doing God's work. That was more than these pious religious leaders could take.

When the Pharisees jumped all over Jesus in John 8, it was because they accused Him (again) of bearing witness of Himself. But Jesus responded that it was well known among all Jews that their law required a matter to come from the mouth of at least two witnesses before it was judged true and legitimate (Deut. 19:15). Then the "I AM" God had the audacity to say, "I am One who bears witness of Myself, and the Father who sent Me bears witness of Me" (John 8:18). Jesus had two witnesses; He was one and Jehovah was the other. That was enough to curdle the blood of any self-respecting Pharisee. What's more, Jesus went on to say, "You know neither Me nor My Father. If you had known Me, you would have known My Father also" (v. 19). Is that plain enough?

"Don't keep us in suspense," they said. "If you are the Messiah, tell us plainly." He had told them plainly time and again, but He told them what they didn't want to hear, so they didn't listen. In fact, they couldn't listen because their spiritual ears were plugged with religious wax.

Actions speak louder

What's more, Jesus not only told them He was the Messiah, the Son of God, He also showed them. You don't have to strain your brain to remember some of Jesus' actions that spoke volumes about who He was.

He changed the water to wine at the wedding feast of Cana (John 2). That was pretty dramatic. He came to the temple at Jerusalem during Passover, made a whip of cords and drove all the moneychangers out of the temple, overturning their tables (John 2). Did the Pharisees forget about that little incident? The whole village of Sychar in Samaria was talking about the town prostitute whose life had been changed—reversed 180 degrees—when she met Jesus. Hadn't that news filtered south to Jerusalem?

Then there was the nobleman's son who was healed in Cana of Galilee (John 4), and the invalid at the Pool of Bethesda in Jerusalem (John 5). Surely the news of the feeding of the 5,000 spread throughout the whole country (John 6). It's hard to keep something like that quiet. Jesus walked on water, a clever feat by anyone's standards (John 6). And there was that uncomfortable confrontation when the Jews brought the adulterous woman to Jesus and He embarrassed them by causing their trap to backfire on them (John 8). Surely the incident of the blind man whom Jesus healed by putting mud on his eyes was still fresh in their minds (John 9). What was wrong with their memories?

What's the problem?

If these religious leaders did not hear Jesus say He was the Messiah and Son of God, certainly they saw Him prove it by His miraculous and wonderful deeds. But they still didn't know, and we have to ask why. Why were they so dull when it came to understanding what Jesus said?

THE SON OF GOD

The "I AM" God had the answer. He said to them, "I told you, and you do not believe. The works that I do in My Father's name, they bear witness of Me. But you do not believe, because you are not of My sheep, as I said to you. My sheep hear My voice, and I know them, and they follow Me" (John 10:25-27).

The problem was not with Jesus' words or His deeds. The problem was with the Jewish leaders' hearts. Jesus did more than enough to announce and demonstrate that He is the Son of God, but they did not believe what they heard nor did they trust what they saw.

These Pharisees were probably still smarting from Jesus' inference at the beginning of John 10 that they were thieves and robbers. Likely they took offense to His reference to a hireling, someone who was in the shepherding business just for the money. The standard of ethics employed by these phony religious teachers was always suspect.

But the real stinger was when the "I AM" God said that the real sheep of God, the real people of God, were the ones who heard His voice and followed Him. The religious leaders were quite familiar with the concept of Israel being the sheep of God (Ps. 78:52; 95:7; 100:3; Jer. 50:17), but they had failed to heed God's warning about the faithless shepherds who had destroyed His sheep (Jer. 23:1; 50:6). Jesus was claiming that an allegiance to the God of Israel required an allegiance to the Good Shepherd of Israel.

That must have made the Pharisees turn green. You can almost hear them grinding their teeth. Could anything be said worse than that? Hold onto your hat. Jesus was about to drop the real bombshell on them.

I and the Father are one

When Jesus made the astounding statement "I and My Father are one" (John 10:30), what did He mean? The Savior was not affirming that the Father and He are the same person. They aren't. In fact, to distinguish between the Father and Himself is to assert there are two persons here, not one. The verb also indicates this; the clause literally reads "I and the Father, we are one." The two persons never become one, so Jesus doesn't say, "We are one person." He says, "We are one."

Bible scholar and prolific author William Hendricksen says of this passage, "Note how carefully both the diversity of the persons and the unity of the essence is expressed here. Jesus says, 'I and the Father.' Hence, he clearly speaks about two persons. And this plurality is shown also by the verb (one word in Greek) "we-are" (*esmen*). These two persons never become one person."[1] Edwin A. Blum adds, "The Son and the Father are two Persons in the Trinity. This is confirmed here by the fact that the word 'One' is neuter."[2]

The Father and Son are one in essence. They are the same sum and substance. They have the same nature (Phil. 2:6; Col. 2:9). Whatever it takes to make the essence of God, the Father and Son both possess it. They are identical with regard to their desire to save the sheep. They are of absolutely identical wills. This is why the "I AM" God of John can claim equality with the "I AM" God of Exodus.

Jesus' claim was the straw that broke the camel's back. John 10:31 records, "Then the Jews took up stones again to stone Him." The word *again* implies they had done this before. In fact they had, when He said, "Before Abraham was, I AM" (John 8:59). But where did they get the stones? They were in the temple area, under Solomon's porch. There would be no stones there.

There are two possibilities. Perhaps they ran from Jesus' presence, fetched some stones from the outside and returned to stone Him. On the other hand, they may have brought the stones with them when they deliberately encircled Jesus to force an answer from Him. I believe this is more likely. The verb John chose implies they brought the stones with them. The word means "to bear" or "to carry." It's the same word used in John 19:17, where, speaking of the crucified Lord, John said, "He, bearing His cross, went out to a place called the Place of a Skull, which is called in Hebrew, Golgotha."

These Jews came "loaded for bear." They were ready to stone Jesus, regardless of His response to their question. Ironic, isn't it? They *bore* stones to kill the Lord of Glory. He *bore* a rugged cross to die for their sins. I never quite get over that thought!

Jesus' brilliant defense of His deity

When Jesus inquired for which of His good works these religious bigots were about to stone Him, they exposed their true feelings. The root of their complaint against Jesus was not His life or works; their complaint was against His person. They snarled, "You, being a Man, make Yourself God" (v. 33).

How would Jesus defend Himself against such a charge? In a word, brilliantly. He asked His religious persecutors, "Is it not written in your law, 'I said "You are gods"'?"

In defense of His words and actions Jesus appealed to the one unalterable constant in Jewish life—the Law. Who of the religious leaders would dare argue with the Law? Normally "the Law" refers to the Pentateuch, the first five books of Moses. But in the broader context, the Law is the Old Testament. Jesus was actually quoting from the Psalms (Ps. 82:6).

In the Jews own "law" God is spoken of as the true Judge (Ps. 82:1, 8) and those men who were appointed as judges were failing to provide true judgment for God (vv. 2-7). The word *gods* in Psalm 82:1 and 6 refers to these human judges. It refers to their superior position among men. Were these judges actually gods? Of course not. They were humans, not gods. But the Bible clearly refers to them in the context of their position before men. It's something like the "lords" of the Houses of Parliament in Great Britain.

In November 1997, a 19-year-old English nanny, Louise Woodward, was convicted by a jury of second-degree murder and sentenced to life imprisonment. The judge in the trial, Massachusetts Superior Court Judge Hiller Zobel, stepped in, however, and reduced the conviction to manslaughter and then reduced her punishment to time served, the nine months she had spent in prison awaiting her trial. The law is "inflexible, inexorable and deaf," Judge Zobel said. By this he meant this decision was his and his alone. Judge Zobel became a "god," just like those of Psalm 82.

Having established what the Bible actually says, Jesus continued to disarm His accusers by establishing that the Bible is the absolute, indestructible, inspired, infallible Word of God. If the Bible said it, Jesus thought the religious leaders ought to believe it. Jesus still thinks the same for us today. If the Bible says it, we ought to believe it. Jesus did. What a testimony to Jesus' faith in the authenticity and authority of the Bible. He said, "the Scripture cannot be broken" (v. 35). The Lord Jesus' view of the veracity of the Word of God is unmistakable. If the Bible said it, it must be true.

Jesus' argument is extremely clever. He established what the Scriptures said. The irrefutable Scriptures refer to the judges of the Old Testament as gods. Strike One. Then He established that if the Bible said it, it must be believed. Strike Two. And yet the Pharisees never protested Asaph using this term in reference to a man. They did not accuse him of an error in his choice of words. They never disapproved of this inspired psalmist calling these judges gods. How could they disapprove of Jesus calling Himself God? Strike Three.

These judges were just men. They were born just like other men. But Jesus was not just a man. He was sent from heaven into the world to become a man. How could the Jews logically accuse Him of blasphemy for calling Himself the Son of God? He was under divine orders from God the Father. He was sanctified, set apart, to engage in the divine rescue of the human race, including these complaining, hypocritical Pharisees. And yet they snarled at Jesus for calling Himself God.

He was sent into the world as the Son of God. He came to die and to save. Only God could do that; only God would do that. The Son of God became a man, so men could become the sons of God. Jesus was not a lunatic, a pretender or an egomaniacal fraud. He was God's Son and everyone in Jerusalem knew that meant He was claiming equality with God.

What does the Son of God mean to you?

Jesus said, "I am the Son of God." What does that claim mean to you? Does this "I am" statement change your life? Does it affect your world today? Does it change the way you do business, the way you treat your family, the way you follow the Savior? It should. If Jesus is God, then God lives within you. If Jesus is God, then you take God with you everywhere you go. That's a pretty scary thought if you've gone some places recently that you think might make God uncomfortable. If Jesus is God, then you have the protection of the Almighty closer than any danger is close to you. All of this and more is true, if Jesus is God. And here's the good part. Everything in the Bible points to the fact that Jesus is God.

Jesus is called "God" in the Bible. The prophet Isaiah said Messiah will be called "Wonderful, Counselor, Mighty God" (Isa. 9:6). The disciple Thomas fell before Jesus and said, "My Lord and my God!" (John 20:28). The apostle Paul said Christ "is over all, the eternally blessed God" (Rom. 9:5). And the apostle John said, "And we know that the Son of God has come and has given us an understanding, that we may know Him who is true; and we are in Him who is true, in His Son Jesus

Christ. This is the true God and eternal life" (1 John 5:20). If anyone says to you that the Bible doesn't say Jesus is God, tell them to go back and read their Bible again.

Jesus exists in "the form of God" (Phil 2:6). He is "the image of the invisible God" (Col. 1:15), and He is "the express image of His [God's] person" (Heb. 1:3). The Son of God manifests divine attributes: omnipresence (Matt. 28:20), omnipotence (Heb. 1:3), omniscience (Col. 2:3), righteousness (2 Tim. 4:8) and more. Jesus claimed to be God. His works proved He is God. His words attested that He is God. And what's more, Jesus did things only God could do, such as forgiving sin (Luke 5:20-21) and giving life (John 5:20-21).

In fact, the "I am" passages in John's Gospel are all about Jesus being God. These are not simply earthly metaphors; they are metaphors of divinity. They show the divine nature of the Vine, the Door, the Good Shepherd. There's something more to this "I AM" God than what the religious leaders saw. There's a sufficiency in Him to sustain us as the Bread of Life, to give us life as the Resurrection and the Life, to open the door to heaven as the Way. He is sufficient because He is God. If He were not God, He couldn't possibly be sufficient for all the things the "I am" statements claim.

Paul knew this. He wrote to the Corinthian believers, "And we have such trust through Christ toward God. Not that we are sufficient of ourselves . . . but our sufficiency is from God" (2 Cor. 3:4-5). God's sufficiency becomes our sufficiency when the Son of God becomes our Savior. Our eternal Savior is not a good man who tragically died; our Savior is God the Son, who laid down His life for us (John 10:18).

What does such a Savior deserve in return for giving His life? What does a God who loved us so much He would come to earth and die for us deserve from us? Here's a start.

Since Jesus is God, He deserves our complete attention

My son-in-law, Barry, is a pretty intense guy. He scares easily, much to the delight of us all. When we are watching a drama on television and the tension is mounting, when you just know something horrible is about to happen, it's almost a contest at my house to see who can say "Boo!" to Barry first. We know there will be a scream, a shake and a stare. It's because he focuses himself so intently on what he is watching. The outside world passes Barry by when he's engrossed in something.

That's the way it ought to be with us and Jesus, the Son of God. He warrants our complete attention. He deserves to be our primary focus.

On the night that Jesus was born, the shepherds were visited by an angel who announced, "For there is born to you this day in the city of David a Savior, who is Christ the Lord" (Luke 2:11). The shepherds decided among themselves, "Let us now go to Bethlehem and see this thing that has come to pass, which the Lord has made known to us" (vv. 15). In the stable that night, Mary was there, Joseph was there, and there were likely some sheep and goats and cattle and even some donkeys. But the attention of these shepherds was fixed on the Babe in the manger.

Later when the wise men came from the East, Matthew 2:11 records, "And when they had come into the house, they saw the young Child with Mary His mother, and fell down and worshiped Him. And when they had opened their treasures, they presented gifts to Him: gold, frankincense, and myrrh." It is exceptionally important to note that the attention of these wise men was riveted on the Child. His mother was there, but they fell down and worshiped the Child, not the mother. They brought gifts, but they presented them to the Child, not the mother. Jesus was the focus of their attention.

In his portrayal of the nativity scene, Rembrandt focused attention entirely on the Babe in the manger. He did this by painting a shaft of light so that it falls exclusively on the Christ-child. Although he included other figures, they are shrouded in shadows. Rembrandt wanted nothing to detract from the significance of that baby—Immanuel, God with us, God in the flesh. The great artist wanted Jesus Christ to be the sole object of our attention.

Just as the shepherds and wise men focused on Jesus at the beginning of His life, so it was on the other end of life. There were at least three people crucified the day Jesus died, maybe more. We are told of a criminal on either side of Him. But all eyes were fixed on that middle cross. Matthew says of the soldiers, "Sitting down, they kept watch over Him there" (Matt. 27:36). Others died, but they watched Jesus die. They gave their attention to Him. So did the Jews who had gathered to witness the crucifixion. Their eyeballing Jesus was a fulfillment of the Lord's prophecy through Zechariah: "Then they will look on Me whom they have pierced" (Zech. 12:10; cf. John 19:37).

Wherever He went, whatever He did, Jesus, the Son of God, was always the center of attention. People watched for Him along the road. They went to the shore to wait for Him where they expected His boat to dock. He was the focus of their attention. And things won't change in the future. "For our citizenship is in heaven, from which we also eagerly wait for the Savior, the Lord Jesus Christ" (Phil. 3:20).

Since Jesus is God, He deserves our complete attention every day. But with the press of daily life sometimes it's hard for Him to get the attention He deserves.

There's a wonderful story about a young family who moved into a new house. The move had been scheduled months in advance, but when the day came, the husband was called away to an important meeting at the office. That left the wife to handle the move by herself. After the truck had pulled away, she stood there in the midst of unpacked boxes, surrounded by appliances that needed to be hooked up. To add to the stress, she had a screaming baby and an active five-year-old, who just threw one of his metal toys through the picture window. With a stiff breeze blowing through the hole, the haggard wife called her husband's office for some help. His secretary informed her that he was tied up and could not be disturbed. "Do you want to leave a message?" the secretary asked. Aware that her husband wasn't very good at getting back to her, the wife said, "Yes, tell him the insurance will cover everything. Call home for details." In a matter of minutes the husband returned the call.

I wonder if the Son of God must feel a bit like that harried housewife. He lived for us and died for us, yet we don't seem to have time to help Him or even talk with Him. Our attention is always on other things. Isn't it time you let some other, less important things go to focus your attention on the One who died for you? The "I AM" God is all you need. He is sufficient. Are you looking elsewhere for fulfillment? If so, you're looking in the wrong place. Jesus deserves your complete attention.

Since Jesus is God, He deserves our complete devotion

Attention is one thing; devotion is a whole other matter. Jesus deserves our complete devotion even more than He deserves our complete attention. If you take a few minutes to focus your attention, I don't think you'll have much trouble focusing your devotion.

On the night of His arrest, soldiers dragged Jesus from a peaceful garden to a palace filled with jealous jurists. They couldn't find any evidence to convict Him, so they paid some no-account stooges to lie about Him. They didn't know what to do with Him, so they sent Jesus to the Roman governor. He didn't want anything to do with Him either, but Pilate thought if he flogged the Savior and beat Him senseless the people would accept that as punishment enough. They didn't. The Roman soldiers pummeled His face. They spit upon Him. They even mocked Him by putting a scarlet robe on His back and feigning worship. They pressed a crown of thorns deep into His brow. They laughed at Him.

The crowded screamed for His crucifixion, so they led Him away to the Place of the Skull. Here they nailed His hands to a cross, as well as His feet. They stripped Him of His clothing. They mocked Him, jeered Him, cursed Him. They raised Him into the air so all could see Him hanging there, naked, bleeding, dying. They did their worst to Him, but He never complained. In fact, while men were at their worst, the "I AM" God was at His best. While they said, "Crucify Him," He said, "Forgive them."

None of this is the worst part about Calvary. It's horrible enough that God the Son died a shameful and incredibly cruel death, but it was there that He took upon Himself the crush of sin—your sin, my sin, the world's sin. The sins of my generation; the sins of all generations. He spiritually absorbed the punishment for all sins, committed by all people, for all time. The burden must have been unimaginable. "For He [God the Father] made Him [God the Son] who knew no sin to be sin for us, that we might become the righteousness of God in Him" (2 Cor. 5:21). That's what really inspires our devotion.

> In the old rugged cross, stained with blood so divine,
> A wondrous beauty I see; for 'twas on that old cross
> Jesus suffered and died to pardon and sanctify me.
>
> — George Bennard

The same "I AM" God who died for you now enjoins you to live for Him. Do you hear His call to the sacrificed life? "My sheep hear My voice, and I know them, and they follow Me" (John 10:27). "If anyone desires to come after Me, let him deny himself, and take up his cross daily, and follow Me" (Luke 9:23). "If anyone serves Me, let him follow Me" (John 12:26).

Jesus continues to muster His army today. His army is the Church, dedicated believers who will march beneath the blood-stained banner of Prince Emmanuel. They have learned to live the sacrificed life. They have heeded Paul's call to "present your bodies a living sacrifice, holy, acceptable to God, which is your reasonable service" (Rom. 12:1). They know no limits to bravery, no depths to deprivation, no heights to self-glory. Their devotion is solely to the One who loved them and gave Himself for them. They are an army—not one that sings, "Onward Christian Soldiers, marching off to war," but one that actually marches off to war. They have walked free from those who, when we don't obey, sing about obeying. These are foot soldiers, grunts, men and women who have devotion to nothing or no one like their devotion for the "I AM" God.

When Giuseppe Garibaldi, the guerrilla general in the mid 19th century who fought for Italian independence, mustered an army of young men to free his country, do you know what he promised them? Nothing. The prospective recruits asked Garibaldi what was in it for them. He replied, "No pay, no position, no quarters. I will offer you hunger, thirst, forced marches, and even death." Then he added, "Let him who loves his country in his heart, and not with his lips only, follow me." Italian peasants flocked to his side.

And so it is with the One deserving of our greatest devotion. The Lord Jesus said, "Foxes have holes and birds of the air have nests, but the Son of Man has nowhere to lay His head" (Matt. 8:20). The army may receive, but shouldn't expect, lavish quarters until the fighting is over. The Lord Jesus said, "Whoever desires to come after Me, let him deny himself, and take up his cross, and follow Me" (Mark 8:34). The army may receive decoration, but shouldn't expect anything but denial until the fighting is over. The eternal sequence hasn't changed: cross first, then crown.

Our salvation belongs to us because of what Jesus did at Calvary. Our devotion belongs to Him for the very same reason.

Since Jesus is God, He deserves our complete jubilation

Jubilation is an expression of joy. When God the Son comes into our lives, joy breaks out. It may take an infinite variety of forms of assertion, but joy can't be contained. It's like making homemade cider. You can put it in a plastic jug, but don't shake it up. The pressure to escape the jug will be enormous. It must vent itself.

Adoniram Judson, a 19th-century Baptist missionary to Burma, was a man of uncontainable joy. So expressive was his love for the "I AM" God that the Burmese used to call him "Mr. Glory-Face." His devotion to the Lord was so evident it was written all over his face.

A Hindu trader in India once asked a Christian missionary there, "What do you put on your face to make it shine?" With surprise the man answered, "I don't put anything on it!" With disbelief the Hindu retorted, "Yes, you do! All you Christians do." Then the missionary understood. It's not something we put on from the outside; it's something that bursts forth from the inside.

This is not a phony, forced jubilation, but a natural expression of the love of Jesus in our hearts. Jesus is in the joy business. At the announcement of His birth, the angel said to the petrified shepherds, "Do not be afraid, for behold I bring you good tidings of great joy" (Luke 2:10). On the other end of Jesus' life, after His resurrection, He led His followers out to Bethany, blessed them and returned to heaven. Luke 24:52 says, "And they worshiped Him, and returned to Jerusalem with great joy." These verses are like bookends to the Gospel of Luke.

But in all the chapters between the beginning of Jesus' days on earth and His ascension into heaven, the Son of God spoke of the joy He gives to those who love Him. "These things I have spoken to you, that My joy may remain in you, and that your joy may be full" (John 15:11). "Therefore you now have sorrow; but I will see you again and your heart will rejoice, and your joy no one will take from you" (John 16:22). "But now I come to You, and these things I speak in the world, that they may have My joy fulfilled in themselves" (John 17:13).

Often we think of our salvation as of future benefit—someday we'll be in heaven with God. And while it's true that there is significant future benefit to your salvation, don't close your eyes now. You'll miss all the present benefits. Romans 5 is a microcosm of current advantages for the Christian: once we have been justified we have peace with God (v. 1), access to the Father (v. 2), happiness even during trials (v. 3), hope that cannot be shaken (v. 5), the presence of the Holy Spirit (v. 5) and proof of God's love (v. 8). The world can't offer these things. Jesus can. He deserves our jubilation.

Robert Louis Stevenson said, "To miss the joy is to miss all." If you have been born again, the joy is in you. It's a part of being saved. You just have to find ways to let it out. Often we don't even have to look for ways to give expression for our joy; we just need to remove the cork. When we uncork our negative attitudes, our demand for answers to the "why" questions of life, our bitterness and envy—all the things that barricade jubilation—we will have a hard time holding back the joy. It will find expression in everything we do.

Someone asked Franz Joseph Haydn, the famous Austrian composer and church musician, why his music was so cheerful. Haydn replied, "I cannot make it otherwise. When I think upon God, my heart is so full of joy that the notes dance and leap from my pen!" That's jubilation.

Was Jesus an historical figure? Yes, a man born in Bethlehem, raised in Nazareth. But more. Was Jesus the Messiah? Yes, the anointed of God, the One promised in so many Old Testament prophecies. But more. Was Jesus the Lamb of God? Yes, God's perfect sacrifice at Calvary to pay for the sins of the world. But more. Was Jesus the Son of God? Yes, the image of the invisible God, the incarnate revelation of God to mankind. But more. Was Jesus God the Son? Yes, He was God in the Person of the Son as much as God is God in the Person of the Father. And this is important: what Jesus was, He always will be.

Jesus is what no other religious leader dare claim to be: He is the Son of God, God in the form of the Son. To the religious leaders of His day He boldly proclaimed, "I and My Father are one." And when they questioned Him further and accused Him of blasphemy He reiterated, "I am the Son of God."

As Christians, we do not serve a dead Savior; we serve a risen Lord. We worship Jesus, not as a man only, but who He in reality is—the incarnate God. He deserves our complete attention, our complete devotion, our complete jubilation.

> Oh, for a thousand tongues to sing my great Redeemer's praise,
> The glories of my God and King, the triumphs of His grace!
> My gracious Master and my God, assist me to proclaim,
> To spread thro' all the earth abroad, the honors of Thy name.
>
> — Charles Wesley

"I am the True Vine; let Me support you."

CHAPTER 7

I Am

THE TRUE VINE

"I am the true vine, and My Father is the vinedresser."
JOHN 15:1

To me, there is no more intriguing form of farming than a vineyard. I love to drive along the highways in the Napa Valley of California or the shores of Lake Erie in western New York. It's fascinating to see the symmetrical and almost perfect rows of grapes growing in a vast vineyard. I can't imagine all the work that goes into planting, pruning and picking just so we can have grapes.

But vineyards are also windows to the soul. You can tell a lot about a farmer or vineyardist by looking at his vineyard. Last year I was traveling over the Alps from Switzerland to Italy. We drove along the eastern edge of Lake Geneva past Vevey and Montreux. From there we ascended the Alps to the St. Bernard Pass and drove through the tunnel to Valle d'Aosta in Italy. I have always been fascinated by the contrast between Switzerland and Italy. You enter the tunnel in one world and exit in another. The Swiss are neat and proper; everything is in order. The Italians, well, they aren't. Italians love chaos; they thrive on it.

Nowhere was this more evident than in the vineyards of Switzerland and Italy. As we passed the vineyards of Montreux and began our ascent to the Alps, I couldn't help but be impressed with the straightness of the rows, the condition of the vines, the almost absolute perfection of the vineyards. The sky was cloudy and a bit chilly as we drove to the St. Bernard tunnel. When we came out the other side, the sun was shining, the air was warm—it was a beautiful day. But the vineyards, oh those vineyards. It looked like the same person who designed a plate of spaghetti also designed the Italian vineyards. There are lessons in life to be learned from vineyards.

The Vine passage

Nowhere are these vineyard lessons more obvious than in John 15. This is one of the most delightful passages in the Gospel of John, perhaps in the entire New Testament. If we are to learn from this vineyard, we must to pay attention to this passage.

There are four players in this beautiful allegory. First, the genuine Vine, who is Jesus Christ, the sufficient "I AM" God Himself. Then there is the fatherly Vinedresser, the great Gardener of the globe, God the Father. Third, there are the diverse branches, some alive and fruit-bearing, others dead and destined for the fire. And finally, there is the luscious fruit, itself the product of the relationship between the first three players.

The allegory is in the larger context of John 15-16. These chapters record part of Jesus' farewell address to His disciples. Soon they would make their way to the Garden of Gethsemane. Soon a band of men would be led by a traitor to the place where Jesus was praying. Soon Jesus would be manhandled and whisked away to Caiaphas and Pilate. Soon He would be senselessly scourged, brutally beaten and mercilessly mocked. Soon He would bear a cross to Calvary and be crucified. Soon Jesus would die. It was all coming so very soon. Jesus knew the time was short, and He had so much to say to His disciples. What He had to say about being the True Vine would be the centerpiece of His farewell comments.

Change is coming

Here's the problem. For three years Jesus had spent almost every waking moment with these men. The disciples and He ate together, laughed together, mourned together, were alternately praised or scorned together. They had always been together. Three intimate years together. But that was all about to change.

With His departure imminent, Jesus was concerned that His disciples maintain proper relationships in three important areas of life. Authentic Christianity is always concerned with these three relationships. First, the relationship of the disciple with his Master. Maintaining intimacy through abiding in Him is primary. Second, the relationship of the disciple with other disciples. Here living the life of love is primary. And third, the relationship of the disciple with the world around him. Responding appropriately to a hostile world is essential.

When Jesus left His disciple band behind, would they rise to their responsibilities? Would they be able to maintain these relationships without Him? Would they still find in Him the sufficiency to do all things? Time would tell, but the "I AM" God would give them at least one more opportunity to see that in Him we find all that we need.

Let's walk along with them and listen in. After all, we are His disciples too. What He said to the remaining eleven, He says to you and me. What does it mean to be a genuine disciple of Jesus the Nazarene? Let's see what Jesus had to say.

Bearing fruit is what the Christian life is all about

Genuine disciples live to bear fruit. It's why we are saved. Salvation is for the long haul; it's good forever. But the immediate purpose of our salvation is obedience, not going to heaven.

Someone has aptly said that we are not saved to sit, soak and sour. I guess what they meant by that is that we are not saved to sit in church, take it all in, soak up all the principles and let everything we learn turn to sour grapes.

If I've said it once, I've said it a thousand times. You should never quote Ephesians 2:8-9 without verse 10. "For by grace you have been saved through faith, and that not of yourselves; it is the gift of God, not of works, lest anyone should boast. For we are His workmanship, created in Christ Jesus for good works, which God prepared beforehand that we should walk in them."

There it is, as plain as day. The *raison d'être* of the Christian life. Our reason to be. What gets us up revived every morning and sends us to bed exhausted every night. The driving force behind our life. The standard to which we hold everything we have, everything we do, everything we are. We are made believers by the grace of God so that we can bear fruit for Christ Jesus that God prepared in eternity past for us to bear. God expects nothing more; He'll accept nothing less.

Vital signs

So essential is fruit bearing to the believer that it is one of God's vital signs for spiritual health. When EMTs arrive on the scene of an accident, one of the first things they do is check for vital signs. Is there a pulse? Is the victim breathing? Is the heart beating? When checking your own spiritual pulse, one of the important vital signs is the evidence of fruit.

Jesus knew this. He said, "By this My Father is glorified, that you bear much fruit; so you will be My disciples" (John 15:8).

Is it possible for a person to be born again and show absolutely no signs of fruit bearing? You be the judge. Jesus said to His disciples, "You did not choose Me, but I chose you and appointed you that you should go and bear fruit, and that your fruit should remain" (v. 16). Jesus Himself said He chose us for the purpose of bearing fruit. If there is no fruit, it's a good indication there is no salvation.

So what kind of fruit should you expect to see as a result of being a disciple of the "I AM" God? A good place to start is with the fruit of the Spirit. "But the fruit of the Spirit is love, joy, peace, longsuffering, kindness, goodness, faithfulness, gentleness, self-control" (Gal. 5:22-23). The list begins with love, which is itself the fruit of being loved by God. Let's use it as an example.

The love factor

When we are born again, vitally connected to the True Vine, the first place that relationship will evidence itself is in how we love others. Love for one another (1 John 3:11, 23; 4:7, 11-12; 1 Pet. 1:22; 1 Thess. 3:12), love for our neighbor (Jas. 2:8; Gal. 5:14) and love for other believers (1 John 3:14; 4:20-21) are all clusters of fruit born from the vine of God. And they are all proof of our new life in Christ.

Ephesians 1:4 declares, "He chose us in Him before the foundation of the world, that we should be holy and without blame before Him in love." The purpose of our salvation is to be holy and blameless in the way we love. This is said even more directly in 1 John 3:14. "We know that we have passed from death to life, because we love the brethren. He who does not love his brother abides in death."

Celsus, a second-century Platonist and critic of Christianity, wrote a work called *True Discourse*. It is one of the oldest literary attacks against Christians (ca. A.D. 178). One of Celsus' criticisms was, "These Christians love each other even before they are acquainted." I wonder if Celsus were alive in this century if he would say the same thing about us?

No love, no fruit. No fruit, no life. That's what the Bible says. We are saved to bear fruit to the glory of God. We are designed by God to be a lean, mean fruit-bearing machine. If there is no evidence of fruit on a tree that's supposed to bear fruit, even if it has breathtaking foliage, the reason for the tree's existence is eliminated.

The fruit business

So how's the fruit business in your life? Is there evidence of self-control in the way you handle unexpected disruptions? How about the way you deal with your emotions, your money or your tongue? What about faithfulness? Do your habits in attending church, tending to family devotions or performing your job at work give any indication you are enjoying new life? What about gentleness? If someone stopped your spouse and children and asked them how gentle you are in dealing with family situations, would they be character witnesses to your new birth?

We also bear fruit when we win others to the Savior (Rom. 1:13). As we grow in holiness and obedience, we are bearing fruit as well (Rom. 6:22). Bearing fruit is not just teaching a Sunday school class, volunteering at the city mission or singing in the choir. It's the spiritual harvest that comes from living for God. It's the kind of Christian character and integrity that glorifies God and makes Christ real to others. It's the fruit of your spirit and mind, the fruit of your charity and contentment. Jesus said, "Take heed and beware of covetousness, for one's life does not consist in the abundance of the things he possesses" (Luke 12:15). Let the abundance of fruit for the True Vine be what your life consists of. It's the path to real joy and fulfillment.

Since bearing fruit is so important in the Christian's life, it makes sense to insure that the fruit just keeps coming, year after year. How will that happen?

The True Vine is the only way to bear fruit

We all know that every branch is dependent upon the vine for its life. If there is no stock, if there is no trunk, if there is no vine, there is no life in the branches. Life originates in the vine, not the branch. Genuine disciples draw their life from the True Vine. Unless we are vitally connected to Jesus, the True Vine, the quality of our fruit will be unacceptable.

But what did the "I AM" God mean when He declared, "I am the true vine" (John 15:1)? Why the "true" vine? Why add the adjective? It's vitally important.

Jesus and His disciples had just finished celebrating the Passover in the Upper Room. There Jesus breathed new life into an old feast and charged His disciples always to remember His broken body and shed blood. In that context He referred to Himself as the True Vine. In just hours they would know what He meant.

An unfruitful vine

The contrast with Israel would have been apparent to the Jews, although not as obvious to you and me. What Jew would not be familiar with the metaphor of the vine as applied to God's people, for it was a frequent characterization of the Jewish nation. "O God of hosts; cause Your face to shine, and we shall be saved! You have brought a vine out of Egypt; You have cast out the nations, and planted it. . . . O God of hosts; look down from heaven and see, and visit this vine and the vineyard which Your right hand has planted" (Ps. 80:7-9, 14-15).

Leon Morris writes, "There seems little doubt that Jesus has in mind passages in the Old Testament which regard Israel as a vine (Ps. 80:8-16; Isa. 5:1-7; Jer. 2:21; Ezek. 15; 19:10; Hos. 10:1). Indeed in time the vine became a symbol of Israel, and it is found, for example, on coins of the Maccabees. Interestingly all the Old Testament passages which use this symbol appear to regard Israel as faithless or as the object of severe punishment. It's against this background that Jesus describes Himself as the 'true' vine."[1]

Things haven't changed much. If you visit Israel today you will quickly recognize the unofficial symbol for the Israel Government Tourist Office. It's a silhouette of Joshua and Caleb carrying a bunch of grapes on the stock of a vine. Ancient Israel saw herself as the vine planted in the Promised Land by God Himself. But the chief value of a vine is the fruit it produces. The fruit produced by the people of God had become unproductive and degenerate, lifeless and soulless.

It would be hard to beat the prophet Hosea's portrait of God's people: "Israel empties his vine; he brings forth fruit for himself. According to the multitude of his fruit he has increased the altars; according to the bounty of his land they have embellished his sacred pillars. Their heart is divided; now they are held guilty" (Hos. 10:1-2). Empty vines. No fruit. Divided hearts. Guilty people. Not a true vine. Israel had failed as the people of God.

Amazing love

And then God did something truly amazing. He sent His only begotten Son from heaven to be the genuine Vine, the Vine Israel had failed to be, the Vine Israel never could be. Jesus said, "I am the true vine." Not that Israel was a false vine, but the chosen people had become degenerate and unproductive for God. There was no fruit from their worship. They had failed to please God or to be a light to the Gentiles. All the things Israel was supposed to be and failed at being (light, vine, shepherd, etc.) Jesus said, "I am."

You don't have to look beyond Jesus to find the true article. He is the true Savior. He is the true Prophet. He is the true Son of God. "That was the true Light which gives light to every man who comes into the world" (John 1:9). When you come face to face with Jesus, you come face to face with reality. He is the true Truth. He is the true Way. He is the true Life. When you're tired of all the phony things this world has to hand you, put your hand in the hand of the True Vine. Then watch yourself grow and bear much fruit.

Being rightly related

So how can you and I be rightly related to this true Vine? How can we be certain that the fruit we bear is the result of His strength and not our own? It all gets back to basics.

First, let's remember the basic difference between Jesus and us. He said it best. "I am the vine, you are the branches" (John 15:5). Until we catch the import of that statement, we will be unfulfilled in our own lives and bear no fruit. He is the Vine; we are the branches. He is the reason we live. Without a vine, branches cannot live. Branches draw their life from the vine. Cut off a branch and the vine lives. Cut off the vine and the branch dies. It's a basic law of agriculture.

If Jesus is not alive today, neither are you. He said, "Because I live, you will live also" (John 14:19). While He was primarily referring to our resurrection life, there is no question but that we have eternal life right now, today, because of Him. He is the Vine; we are the branches. Don't lose that. It's the difference between bearing fruit and being barren. It's too crucial to let slide by. He is the Vine; we are the branches. If He isn't alive, neither are we. The branches are inexorably tied to the life of the Vine.

In Howard Ferrin's book *Unto All*, he described the relationship between the life of the Vine and the branches in graphic terms:

> If a small section of a true grapevine with an extended branch is cut off and split open, something most illuminating will be ob-

served. The pith line of the vine extends up to the point where the branch begins; likewise the pith line of the branch extends down to the place where the union with the vine is made; but at the point where the vine and the branch become one and are united, both pith lines cease so that only solid wood exits at the union.

Furthermore, if the grain of the vine and the branch is traced carefully, it will be observed that as the vine approaches a point where a branch is to extend, the right side of the vine crosses over and becomes the left side of the branch and the left side of the vine becomes the right side of the branch, making a perfect cross of strong wood at the place of the union. The vine and the branch become one at the cross.[2]

What Ferrin observed is the absolute necessity of union between the vine and the branch if the branch is to remain alive. That union takes place at the cross. So it is with the True Vine and us. If we are to be alive in Christ, our very life depends on our union with Him, and that takes place at Calvary's cross.

Second, let's remember that the life we experience isn't even our own. Not only do we not live if He doesn't live, but when we do live it's His life that sustains us. We don't live for Him; He lives through us. It's that critical "Christ in you" principle found in Galatians 2:20: "I have been crucified with Christ; it is no longer I who live, but Christ lives in me; and the life which I now live in the flesh I live by faith in the Son of God, who loved me and gave Himself for me."

Often I hear Christians talk about what they are doing for the Lord. Anything I do *for* the Lord is of no eternal value. I can do nothing without Him. What is important, and what brings eternal reward, is what I permit Him to do *through* me. I'm just a vessel; He's the juice. I'm just a conduit; He's the Living Water. I'm just a branch; He's the Vine.

Here's an incredible thought. As a branch drawing my life from the Vine, I'm not living my own life; I'm living His life. He is living through me. That's why He can say, "I give them eternal life, and they shall never perish" (John 10:28). "And this is the testimony: that God has given us eternal life, and this life is in His Son" (1 John 5:11). If eternal life is found in the "I AM" God and I am vitally attached to Him, then eternal life is found in me. It is His gift to you and me (Rom. 6:23), and it is always ours because we are always His.

Third, His life is our life, so our fruit is His fruit. He is the Vine; we are the branches. We are extensions of His life in the world, and the fruit that is born on our branches is not really our fruit. It belongs to the Vine. As branches we bear the fruit, but we do not generate it. The life juices that cause fruit to flourish come from the Vine and are transported through the branches to the fruit. The beauty of the fruit is His beauty. The tastiness of the fruit is His tastiness. We aren't the Vine nor are we the fruit. We are just the connector between the True Vine and His eternal fruit. We are but a channel; He is the life that flows through that channel.

> Channels only, blessed Master,
> but with all Thy wondrous power
> Flowing thro' us, Thou canst use us
> every day and every hour.
> — Mary E. Maxwell

One of the finest biblical expositors of the 19th century, Bishop J. C. Ryle, described the relationship between Christ and believers as follows:

> The union between the branch of a vine and the main stem, is the closest that can be conceived. It is the whole secret of the branch's life, strength, vigor, beauty, and fertility. . . . The union between Christ and believers is just as close, and just as real. In themselves believers have no life, or strength, or spiritual power. All that they have of vital religion comes from Christ. They are what they are, and feel what they feel, and do what they do, because they draw out of Jesus a continual supply of grace, help, and ability. Joined to the Lord by faith, and united in mysterious union with Him by the Spirit, they stand, and walk, and continue, and run the Christian race. But every jot of good above them is drawn from their spiritual Head, Jesus Christ.[3]

To bear fruit for time and eternity, we must draw all our strength from the vine. If we "muscle" through a job, if we do some service in our own strength and ability, we may get it done, but God will not have done it. What He does not do does not last. It doesn't bring good to others or eternal reward to us. Only as we are rightly related to the True Vine will we bear true fruit.

Needing the Vinedresser's care

But even when we are rightly related to the Vine, it isn't easy. Sometimes our lives seem to be out of control. Our thoughts run wild. Our spending habits don't reflect eternal values. We grow cold and lifeless. Our branches get a bit gangly and full of ourselves. That's when we need a Heavenly Gardener.

Genuine disciples always benefit from pruning. We know we need it, and even if it hurts for a little while, we all understand that it makes us healthier and more useful to the Vine. Still, the idea of having our foliage trimmed is not engaging to us. The only thing that makes it palatable is knowing that success in raising any crop depends largely on the skill and care of the farmer. In our case, our vinedresser is our Heavenly Father. Talk about skill and care! Some trees can take a lot of pruning; others cannot. Each fall I watch Linda prune her rose bushes around our house. I am amazed at how much she can prune away and still have them come back healthy and beautiful in the spring. I have seen olive trees in Israel pruned right back to where you can hardly see the trunks sticking out of the ground. Yet when I would see those same trees a year later, they had amazingly healthy limbs shooting out of them. The secret is in the wisdom of the vinedresser. If the farmer is caring and knows what he's doing, he can cut back branches or a bush and make it healthier than it had been before. All that overbearing growth is cut away to stave off bugs and disease and allow new growth to take its place.

I have a next-door neighbor who trimmed his tree. He's not a farmer or a horticulturist by any stretch of the imagination. In fact, the best way I can describe him is, well, he's a tree killer. He committed arbor homicide on his tree and now it has gone up in smoke. The difference between the farmer and my neighbor is the difference between a professional and an amateur. God is a professional gardener. He is the most loving, caring Vinedresser we'll ever know. If my life is to be trimmed by anyone, I want it to be the God who has loved me with an everlasting love (Jer. 31:3).

Two kinds of pruning

It's true. Genuine disciples always benefit from pruning, just like healthy trees do. But what if the tree isn't healthy? What if the disciple isn't genuine? What happens then? Listen again to the words of the "I AM" God. "I am the true vine, and My Father is the vinedresser. Every branch in Me that does not bear fruit He takes away; and every branch that bears fruit He prunes, that it may bear more fruit" (John 15:1-2).

126

The Father Vinedresser does two kinds of pruning in His vineyard. The first kind is when He prunes those branches that are healthy, cutting away excess so that the fruit may get more sunlight and grow bigger and tastier. Not all branches are created equal, and thus not all fruit is created equal. But all branches that are vitally linked to the vine bear fruit and thus need to be purged from time to time.

Do you know what is the greatest judgment God could allow to fall to us as believers? It would be to leave us alone. If He let us grow as we wanted to, grow our own way, grow wild, reckless and untamed, soon our foliage would overshadow our fruit and the fruit would die. But by pruning us He can cut away decay, remove wood that breeds disease and insects, carve away tissue that is useless and remove excess foliage that hides the fruit. The Father Vinedresser doesn't jeopardize our lives by pruning us. He would jeopardize our lives if He didn't.

But the Father Vinedresser does another kind of pruning that is more akin to radical surgery than a little snip here or there. "Every branch in Me that does not bear fruit He takes away."

This verse has been the scene of a great deal of theological bloodshed over the generations. What exactly is the "I AM" God saying here? Some have thought that He was talking about believers—branches who once were alive but had died, believers who had been saved but lost their salvation and were cast into the fire and burned. But that view is impossible. It contradicts the clear teaching of Scripture in too many other places.

The phrase "in Me" (v. 2) does not mean the same as Paul's words "in Christ." "In Christ" is always used of our vital relationship to the Savior (Rom. 8:1; 1 Cor. 1:30; 2 Cor. 5:17; Phil. 1:1; Col. 1:2). We are placed "in Christ" at the moment we believe, never to be removed "out of Christ." But here, "in Me" is part of the metaphor of the Vine. It seems to mean "every person who professes to be My disciple." Remember, there's a much greater difference between profession and possession than mere spelling. Not every one who professes to know Christ really does. Not every one who professes to be a follower of Christ really is.

The True Vine said, "Many will say to Me in that day, 'Lord, Lord, have we not prophesied in Your name, cast out demons in Your name, and done many wonders in Your name?' And then I will declare to them, 'I never knew you; depart from Me, you who practice lawlessness!'" (Matt. 7:22-23).

What Jesus was saying is that every branch entwined with Him is treated by the Father Vinedresser in one of two ways. Those that are vitally linked to the Vine but need purging will be pruned, so they may bear even greater fruit. Those that are dead are not simply presumed dead. They are known to be dead by their lack of fruit. These branches are fruitless hangers-on, headed for an appropriate fate. They are cast out because their branch is withered. The workmen gather them and throw them into the fire, and they are burned (v. 6).

Is anyone better qualified than God to judge the life of those branches that hang out around the True Vine? The Father Vinedresser is a caring, loving, just God. If there were any life in these dead branches, He would know and He would prune them to enhance their life. But these are not branches that have been in union with the Vine and died. These branches are not now, nor have they ever been, vitally linked to the True Vine. Our link with the eternal "I AM" God is an eternal link and can never be severed. The Bible says so!

Entwined, but no life

A couple of weeks ago I walked beside a tree line. It ran along the edge of a field with a barbed wire fence at the base of the trees. All the trees were tall and healthy. But one of the trees looked like it had some dead branches. Part of it looked green and vital; part of it was brown and lifeless. As I got closer to the tree, however, I discovered that there were actually two trunks on that tree. One led to the green part of the tree, and from it all the green branches stemmed. The other entwined itself around the healthy trunk, but its limbs were lifeless and leafless. It wasn't one tree, but two. One was alive and one was not. One was fruitful and one was not.

So it is with those who claim to be Jesus' disciples. Some are alive; they are vitally linked to the True Vine. Their leaves flourish and their fruit is evident. Others who claim to be His disciples have roots elsewhere. They are not connected to the True Vine. They have never been born again. They may wear the clothes of a Christian, carry the Bible of a Christian and talk the language of a Christian, but the only thing that makes a Christian is a living relationship with Jesus Christ, the "I AM" God, and they don't have it.

The work of the Vinedresser is important in the life of the vineyard.

After all, it's His vineyard. He wants to keep it trim, well-maintained and free from phonies.

Jesus Christ is the True Vine. Only the True Vine is sufficient to give life to the branches and ultimately fruit to their limbs. His Father is the Vinedresser. He prunes the branches attached to the Vine and makes them healthier. He also removes the dead wood, those who are not attached to the vine. He cuts the live wood back. He cuts the dead wood away. If you are to find life, abundant life, eternal life, you must find it in a vine sufficient to support your branches. Only Jesus can do that. Find your sufficiency in Him and you will never be weak, limp or lifeless.

This whole allegory is about relationships. What is our responsibility in this relationship with the True Vine and the Father Vinedresser? What is the True Vine looking for from His branches? What does the Vinedresser look for when He is pruning His branches? What is the key to maintaining a healthy relationship with the True Vine and the Vinedresser? Jesus gives us the answer. "I am the vine, you are the branches. He who abides in Me, and I in him, bears much fruit; for without Me you can do nothing" (v. 5).

What does Jesus the True Vine mean to you?

Genuine disciples are obedient if they want to be productive. We know that without the True Vine we have no life, no productivity, no fruit. We really don't have to do much in order to be productive. God the Father and God the Son do pretty much everything that needs done. But there is one thing they expect us to do—abide.

Fruitfulness is the result of the True Vine producing His life through His disciples. Our duty is simply to remain in Him, to abide in Him. That word *abide* (Gr. *meno*) must be pretty important in John's theology. It occurs 11 times in this chapter, 40 times in the Gospel of John and 27 times in John's epistles. So what does it mean?

To abide in the True Vine means to trust Jesus Christ as your Savior

"Whoever eats My flesh and drinks My blood has eternal life . . . . He who eats My flesh and drinks My blood abides in Me, and I in him" (John 6:54, 56). To eat Christ's flesh and drink His blood is not as gruesome as it sounds. It's just a poetic way of saying we trust the breaking of His body on Calvary's cross and the atonement of His blood as payment for our sins. It's the same analogy used in the Lord's Supper (Matt. 26:26-29).

We cannot possibly abide in the True Vine if we do not have a vital union with Him. That union is salvation. Every union must have an entry point. There must be a beginning before there can be an abiding. In fact, abiding implies a beginning before it implies a continuance.

It was a warm Saturday evening in June 1965. I had anticipated that evening for years and when it finally came I was thrilled. It was on that day, June 26, that I entered a union with Linda and we became husband and wife. My father, our pastor, said, "Wilt thou?" and I wilted. We said our vows before hundreds of other people and began a life together.

That's the way it is when we begin a relationship with Jesus Christ as Savior. Before we respond to the call to salvation, before we say "I do," we have no relationship; therefore we have no union. Our relationship with God was non-existent. In fact, we were at war with God (James 4:4). But then we believed the Gospel and trusted Jesus Christ as our Savior, and He became our peace treaty with God (Rom. 5:1). No longer are we under divine judgment; now we are under the protection of divine grace.

"He who believes in the Son has everlasting life; and he who does not believe the Son shall not see life, but the wrath of God abides on him" (John 3:36). The word translated "abides" here is exactly the same as "abides" in John 15:6. The only difference is where we are abiding. Before salvation we abide under the sentence of God's wrath; after salvation we abide under the umbrella of God's grace.

To abide in Christ requires an entry point, a place to start abiding. That place is trusting Him as Savior. When you believe with all your heart that only Jesus is sufficient to save you from your sins (Acts 16:31), then you enter into a new relationship with Him and begin abiding as the branch abides in the vine.

To abide in the True Vine means to continue in Him

"Then Jesus said to those Jews who believed Him, 'If you abide in My word, you are My disciples indeed. And you shall know the truth, and the truth shall make you free" (John 8:31-32). Abiding in Christ means throwing your lot in with Him, trusting Him so completely that regardless of what happens in your life, you know that you are eternally and vitally connected to the True Vine. But it means more.

Abiding in Christ also means staying in Him, living in Him, remaining in Him, continuing in Him. You cannot abide in Christ and run to Him only when you're in a jam. That's not abiding; that's manipulating, and the True Vine will not be manipulated by a branch.

The promise of God's blessing and protection is always made only to those who abide, not to those who live life their own way and then run to God for protection. "He who dwells in the secret place of the Most High shall abide under the shadow of the Almighty. . . . Surely He shall deliver you from the snare of the fowler . . . . He shall cover you with His feathers, and under His wings you shall take refuge" (Ps. 91:1, 3-4).

Abiding requires an entry point, but it also requires a continuing path. You can see that meaning in the way John uses the word *meno* as he records the words of the "I AM" God. "Do not labor for the food which perishes, but for the food which endures (*meno*) to everlasting life (John 6:27). "I have come as a light into the world, that whoever believes in Me should not abide (*meno*) in darkness" (12:46). "And I will pray the Father, and He will give you another Helper, that He may abide (*meno*) with you forever" (14:16). "As the Father loved Me, I also have loved you; abide (*meno*) in My love" (15:9). "These things I have spoken to you, that My joy may remain (*meno*) in you, and that your joy may be full" (15:11).

The secret to bearing fruit is to continue a healthy union with the Vine, for without continuing in intimacy with Him, you and I can do nothing of eternal importance. Little wonder Jesus spoke so frequently about our abiding in Him.

To abide in the True Vine means obedience

Abiding is giving loving obedience to Him as the "I AM" God, the all-sufficient Jesus. "As the Father loved Me, I also have loved you; abide in My love. If you keep My commandments, you will abide in My love, just as I have kept My father's commandments and abide in His love" (John 15:9-10).

The surest test of abiding in Christ is obedience—explicit, immediate, enthusiastic obedience. Wild branches don't obey the Vine. Unhealthy branches may obey, but not willingly. Only the heartiest branches give enthusiastic obedience to the One from whom they draw their life.

I can remember Linda teaching our children, when they were very young, this definition of obedience: "Obedience is doing what you're told, when you're told to do it, with the right heart attitude." The three elements to that definition are important for healthy branches.

Obedience is doing explicitly what the True Vine tells us to do, immediately when we're told to do it, with an enthusiastic attitude about doing it. Disobedience is not doing what we're told to do. Disobedience is doing what we're told to do, but only when we feel like it. Disobedience is doing what we're told to do immediately, but grumbling about it the whole time.

The Vine is our lifeblood. He gives us life and the nutrients to sustain continued life. To disobey the biological or spiritual messages sent to us by the Vine is to destine ourselves to disease.

Growth patterns

There is a chain reaction going on here. Without faith, there is no life because without faith it is impossible to please God (Heb. 11:6). And without the life of Christ giving spiritual life to His branches, there is no fruit. "Neither can you [bear fruit], unless you abide in Me" (John 15:4). But if we abide in Christ, a strange and wondrous thing happens. Not only do we bear fruit, but when we are pruned by the Father Vinedresser, we "bear *more* fruit" (v. 2, emphasis mine). And when He abides in us and we abide in Him, we bear "*much* fruit" (v. 5, emphasis mine).

Jesus Christ is sufficient not only to give us life, but to give us the opportunity, the ability and the love to bear fruit for Him. Nobody else does that for the believer, nor can anyone else. It is only the sufficiency of Christ that gets it done for us.

If you're vitally related to the True Vine, you never need fear the pruning of the Vinedresser. Sure it hurts. When God prunes something or someone from our lives we have come to depend on, it's bound to hurt. But we must never forget that it's our vital union with the Vine that can never be severed, not our union with other people or other things.

132

The next time you feel the pruning of the Heavenly Gardener and you don't understand why, remember this little rhyme:

> He knows, He loves, He cares,
> Nothing this truth can dim;
> He does the very best for those,
> Who leave the choice with Him.

Enjoy your life as a branch, vitally related to the True Vine. When Jesus said, "I am the vine," He was saying to you, "I am all you need for life, for health, for happiness."

"I am the Resurrection and the Life;
let Me give you hope."

CHAPTER 8

I Am

THE RESURRECTION
AND THE LIFE

*Jesus said to her, "I am the resurrection and the life. He who believes in Me,
though he may die, he shall live."*
JOHN 11:25

Like you, I have stood in somber silence at the graveside of loved ones.
I have experienced the trauma and tragedy of death—the trauma of suddenly losing someone I loved and the tragedy of knowing this meant
years of separation. Death hurts, and time is a slow healer. But as a
Christian, I also have experienced the tribute and triumph of death—
the tribute to the grace and goodness of God and the triumph of life beyond death. I know that resurrection is a sure thing and Jesus is coming.

The Preacher said there is "a time to be born, and a time to die" (Eccl.
3:2). But there is no time that proves the sufficiency of Christ like the
time of death. The story that focuses on Jesus' statement "I am the resurrection and the life" is a common one. It's a story of a family, of loss,
of tears and of grief. It's also the story of hope in the midst of despair.

Friends and family

The story of Lazarus is about friends and family. While we are introduced to Mary and Martha elsewhere (Luke 10:38-42), we are acquainted with their brother, Lazarus, only because of this chapter and
the next. (The Lazarus of Jesus' parable in Luke 16 is a beggar, full of
sores, and not the brother of Mary and Martha.) Lazarus and his sisters
lived in Bethany, not the village by that name across the Jordan River,
but the one just two miles outside of Jerusalem on the southeastern slope
of the Mount of Olives. They were suburbanites, if you will.

One day, shortly before Christ's own death, Lazarus, a friend of Jesus, became extremely ill. His sickness was so life-threatening that Mary and Martha sent for Jesus to heal their brother, even though everyone knew there was a price on Jesus' head and it was extremely dangerous for Him to return to Judea. Jesus and His disciples were in Perea, which is the land east of the Jordan River in the present Hashemite Kingdom of Jordan.

The first-century Jewish historian Josephus described Perea as the region between the Jabbok and Arnon rivers. The Jabbok flows westward into the Jordan River about a third of the way between the Dead Sea and the Sea of Galilee. The Arnon flows westward into the Dead Sea at about its center. The location of Perea is important, as will become evident later.

When the news of Lazarus' illness reached Jesus, the Master delayed leaving for two days. When He finally arrived at Bethany, Lazarus had already been buried four days. When the sisters heard that Jesus was coming and that He was near Bethany, each reacted in their characteristic way. Mary, likely the younger of the two and the more sensitive, remained at home, weeping and being consoled by friends who had come to mourn her loss. This squares marvelously with the portrait Luke paints of Mary (Luke 10:38-42). Martha, on the other hand, was more proactive, more aggressive, more the take-charge type. She rushed out to meet Jesus before He was able to enter the village.

It was here, in His encounter with Martha, that the "I AM" God spoke again of His eternality and sufficiency. When Martha lamented, "Lord, if You had been here, my brother would not have died" (John 11:21), Jesus confidently responded, "Your brother will rise again."

The woman immediately replied with a flash of insight into the Old Testament understanding of resurrection: "I know that he will rise again in the resurrection at the last day" (v. 24). That gave Jesus opportunity to voice one of the great "I am" statements of Scripture. He said, "I am the resurrection and the life. He who believes in Me, though he may die, he shall live. And whoever lives and believes in Me shall never die" (vv. 25-26). With this Jesus continued, "Do you believe this?"

Do you believe this?

While the raising of Lazarus from the dead was perhaps the most dramatic element to this story of family and friends, what Jesus said to

Martha was by far the most important. It touched both time and eternity.

Jesus asked Martha, "Do you believe this?" Would Martha believe in more than the typical Jewish understanding of resurrection? Would she believe that, as the Resurrection and the Life, Jesus had the power to give life beyond death? Would she believe that one who trusts Jesus has the power to live forever? More to the point for you and me, do we believe this? Do you believe that Jesus has the power to raise you from the dead and to give you eternal life? Has the truth that Jesus is the Resurrection and the Life affected both your eternal destiny and your present duty?

What does it mean that Jesus is the Resurrection and the Life? What are the results of placing faith in Jesus' resuscitation power and subsequent eternal life-giving power? What did it mean to Mary, Martha and Lazarus? What did it mean to the Jewish mourners at Bethany that day? What does Jesus the Resurrection and the Life mean to you today? Here's what this "I am" statement means.

Jesus the Resurrection and the Life makes death transitional, not terminal

Today most people believe death is terminal. When you die, that's it. There's nothing more. You just go back to the earth, dust to dust and all that. That's why we talk about terminal illness. But death is not terminal when we place our faith in Jesus the Resurrection and the Life. The Christian view of death is that it is transitional.

Of course, when you die, your physical life (as we know it on this earth) ends. You stop breathing. Your body begins the natural process of decomposition. You leave your friends and family behind. But while death means separation, it doesn't mean termination. The reason is Jesus, the Resurrection and the Life.

When my wife's mother died some years ago, it was a time of sadness for all of us. Stand-up comics may make their living from mother-in-law jokes, but I loved my mother-in-law, and she loved me. She had a cerebral hemorrhage and was in a comatose state for about a week. Linda sat at her side. Her mother was there, but not really there. Finally, her mother died. When we placed her coffin in the ground, it began a time of separation. Some years later Linda's father died as well and our separation from him began. Death means separation, but because Jesus is the Resurrection and the Life, we have the confidence that we will see them again!

139

Death and O'Hare

When I think of death I think of Chicago's O'Hare Airport. I know that sounds a bit strange, but stay with me on this. Since I live in Lincoln, Nebraska (a city from which you must fly somewhere else to fly most places), almost all of my flights to the East go through Chicago. When I fly to O'Hare Airport, Chicago is almost never my destination. I'm going on to Tampa or Raleigh or New York or Pittsburgh or some other city. O'Hare is where I catch a connecting flight. In Lincoln, the airline people tag my luggage all the way to my final destination, not just to Chicago.

Death is like that. It's not terminal; it's only where you change planes to continue on to your final destination. Your final destination is not the grave; it is a joyous eternity with God. Life doesn't end at death; only life on this side of Chicago, life on this side of the grave. Because Jesus is the Resurrection and the Life (which means life on the other side of the grave), we continue on a connecting flight well beyond the grave.

In many ways I dread flying to Chicago because I know it means separation from my friends and family back home. But the joy of flying through Chicago is that I will board a bigger, more comfortable, faster jet to my final destination. That's what death is like—separation but not termination, because there's more to the journey than the flight to Chicago.

Plus Ultra

For many years the national motto of Portugal was "*Ne Plus Ultra*" ("Nothing More Beyond"). Portugal is situated on the Iberian Peninsula of Europe, west of Spain. It is the westernmost land mass of the Continent. When you sail from one of the harbors of Portugal, there's not much out there but the Atlantic Ocean—hence the national motto.

But Christopher Columbus believed there was more out there. He didn't know what he would find, but he sailed into the expanse of the Atlantic in search of whatever was out there. He thought it would take him around the globe to the East Indies. Was he ever wrong. No one dreamed there was a couple of continents between Europe and Asia.

When Columbus discovered the new world, he proved three things wrong. First, he proved the earth wasn't flat; it was spherical. Second, he proved that you wouldn't drop off the end if you sailed too far. You just kept on sailing. And third, he proved the Portuguese motto was wrong. It had to change. So it became "*Plus Ultra*" ("More Beyond").

That's what the "I AM" God means to us. Jesus said, "I am the resurrection and the life." There is more beyond the grave. Death isn't terminal; it's transitional. Our Lord's great words of comfort to His disciples were, "A little while longer and the world will see Me no more (separation), but you will see Me (resurrection). Because I live you will live also (life)" (John 14:19). Can anything be plainer than that?

At the end of this story, Jesus stood before the tomb of Lazarus and shouted, "Lazarus, come forth!" It was Augustine in the fourth century who first noted that it's a good thing Jesus called Lazarus by name, or else everybody in that family tomb would have come out. When Jesus said, "Lazarus! This way out!" it's as if He was directing someone lost in the deep recesses of a cavern. Jesus was leading the way to life beyond the grave. The creative power of God reversed the process of corruption and changed a corpse into a witness.

As the Resurrection and the Life, the "I AM" God proved there is more to life than what we know on this side of the grave. There is a connecting flight beyond. In fact, the best is beyond Chicago!

Jesus the Resurrection and the Life illustrates the perfect timetable of God

Since I just mentioned flying, please allow me to continue in that vein. Have you noticed that airlines aren't all that tolerant if you're late for your flight? I have missed flights in London, Amsterdam and some of the finest cities in America. Airlines don't put up with much when you're late. But they seem to have no problem delaying your flight when you're on time.

Some years ago I was to fly from New York to Santo Domingo, the capital of the Dominican Republic. I was flying Dominicana Airlines, the national airline of that country. Now I know that the pace of life in the Caribbean is somewhat slower than the pace of life in New York. Well, who am I kidding? It's not somewhat slower; it's more like a full stop. But that's my point. I arrived at JFK International in time for my flight, made my way through a mountain of oversized suitcases and bags to the check-in counter, and was told to go sit down and wait patiently. There would be a delay in the flight.

I waited one hour. Time for our departure came and went. While I was waiting, I couldn't help but notice that passengers continued to arrive, laden with oversized suitcases and bags. They checked in as they arrived. I waited another hour. Passengers trickled in. Finally, I went to the young lady at the check-in counter and inquired, "What's the problem? Why this long delay? Is it mechanical?" She politely replied, "Oh no, nothing is wrong with the plane. We're just waiting because all the passengers haven't arrived yet!" My eyes rolled up into my head. I resigned myself to more waiting.

On God's schedule

Like flight schedules, timetables of all sorts aren't perfect. Deadlines come and go. Sometimes we make them; often we miss them. Our team is on the seven yard line and it's goal to go, but time runs out and we lose, complaining, "If only we had a little more time" (apparently oblivious to the 60 minutes of playing time our team already had).

Once the well-known preacher Phillips Brooks was nervously pacing the floor of his study. The usually sensitive Brooks, who wrote the Christmas hymn "O Little Town of Bethlehem," was like a caged lion. When a friend asked what was troubling him, the preacher replied, "The trouble is that I'm in a hurry and God isn't."

Getting on God's timetable is one of the most enlightening and fulfilling activities of life. It can change our whole attitude about God, about ourselves and about our circumstances. In this story, Martha and Mary are good examples of believers who needed to get on the timetable of God.

Day-by-day account

It's not possible to piece together this story in its entirety. That makes it difficult to be certain of Jesus' timetable for proving He is the Resurrection and the Life. Many have tried. Good men and women disagree. Some believe that by the time the news reached Jesus concerning Lazarus' illness, His friend was already dead. Others believe he died two days later. All this speculation revolves around why Jesus waited two days before setting out to comfort the dead man's sisters. Here's my best guess at how all this played out.

Jesus was in Perea, across the Jordan River. Lazarus fell gravely ill and thus Mary and Martha sent a messenger to tell Jesus. When the messenger arrived, he announced, "Lord, behold, he whom You love is sick" (John 11:3). The messenger delivered the right message. Lazarus was sick (Gr. *astheneo*), not dead. The word means "weak" or "feeble." It's the same word used for the weaker brother—those who are weak in the faith (Rom. 14:1; 1 Cor. 8:9). The messenger left Bethany to run to Perea and tell Jesus that Lazarus was weak, near death, but not already dead.

But by the time he arrived in Perea, however, Lazarus had indeed died, and Jesus knew it. The Master delayed two more days. Then He announced to His disciples that Lazarus had died and they would make the journey up to Bethany. The disciples objected that it was too dangerous, but Jesus was operating on His Father's timetable and under His Father's protection. They trekked up the mountain to Bethany on the fourth day. Thus, when he arrived, Martha and Mary both lamented, "Lord, if You had been here, my brother would not have died" (John 11:21, 32). This is the only time these two very different sisters felt and said the same thing.

After a private meeting with Martha and then a meeting with Mary, Jesus made His way to the family sepulcher. It wasn't much—just a cave carved out of the rock (v. 38). The "I AM" God commanded the stone to be removed from the mouth of the cave. Martha protested, "Lord, by this time there is a stench, for he has been dead four days" (v. 39).

Embalming was an Egyptian practice, not Jewish. The Jews anointed or perfumed the bodies of their dead, wrapped them in cloths and buried them the same day they died. By the fourth day, surely the body of the Lord's friend would have begun to decay and decompose. But Jesus knew we could handle the stench of death because He could remove the sting of death.

Why the delay?

Here's the real question. Why did Jesus take so long? Why did He not rush to Bethany the moment He heard that Lazarus was ill? Why delay two days? Whose timetable was He operating on anyway? Didn't He know how anxious Mary and Martha would be?

It does seem a bit cruel for Jesus to wait so long, unless, of course, He understands better than we do the timetable of God. That Jesus' delay was purposeful and well-timed is seen in several statements recorded by the apostle John. Think about them.

"This sickness is not unto death, but for the glory of God, that the Son of God may be glorified through it" (v. 4). God had a higher agenda than comforting those who mourn.

"Are there not twelve hours in the day?" (v. 9). God has a time fixed to accomplish everything; don't get in a hurry!

"I am glad for your sakes that I was not there" (v. 15). God the Son was totally in tune with the timetable of God the Father.

"Your brother will rise again" (v. 23). God had a resurrection plan that preceded the timetable for the resurrection at the last day.

"Now Jesus had not yet come into the town" (v. 30). God is still delaying to coordinate Jesus' arrival at Lazarus' tomb with the crowd's arrival to witness Lazarus' resurrection.

"Could not this Man, who opened the eyes of the blind, also have kept this man from dying?" (v. 37). God doesn't always choose to heal just in the nick of time. Sometimes He has something even more spectacular in mind.

What's wrong with God?

Is it easy to live with the timetable of God? If you say yes, you probably aren't doing it. Why did your child die before you could get him to the hospital? What's wrong with God's timetable? Why has God not yet answered your prayer that He save your husband? What's wrong with God's timetable? Why does God seem to be taking His good old time with your recovery from bypass surgery? What's wrong with God's timetable? Why was your wife taken so quickly after being diagnosed with cancer? What's wrong with God's timetable?

If you haven't struggled with these or similar questions, you haven't struggled. Almost every question that we ask of God or every complaint we voice to Him has to do with His timing. If you have struggled with such questions, cheer up. You're not alone.

If you've asked, "Lord, how much longer do I have to lie here in my weakened condition, unable to care for myself, before You take me home?" read Psalm 6:3.

If you've asked, "Lord, how much longer do I have to pray before You listen to me and I get an answer?" read Psalm 13:1.

If you've asked, "Lord, how long are You going to put up with that filthy language on television?" read Psalm 74:10.

If you've asked, "Lord, how much longer are You going to be angry with me for what I did?" read Psalm 79:5.

If you've asked, "Lord, how long are You going to let the Supreme Court go before they overturn *Roe v. Wade*?" read Psalm 94:3.

Adjusting ourselves to the timetable of God is not easy, but it is necessary. Jesus knew that healing Lazarus would bring glory to God. Anybody who was as sick and as close to death as Lazarus was and was healed by the power of God would make a great guest on some Christian talk program. Couldn't God see that? Doesn't He want us to praise Him?

But Jesus also knew that by delaying His arrival at Bethany, God would be given even greater glory. "This sickness is not unto death, but for the glory of God" (v. 4). Only by following God's timetable could Lazarus' story end with the glory of God and not the death of Lazarus. That's true in your life too.

No answer? Trust God!

When you are facing a delay, trust God. When things aren't going as you planned, trust God. When you are wondering why He hasn't healed you as you've asked, trust God. When you are looking for a job and can't find one, trust God. He has a timetable.

When you've asked God to bring that certain someone into your life and there's no one on the horizon, trust God. When you've prayed that God would give you a family and there's still just the two of you, trust God. When you've asked Him to take you home, yet you linger in pain, trust God. He has a timetable.

When you've prayed that God would bring your runaway daughter home, trust God. When you've been without a pastor for more than two years and the pulpit committee is about to throw in the towel, trust God. When you've asked God to change your spouse and give you a more peaceful home, trust God. He has a timetable.

Do you believe this?

Isn't that exactly what Jesus asked Martha when He announced that He was the Resurrection and the Life? Do you believe this? Do you think His delay was purposeful and not just unavoidable? Do you trust God to do what is best for you?

So, all you Marthas, do you believe this? Do you believe it is better to wait for God to work than to take matters into your own hands? Do you believe it is better to allow God to change your situation in His divine time, or to try to influence His timetable?

Jesus the Resurrection and the Life illustrates the perfect timetable of God. He came and He acted in consort with a plan that was drafted before the world began. Isn't it time you adapted your life to His schedule? The alternative is to miss your plane.

Jesus the Resurrection and the Life gives meaning to death

If death is not terminal and if everything is progressing according to a divine schedule, what do we have to look forward to in God's future?

The subjects of heaven, hell and eternity usually produce more questions than answers—at least good answers. We are all interested in what life will be like when we board our connecting flight. It's easy to see why people misunderstand; just look at the disciples.

When Jesus announced to His disciple band that Lazarus was ill and they were going to Bethany, He said, "Our friend Lazarus sleeps, but I go that I may wake him up" (v. 11). Their natural reasoning powers caused them to think something like this: "If it is so dangerous for Jesus to return to Judea right now, and if Lazarus is sleeping, resting well, why would Jesus want to risk His life just to wake him up?" They responded, "Lord, if he sleeps he will get well" (v. 12). That sounds reasonable enough.

But Jesus knew Lazarus was dead, either because His divine nature imparted that knowledge to His human nature or because God the Father had revealed it to Him. Thus, to make sure the disciples understood the gravity of the situation and why He must return to Bethany, "Jesus said to them plainly, 'Lazarus is dead'" (v. 14).

Good night, Sweet Prince

The death of the faithful is often euphemistically referred to in the Bible as sleep (especially in the authorized version, from which these references are taken). "And the LORD said unto Moses, Behold, thou shalt sleep with thy fathers" (Deut. 31:16). To David, God said, "And when thy days be fulfilled, and thou shalt sleep with thy fathers, I will set up thy seed after thee" (2 Sam. 7:12). Job said, "For now shall I sleep in the dust" (Job 7:21). Psalm 13:3 refers to sleeping the "sleep of death." And all those passages that show the transition from one king to the next use the euphemism "slept with his fathers": David (1 Kings 2:10), Solomon (1 Kings 11:43) and Rehoboam (1 King 14:31), for example.

The New Testament uses the same figurative language. At Jesus' crucifixion there were earthquakes, the veil of the temple was torn in two, and "graves were opened; and many bodies of the saints which slept arose" (Matt. 27:52). Paul affirmed both the death and resurrection of Christ when he said, "But now is Christ risen from the dead, and become the firstfruits of them that slept" (1 Cor. 15:20). The great hope of the Christian is that "we shall not all sleep, but we shall all be changed" (1 Cor. 15:51). If that refers to actual sleep, Christians must be the biggest group of insomniacs in the world. "For if we believe that Jesus died and rose again, even so them also which sleep in Jesus will God bring with him" (1 Thess. 4:14).

The clear teaching of the context in each of these passages is that sleep refers to death, not to a catnap. Today, people euphemistically, if not crudely, refer to death as a "dirt nap." But none of the passages about sleeping as death refers to the unbiblical teaching of "soul sleep." There is no reference here to a state of total unconsciousness. In fact, the Bible teaches just the opposite. Jesus' illustration of the rich man and the other Lazarus, the beggar, speaks of complete consciousness after death (Luke 16:19-31).

A necessary tandem

This story demonstrates the importance of Jesus' statement "I am the resurrection and the life. He who believes in me, though he may die, he shall live. And whoever lives and believes in Me shall never die. Do you believe this?" (John 11:25-26). There are two separate scenarios here. Jesus is the Resurrection. If we believe in Him, though we may die, we shall live again. Jesus is also the Life. If we believe in Him, we will never truly die.

That there are two scenarios is important. C. H. Dodd explained, "The former of the two elucidates the claim 'I am the resurrection', while the latter elucidates the claim 'I am the life', thus: 'I am the resurrection: he who has faith in me, even if he dies, will live again. I am the life; he who is alive and has faith in me will never die.'"[1]

Without resurrection from the dead, we are a pathetic people. "If in this life only we have hope in Christ, we are of all men the most pitiable"

(1 Cor. 15:19). Jesus is our Resurrection. Only He has the power to raise you from the dead. But Jesus is also our Life. Only He has the power to give you life that never ends.

What does Jesus mean? He means life is not the end. Jesus means death is not so cruel. Jesus means hope continues on the other side of the grave. Jesus means that even if we do die, we don't stay dead. Jesus means resurrection from the dead because Jesus is the Resurrection and the Life.

The only way death can open up into life is for resurrection and life to be inextricably connected, and they are in Jesus. Here's how it works.

We are born alive physically, but dead spiritually (Eph. 2:1). When we trust Jesus Christ as our Savior, we are born again (John 3:1-7), made alive spiritually, never to die spiritually. Unless the Lord returns for us first, we, too, will die and "sleep the sleep of death," as all our ancestors have before us. Our body goes to the ground; our soul goes immediately to be with the Lord (2 Cor. 5:8).

Yet because Jesus is the Resurrection *and* the Life, our dead bodies will be raised, rejoined with our soul, and our life will continue eternally. I believe this happens at the Rapture for church saints (1 Thess. 4:16), and at His return for Old Testament saints (Dan. 12:2) and Tribulation saints (Rev. 20:4, 6). Others may disagree, but God controls the timetable.

Death means separation, but once our bodies have been raised from the dead, body and soul will never be separated again. We will also never be separated from our Savior and God. That's why Jesus the Resurrection and the Life gives meaning to death. Without Him, the "I AM" God, death would be the end. Without Him, the "I AM" God, resurrection would not be possible. It's only because He is the Resurrection and the Life that we can face death with confidence.

What does Jesus the Resurrection and the Life mean to you?

As I write this I have a dear friend, a member of our Back to the Bible team, who is bedfast, in excruciating pain, being eaten alive by cancer. By the time you read this, He will be in heaven. Every time I face death, either the potential of my own or the reality of a friend's death, I ask myself, "What does Jesus the Resurrection and the Life really mean? What are the real issues beyond my own salvation that I must think about in preparing to die?" Here are some of my thoughts.

Death is the Christian's ultimate opportunity to glorify God

Jesus viewed the dark times of our lives, the really difficult times, not as something to be avoided or cursed, but as opportunities to glorify God (1 Pet. 1:7). If the dark times of life can be used to glorify God, what can be said of the darkest time—death?

When the messenger from Mary and Martha announced Lazarus' death to Jesus, the Master responded, "This sickness is not unto death [ending in death], but for the glory of God" (John 11: 4). And to Martha He said, "Did I not say to you that if you would believe you would see the glory of God?" (v. 40). Even death is a wonderful opportunity to glorify God. In fact, it's the ultimate opportunity.

My dying friend told me on many occasions during the stress of the dying process, "I only want to bring glory to God through all of this." He got his wish. That's an attitude that characterizes maturity of faith.

Have you given any thought to how your death will glorify God? Do you have a will? Does it reflect that you "were not redeemed with corruptible things, like silver or gold . . . but with the precious blood of Christ?" (1 Pet. 1:18-19). Your death is your ultimate opportunity to glorify God on this leg of your flight. Will you do it?

How often Christians, even those who are good stewards in life, are very poor stewards in death. You must take care of your family; God's Word commands it (Prov. 13:22). But often our children are miles ahead financially of where we were at their age. Don't forget to glorify the Lord with what He has entrusted to you in life. "Honor the LORD with your possessions" (Prov. 3:9).

There are other ways to glorify God in your death. What about your memorial service? Will it be mostly about you or mostly about Him? Will it be structured to glorify your life or reflect that glory back to the Resurrection and the Life? Have you taken the time to plan your memorial service, listing exactly the ways you want those who conduct it to glorify God? Why not think about that. And why not do something about it. Make your final act of witness your ultimate act of witness.

Resurrection life is not a future hope, but a present reality

When the Jews came to mourn the death of Lazarus, they did so without hope. It was a time of wailing, of cultural commiseration. It was not a time of hope. You've seen that on the television. When Jews and Arabs battle it out in the Holy Land, the TV cameras always show a group of wailing women almost overcome by grief.

But we Christians do not sorrow as those who have no hope (1 Thess. 4:13). Jesus is our hope. He is everything to us. He is our hope for every occasion. Jesus gives us living hope (1 Pet. 1:3), dying hope (1 Cor. 15:19-20), resurrection hope (1 Cor. 15:54), the blessed hope (Titus 2:11-13), even eternal hope (Titus 3:7).

But hope in life is not a future hope only. It is a present hope as well. Jesus the Resurrection and Life is with us right now. He is the Lord of life (John 1:4). While it is true that a believer's death will issue in new life, it is also true that we will never die. Spiritually, once we are made alive in Christ, we can never die. That's God's promise to us (John 3:16; 5:24; 10:28). Eternal life doesn't begin when time ends; eternal life begins when Christ comes into our life. That is truly the first day of the rest of our eternal life.

Don't spend your time speculating on what eternal life will be like. You're living it right now. Shape it. Mold it. Make it a reality in the way you live every day, and you'll have a greater appreciation of the power of Jesus the Resurrection and the Life.

Trusting Jesus as the Resurrection and Life means
you don't have to have answers to all your questions

Can't answer all the "why" questions in your life? Neither could Mary and Martha. Can't get comfortable with the "how long" questions of your life? Neither could Mary and Martha.

Trying to answer those questions will drive you crazy. God has a better idea. It's called rest, trust, faith, confidence. The psalmist David said, "Trust in the LORD . . . Delight yourself also in the LORD . . . Commit your way to the LORD . . . Rest in the LORD" (Ps. 37:3-5, 7). Those verbs are power words. Trust Him with your future. Delight in Him in the present. Commit your unresolved questions to Him. Rest in His ability to do more than you can ask or think.

Have faith in God's ability to make "all things work together for good to those who love God, to those who are the called according to His purpose" (Rom. 8:28). That's not a crutch; that's a promise of God. Have confidence that God's timetable will bring His best to you. And if you don't get answers to all your questions, trust the Resurrection and the Life to be withholding answers for your good.

We don't always understand the way God does things, especially when it comes to death. Let's not kid ourselves; we rarely understand the way God does things. But Jesus is the Resurrection and the Life. He can do for you and your loved ones what no one else can do. He can make it possible for you to live forever.

Take comfort in William Cowper's insightful poem:

> God moves in a mysterious way
> His wonders to perform;
> He plants his footsteps in the sea,
> And rides upon the storm.
> Ye fearful saints, fresh courage take;
> The clouds ye so much dread
> Are big with mercy, and shall break
> In blessings on your head.
> His purposes will ripen fast,
> Unfolding every hour;
> The bud may have a bitter taste,
> But sweet will be the flower.

William Barclay demonstrated good insight when he noted, "The last words of Edward the Confessor were: 'Weep not, I shall not die; and as I leave the land of the dying, I trust to see the blessings of the Lord in *the land of the living.*' We call this world the land of the living; but it would in fact be more correct to call it *the land of the dying.* Through Jesus Christ we know that we are journeying, not to the sunset, but to the sunrise."[2]

"I am the King; let Me share My kingdom with you."

IAM

CHAPTER 9

THE KING

Pilate therefore said to Him, "Are You a king then?" Jesus answered, "You say rightly that I am a king."
JOHN 18:37

As mentioned in the introduction to this book, there are seven "I am" statements in which the subject and the predicate are interchangeable. Those seven include I am the Bread of Life, the Light of the World, the Door, the Good Shepherd, the Way, Truth and Life, the Resurrection and the Life, and the Vine. But there are other "I am" statements that identify the person and work of Jesus Christ even though grammatically they do not consist of a subject and predicate nominative. One of these is "I am a King."

The account of Pilate's interrogation of Jesus is recorded in all four Gospels (Matt. 27:11; Mark 15:2; Luke 23:3; John 18:33). Each of them mentions that Pilate asked Jesus, "Are you a king?"

Here in the Gospel of John the author does not describe the early-morning session of the council, with Caiaphas presiding. There Jesus was condemned to death, but because the high priest had no authority to carry out an execution, the Jewish religious leaders had to hatch another plan. Somehow they had to force Pilate into pronouncing a death sentence on Jesus and then carry it out. But how? This would be tricky; they hated Pilate and he hated them.

Pontius Pilate was the Roman governor or procurator of the province of Judea (A.D. 26-36). As the procurator he had absolute authority over the non-Roman citizens of the province. Normally he lived in Caesarea, but during the Jewish festivals it was prudent for him to be in Jerusalem. His presence was necessary should there be a riot or insurrection.

Passover was a particularly dangerous feast because Jewish emotions ran so high.

But Pilate and the Jews had a longstanding, running feud. It was a battle of wills. Neither respected the other. Neither trusted the other. As often as they could, they would try to paint each other into a corner. Frequently the Jewish leaders attempted to create a situation that would put pressure on the Roman governor. That's what they intended to do with Jesus the King. They wanted rid of Him and His threat to their influence over God's people, but they wanted Pilate to do the job for them. Let him take the heat; let him have the blame.

The key to their plan was the right to execute. The issue was not whether the Jews had the right of capital punishment under Roman law, but whether or not their own law permitted it. The Sanhedrin apparently interpreted the sixth commandment ("You shall not murder") with extreme literalism in this case. If they executed someone not formally convicted of a crime, that would be murder according to the Law of Moses. But they were unwilling to press the Jesus case for fear of a popular uprising, so they turned to their archenemy, Pilate.

Sad observations

There are four very sad observations one can make about this whole incident. These conclusions reflect just how much a world that is no friend of grace hates our Savior.

First, it is evident that the Jews' claim not to be empowered both to condemn a person to death and carry out the execution didn't stop them from capital punishment when they chose. How else can we explain the stoning of Stephen (Acts 6:8-7:60)? It was men from the synagogue who secretly induced false witnesses to lie about Stephen. So their claim not to be able to carry out a death sentence was used as a pathetic ploy to get Pilate involved. Jesus' popularity was their real concern.

Second, when asked what accusation they brought against Jesus, the religious leaders told Pilate they had concluded that Jesus was a politically dangerous man after due investigation of the facts. "If He were not an evildoer, we would not have delivered Him up to you" (John 18:30). But there were no facts; there was no due process. The so-called witnesses were bribed and paid off for their fabrications. There was nothing but an illegal lynch-mob trial. They lied to Pilate.

Third, the intention of the Jewish accusers was not justice, but execution. They didn't want Pilate to try Jesus, to give Him a hearing, to invite witnesses who could testify either on His behalf or against Him. They weren't interested in due process. Their sole intent was for Pilate to kill Jesus. It was a very telling admission when they said to the governor, "It is not lawful for us to put anyone to death" (John 18:31). Their true colors were showing. Jesus' execution was the only thing they had on their mind.

Fourth, these men refused to enter Pilate's residence because entering a Gentile home or business entailed seven days of defilement under the Levitical law. Inasmuch as the Passover was imminent, they did not wish to be excluded from the festivities because of ceremonial uncleanness. So they maintained their religious scruples. They kept up a good front. Their outward whitewash of religion remained in tact. But during the whole time, they were lying about Jesus, plotting His murder and duplicitously involving Pilate. They not only wanted to avoid the stigma of stoning a very popular miracle-worker, but they also wanted to place that stigma on their old nemesis. So much for their religion.

These envious religious leaders thought if they could induce Pilate to sentence Jesus, knowing that crucifixion would result, that this would place Jesus under the curse of God (Deut. 21:22-23; cf. Gal. 3:13). His messianic claims would thus be discredited in the eyes of the people. They thought they could get rid of Jesus and stick Pilate with the rap. Little did they know that they were playing right into the perfect plan of God. They were being used to deliver Jesus as the Suffering Savior of Isaiah 53.

Let's see how this story unfolds and how the "I AM" God handles the declaration that He was indeed the King of the Jews. Because of the political intrigue involved and the timing of this "I am" statement, this becomes one of the more controversial of Jesus' claims. Still, it proves Him to be sufficient to be the King of Kings.

Setting the scene

Representatives from the Sanhedrin accompanied Jesus across town from the house of Caiaphas to the Praetorium. It was early in the morning. The Jews remained out in the courtyard of Pilate's residence while their political games with the governor began.

Pilate went out and asked what the problem was. Did they have an accusation to bring against Jesus? Pilate's response, "You take Him and judge Him according to your law" (John 18:31), reflects the fact he didn't want to get involved. The Jews reminded the governor that state execution was Rome's business and they saw Jesus as a politically dangerous person.

Undoubtedly Pilate was aware of the events on Palm Sunday just days earlier. The crowds lining the streets gleefully shouted, "Hosanna! 'Blessed is He who comes in the name of the LORD!' The King of Israel!" (John 12:13). Unwillingly Pilate began to be sucked into the Sanhedrin's plan to pin Jesus' crucifixion on him.

Pilate returned to the Praetorium, where he was accustomed to hearing judicial matters and making judgments while in Jerusalem. Jesus was brought in and Pilate asked Him point-blank, "Are You the King of the Jews?" (John 18:33). It's here that we begin to see the Governor of Judea interacting with the King of the Jews. It's also in this context that we hear Jesus say, "I am the king." Let's enter the judgment hall and listen in.

Jesus asks for a clarification

Jesus' response to the governor's question was entirely justified. It was asked for the sake of clarification. The reason Pilate asked the question would determine how Jesus framed His answer. If Pilate was asking, "Are you intending to lead a revolution against the Roman Empire and set up your own kingdom here in Judea?" Jesus' obvious answer would be "no." But if Pilate was asking, "Are you really a king?" Jesus could not lie and thus the answer would have to be "yes." A clarification was necessary because a simple yes or no answer would not suffice.

Jesus responded, "Are you speaking for yourself on this, or did others tell you this about Me?" (v. 34). If I could paraphrase what I think Jesus' question meant it would be, "Do you really want to know the answer for your own sake, or are you simply carrying out your duty as magistrate?" Was Pilate really interested or was he simply doing his job? Maybe the intent was, "Are you asking this of your own accord, or did others put you up to it?"

If Pilate had a sincere interest in who Jesus was and why He had come, this would be the perfect opportunity for Jesus to explain God's eternal plan for saving the world. But if Pilate was trying to trick Jesus into admitting He was an insurrectionist, the outcome would have been much different. Jesus' question clearly was to reveal Pilate's intent.

Apparently Pilate was shocked by Jesus' reply. This was the duly appointed Roman governor asking a direct question to one of his subjects (or so he thought). Pilate was accustomed to receiving answers to his questions, not challenges. When Pilate's question was answered with a question, he indignantly retorted, "Am I a Jew? Your own nation and the chief priests have delivered You to me. What have You done?" (v. 35).

To the "What have You done?" question Jesus could have replied, "Nothing. I am innocent. I have healed the sick, helped the poor, fed the hungry. I have preached of love and for this I am hated." But Jesus was not there to defend Himself. He was there to receive a sentence that was determined before the world began. So instead of addressing the "What have You done?" question, Jesus' response returned to the "Are you the King of the Jews?" question.

Pilate must have been stunned at this. What is wrong with this Galilean? Why does He come as a lamb before the slaughter without uttering a word in His defense? It was all too much for the governor.

Jesus doesn't fit the profile of a king

Pilate was baffled. His bewildered mind must have thought that Jesus had all the qualities of a king. He was kingly, He had a huge following, He was quite popular with the common people, He would be perfect in the role of insurgent. Jesus was certainly sufficient to be all that an insurrection would need.

And yet there was something about this Jesus that clearly did not fit the role of revolutionary. He was humble and meek. He was kind and mannerly. He was kingly, yet not defiant. He was not eager to be in Pilate's judgment hall, and yet He seemed to know that it was right for Him to be there. Jesus was sufficient to be whatever He intended to be.

If Jesus intended to lead the people against Rome, He was off to a bad start. Surely alienating the religious establishment was not the way to lead an army of Jewish zealots against the Roman eagle. Was this Jesus a king or was He just a pathetic failure? You can almost see Pilate's one eye raised in suspicion and hear the wheels grinding in his head. What did Jesus want? Why was He here? More to the point, what would Pilate do with Him?

Likely the problem for Pilate was expectation. Jesus was not what Pilate expected. Against Pilate's ingrown political interpretation of the word *king* was Jesus' definition of the term. Pilate knew what a *kingdom* was; he was a political appointee of Rome. But what did Jesus envision as His kingdom? Pilate worked indirectly for the emperor. He knew what a king should be. But how was Jesus defining what a king should be? The answers were forthcoming from the King.

Jesus knew Pilate was having a tough time understanding. In essence, Jesus was redefining terms right before Pilate's ears. What Jesus said about His being the King and the way He described His kingdom introduced foreign concepts to Pilate. Jesus said, "My kingdom is not of this world. If My kingdom were of this world, My servants would fight, so that I should not be delivered to the Jews; but now My kingdom is not from here" (v. 36). That must have blown Pilate away. He didn't understand any of that.

Kings are defined, at least in Roman terms, by two elements: a king has a definable territory over which he rules, and a king has a conscripted army who will defend him and his territory to the death. If you feed the Roman understanding of a king into your computer and try to match it with what Jesus just said, it will not compute. Jesus and Pilate weren't reading off the same page. How Pilate understood kingship was very different from the way Jesus understood it. So Jesus moved swiftly to redefine the terms and provide a new context in which to describe His kingship and His kingdom. Jesus spoke and Pilate listened, but he did not hear.

Jesus' kingdom originates in heaven

Notice that Jesus did not deny that He is a king. He couldn't deny it. To this point He simply clarified the issues because He knew Pilate was thinking politically and not spiritually. Thus Jesus began to define His kingdom in His own terms.

"My kingdom is not of this world" (v. 36). By this Jesus did not mean that His kingdom's presence is otherworldly. He meant its origin was otherworldly. If you read the Book of Revelation, especially chapter 19, you'll see very clearly that Jesus' kingdom has a great deal to do with this world. One day He will ride out of heaven on a white stallion. His eyes will be like a blazing fire. His robe will be dipped in blood. And His armies will follow Him, all wearing fine linen. He will conquer all nations as King of Kings and Lord of Lords. He will establish a kingdom that will last for a thousand years, longer than any in recorded history. His kingdom is for this world all right, but not yet. And it doesn't originate here.

As proof that His kingdom is not presently of this world, Jesus referred to the lack of an army, the lack of soldiers and officers, and all the trappings of kingship. Where was His military support? Where was the geographical territory that He called His power base? "If My kingdom were of this world, My servants would fight, so that I should not be delivered to the Jews" (v. 36).

No history of resistance

A quick check of the events of the last 24 hours in Jesus' life proves that Pilate's concept of kingdom needed to change if he was to understand Jesus' "I am" statement. When Jesus was praying in the Garden of Gethsemane, His time alone with God was interrupted by Judas, the betrayer, and a detachment of troops from the chief priests and Pharisees. They came with torches and lanterns and weapons (John 18:3). They came to take Jesus away. Rather than take a defensive posture, Jesus approached them and asked who they were looking for. When they said, "Jesus of Nazareth," the Lord responded "I am He." Not a textbook military maneuver.

In fact, He said it twice, and twice He asked them who they were looking for. And then the most amazing thing happened. He said, "I have told you that I am He. Therefore, if you seek Me, let these go their way" (John 18:8). Kings don't release their armies when their enemies come looking for them.

And when Simon Peter impetuously drew his sword to defend Jesus, cutting off the ear of the high priest's servant, Jesus rebuked the closest thing He had to a general: "Put your sword in its place, for all who take the sword will perish by the sword. Or do you think that I cannot now pray to My Father, and He will provide Me with more than twelve legions of angels?" (Matt. 26:52-53). It was clear that Jesus was a King, but the disciples and His followers in Israel were not His army. His troops were stationed elsewhere.

No noise of rebellion

That's the past 24 hours. What about now? What about while Jesus was being interrogated by Pilate? Did the governor hear the noise of rallying troops out in the dark streets of Jerusalem? Were there rumblings of revolution even as they spoke? Were the chants outside, "Down with Pilate"? Not at all. Jesus did not have troops maneuvering into position to assault the Fortress of Antonio. His kingdom was not of this world— not for now anyway.

So if Jesus is the King as He says, where does His kingdom originate? Where does Jesus of Nazareth get the authority to say, "I am King"? Who made Him king anyway? Those are legitimate questions because every king must either be invested with authority or take it upon himself.

Jesus' answer was splendid in its simplicity but sublime in its sagacity. "My kingdom is not of this world. . . . My kingdom is not from here" (John 18:36). What Christ meant was that the origin of His kingdom was from above. The authority for Christ's kingdom was from the Father in Heaven. His kingdom was not from this world; it was from another world. Like Jesus Himself, it was "from above" (John 8:23), and currently He reigns in the hearts of His followers. To see His kingdom, to enter His kingdom, one must be "born again" or "born from above" (John 3:3). Jesus' kingdom is a great kingdom. Its source is God, just as Jesus comes from God. "Every good gift and every perfect gift is from above, and comes down from the Father" (James 1:17).

One day Jesus' kingdom will take its place on this earth. But for now, His kingdom is in every one who has trusted Him as their Savior and Lord (Luke 17:21). It's a kingdom unlike any other. It would be hard for a politician like Pilate to grasp a kingdom of love and joy and peace. He was only used to kingdoms of bloodshed and slaughter and unbridled power. But then Pilate was exclusively accustomed to kingdoms that originated on earth, in the lust and greed of men. Christ's kingdom originates in heaven, in the loving heart of God.

As hard as this must have been for Pilate to understand, the other shoe was about to drop. There was more about the "I AM" God that Pilate needed to know. For clarification Pilate then said, "Are You a king then?" He was saying, "So you are a king, right? Does this mean you are saying you are a king?" Jesus responded, "You say rightly that I am a king." The "I AM" God, who has already said "I am the Door," "I am the Vine," "I am the Good Shepherd," now says "I am King"!

Jesus exclusively was born king

Jesus was not intentionally being noncommittal. He was leading Pilate into paths of truth where the governor had never walked before. Pilate was beginning to understand slightly. Jesus was a king, but not in the conventional sense, not in the immediate sense. Pilate was correct in inferring that his prisoner possessed and claimed royal authority. But there was more.

Jesus announced, "For this cause I was born, and for this cause I have come into the world" (v. 37). Was Jesus a man born to be king? Not exactly. He is much more. Jesus was not born to be king; Jesus was born King.

The men wise in astrology who came from the East to find the young child Jesus made their arduous journey on camel back over hundreds of miles to Jerusalem. When they arrived they wasted no time in asking, "Where is He who has been born King of the Jews?" (Matt. 2:2). "When King Herod heard these things, he was troubled, and all Jerusalem with him" (v. 3). Little doubt Herod was troubled. You can almost hear him saying, "Born King of the Jews? I thought I was king of the Jews!" But a babe had been born in a Bethlehem stable who was born King of the Jews.

One can either seize the throne and proclaim himself to be king, or one can be born the heir to the throne and succeed his father. But when you are born the heir to the throne, you are not born king; you are born a prince. Jesus, however, was not born Prince Jesus; He was born King Jesus!

> What Child is this, who, laid to rest,
> on Mary's lap is sleeping?
> Whom angels greet with anthems sweet,
> while shepherds watch are keeping?
> This, this is Christ the King,
> whom shepherds guard and angels sing;
> Haste, haste to bring Him laud,
> the Babe, the Son of Mary.
>
> — William C. Dix

"For this cause I was born." Jesus is King. Nathaniel knew it the first time he met the Master. "Rabbi, You are the Son of God! You are the King of Israel!" (John 1:49). Many in the crowds knew it. Once "Jesus perceived that they were about to come and take Him by force to make Him king," so He stole away to the mountain to be alone with His Heavenly Father (6:15). People who lined His path at the triumphal entry into Jerusalem were convinced Jesus was King. They shouted, "Hosanna! 'Blessed is He who comes in the name of the LORD!' The King of Israel!" (12:13).

But all the skeptical Pilate could manage were four semi-cynical references to Jesus as King. At first he questioned, "Are You the King of the Jews?" (18:33). Then to clarify he asked, "Are You a king then?" (v. 37). In desperation he asked the people, "Do you therefore want me to release to you the King of the Jews?" (v. 39). And finally he presented the beaten, bloodied, bruised Messiah and said, "Behold your King!" (19:14).

Pilate never really believed Jesus was King. He saw Him as a pathetic man, perhaps deluded into believing He was king of something. But if Pilate didn't believe the world was round, would that make it any less so? Most Jewish people today do not believe Jesus is Messiah. But denying Jesus' messiahship doesn't nullify it. We can say Jesus was not King, but the facts remain the same. Truth doesn't become truth when we believe it; it's truth whether we believe it or not. As Winston Churchill once said, "Truth is incontrovertible. Panic may resent it; ignorance may deride it; malice may distort it; but there it is."

Here is truth. Jesus is King, today in our hearts, one day in our world. All hail, King Jesus! All hail, Emmanuel!

Jesus' kingdom is governed by truth

One of the cornerstones of Jesus' kingdom is that it is not governed by brute force, but by the force of the truth. The King said, "For this cause I have come into the world, that I should bear witness to the truth. Everyone who is of the truth hears My voice" (11:37).

Most civilizations have been built on the assumption that truth and power are opposites. Most people believe they are incompatible. Either you have truth or you have someone who crushes the truth with power. Do you remember those scenes from Tiananmen Square in Beijing? A young dissident standing in front of a tank, impeding its progress. I have stood in Tiananmen Square and wondered what it would have been like to be that young protester. What courage in the battle for truth! But, at last, power put down the truth. Truth angers those whom it does not fully convince.

Truth rules

In Jesus' kingdom, however, power and truth are not incompatible. In fact, the power of His kingdom is the truth. As King, Jesus' instrument is not a sword but the truth. He fights the lies of Satan with the truth (John 8:44). He frees those enslaved by sin with the truth (v. 32). He elevates our steps from darkness with the light of the truth (1 John 1:6-7). He bears testimony to God's truth, unadulterated truth, the only kind of truth that matters eternally.

Jesus' kingdom of truth overshadows all other kingdoms. He recruits His army from those who discover the truth and are freed by it. His troops are those who once were enslaved to sin and the big lies of immorality, idolatry and self-indulgence. Once they were fornicators, adulterers, homosexuals, thieves, extortioners. But these can never inherit the kingdom of God. One day they came face to face with Jesus, however, and believed the truth of the Gospel. They have been washed, sanctified and justified in the name of the Lord Jesus (1 Cor. 6:9-11). They're in the army now. They've joined up with the King.

While in most kingdoms power and truth are antithetical, in Jesus' kingdom they are congenial. In most kingdoms power is irrational and truth is impotent; in Jesus' kingdom truth is power.

What's more, Jesus flatly asserted, "Everyone who is of the truth hears My voice" (John 18:37). Where does that leave Pilate? Did he hear what Jesus was saying to him? Do you? Did Pilate come to a knowledge of the truth? Have you? Paul said that God "desires all men to be saved and to come to the knowledge of the truth" (1 Tim. 2:4).

Jesus' kingdom is not made up of power-hungry barons; it's made up of truth-seekers, men and women who have asked honest questions and found honest answers in the sufficiency of Jesus Christ. He said, "I am the way, the truth and the life. No one comes to the Father except through Me" (John 14:6).

Your response to Jesus as the truth determines whether or not you find the truth and enter His kingdom. Whatever that response is, make sure it's genuine. Pilate responded to Jesus' kingdom of truth by asking, "What is truth?" (18:38). How did he mean this? Was he facetious, scornful, impatient, despairing? Was he sincere, seeking an honest answer? It's impossible to know, even from the context. But it is possible for you to know what motivates you to seek Jesus as the King of truth. Make sure you are a genuine seeker after the kingdom that is governed by truth. When you are, you will find the One who said, "I am a king."

Have you seen the sufficiency of Jesus Christ to be your King? Have you found Him to be Lord and Master in a way that brings good to you and glory to God the Father? He has the right credentials, the right attitude, the right demeanor to be King. He has the right to be King of your life. As King He is more than able to meet the needs and care for the welfare of His subjects. Here's why.

Jesus' kingdom supersedes all other kingdoms

When Pilate washed his hands of Jesus and sent him away with the mob to be crucified, the kingship controversy was not yet over. It was customary to put a placard on the cross when someone was crucified that indicated to all passersby the crime for which this person was receiving such torture. Jesus was no exception. The game of cat and mouse that Pilate had been playing with the priests and Sanhedrin came to a climax here.

Their hatred for each other was evident. That they tried to pass responsibility for the death of Jesus back and forth is also evident. And it appeared that the Jews had won. Pilate agreed to sentence Jesus to death by crucifixion. But if you think the religious leaders won, you do not know how foxy this old Roman was.

When Pilate placed the title on the cross over Jesus' head, he had his soldiers write: "Jesus of Nazareth, The King of the Jews" (John 19:19). The religious leaders were outraged. What an insult. The chief priests angrily said to Pilate, "Do not write, 'The King of the Jews,' but, 'He said, "I am the King of the Jews"'" (v. 21). If the title were allowed to stand, it would say to the world that Jesus' crime was that indeed He was the King of the Jews.

What's more, writes commentator Merrill Tenney, "the placard was written in three languages, in order to make the inscription plain to all: Aramaic, for the local inhabitants; Latin, for the officials; Greek, the lingua franca of the eastern Mediterranean world. Its content was Pilate's psychological revenge on the Jewish hierarchy for forcing his decision."[1]

And since Jesus was crucified in a public place, in broad daylight, everyone who passed by that busy place would know what the title read.

But the religious leaders' protest fell on deaf ears. Pilate had the last laugh. "What I have written, I have written" (v. 22). The title would stand. It was Pilate's way of saying, "Take it or leave it!" The King was crucified on the cross of Calvary.

What does King Jesus mean to you?

There is incredible irony in this "I am" account of Jesus. He could have called 12 legions of angels, but He stood alone before Pilate the governor. At one point, agitated by Jesus' silence, Pilate exploded, "Are You not speaking to me? Do You not know that I have power to crucify You, and power to release You?" (v. 10). Jesus' answer must have rocked Pilate back on his heels. "You could have no power at all against Me unless it had been given you from above" (v. 11). Where Jesus came from is where the power comes from. Here we begin to understand who was really in control of these proceedings.

Charles R. Erdman describes the irony. Speaking of Pilate writing the inscription over Jesus' head, he says, "He did so in bitter irony; he meant that the only king, or deliverer, the subject Jews could boast or need expect was a helpless sufferer, dying the death of a malefactor. Pilate, however, like Caiaphas, was affirming more than he intended. What he stated was the truth, and the very truth John wished to establish by His Gospel, namely, that Jesus was 'the Christ,' that is, the King of the Jews. Here, too, was a prophecy; the only Saviour of the Jews, their only hope now and ever, is the same crucified Jesus."[2]

What does it mean to you that Jesus is King? How does His kingship affect the way you do your work, spend your money, plan your future? Does King Jesus change the way you view the unexplained or unexpected things that happen to you? What does His kingship mean in everyday life? Think about two things.

Because Jesus is king in the heart of every believer,
we are all under authority of a heavenly kingdom

All the work I do is kingdom work. All the work you do is kingdom work. All the work every subject of the King of Kings does is kingdom work. That work may be changing a spark plug or data entry or military

167

service or raising a family, but for subjects of the King, all we do, we do for Him. That makes it kingdom work.

Paul was right when he said, "Whatever you do in word or deed, do all in the name of the Lord Jesus, giving thanks to God the Father through Him" (Col. 3:17). Because what you do is done for your King, it gives meaning to all that you do. Every task you perform with your hands is a task done for the kingdom. Every brain function you execute is done for the kingdom of Jesus Christ. When you and I remember that, it gives infinite, eternal meaning to our every task.

When you next go to work, remember that whatever you do will touch eternity if you do it for your King, as a member of His kingdom. Do it cheerfully. Do it well. Do good work because it's kingdom work.

Because Jesus is King, we can see the hand of God behind the scenes in every area of our life

The story of Jesus' death and crucifixion is tragic from the human perspective. But behind it all, using the envy of the Sanhedrin and the spineless character of Pilate, God was somehow making all these proceedings fit His divine plan. Although ill-motivated, the Jews had to succeed in getting Pilate involved because it was prophesied that Jesus' hands and feet would be pierced (Ps. 22:16). Though it irritated Pilate that Jesus was not more vocal in His answers and mystified the governor that Jesus would not defend Himself, that, too, was prophesied (Isa. 53:7).

Because Jesus is King, we realize that His kingdom in our hearts is no meaningless expression. He is King and He is in control. Even in the events of our lives that don't seem to go the way we choose, the King is still in charge.

It may be difficult sometimes, but seek to look behind the faces and events of your life to discern why God put them there. In our King's kingdom, we are not left to chance. When you take the King with you everywhere you go, you take His kingdom rule as well. Enjoy that rule.

Jesus is sufficient to give meaning to every meaningless event of your life. See Him as your King and you'll have no difficulty seeing Him as your sufficiency. Because Jesus is King, the future of the kingdom is not in doubt.

"*I am the Way; let Me show you.*"

CHAPTER 10

I Am

THE WAY

Jesus said to him, "I am the way, the truth, and the life. No one comes to the Father except through Me."
JOHN 14:6

Apart from death, there is probably no more sorrowful time than when you must move. On more than one occasion my family and I have loaded a U-Haul truck with all the stuff we owned and left friends and acquaintances behind to move to a distant city. It wasn't easy. It never is.

In August 1990, my family and I moved from New York to Nebraska to become part of the international ministry of Back to the Bible. Our two youngest daughters, Tina and Tiffany, moved with us because they were still in high school. Tim and Lisa, my son and daughter-in-law, were married and Tim was attending seminary in Virginia. But my oldest daughter, Tracy, and her husband, John, were left behind in New York State. I'll never forget the look on her face as we pulled away. We left her! I have seen the sad eyes of a Beagle puppy that weren't as sad as hers.

Jesus' disciples were feeling that same sense of loss as Jesus prepared them for His death at Calvary and His imminent departure. They were completely bewildered and discouraged. Jesus had assured His little band that one would betray Him (John 13:21), one would deny Him (v. 38), and all of them would forsake Him (Matt. 26:31). Most distressing of all, He was about to go where they could not immediately come (John 13:33). It was the emotional equivalent of stepping on the teeth of a rake and getting whacked in the face time and time again. His disciples were depressed and not a little uncertain about the future.

Stay calm

It is in this context that John 14 opens with the comforting words,

"Let not your heart be troubled." Jesus was telling His disciples, "Don't continue to be distressed and stirred up." That's what the word (Gr. *tarassestho*) means—to be stressed out or agitated. John had used this same word several times already to describe stressful situations.

In John 5, Jesus encountered a crippled man who struggled to get into the Pool of Bethesda, but someone always beat him. The man explained that the reason he so wanted in the water was because an angel often came down to the pool and stirred the water, and whoever made it in first was healed (5:4). The word *stirred* is the same word as translated "troubled" in John 14:1.

And when Jesus struggled with fears about His own crucifixion, He admitted, "Now My soul is troubled, and what shall I say? 'Father, save Me from this hour'? But for this purpose I came to this hour" (12:27). Jesus' agitated soul was quieted because of the sovereign God's comfort. Now He bid His disciples to quiet their hearts using the same source.

Yes, Jesus would go away and prepare a place for them to live forever, but He would also come back (14:3). That was the basis for the disciples' comfort. Jesus must go, but He would return. That was His promise, not only to these disciples, but to you and me as well. This is one of Jesus' few allusions to His return in John's gospel. He wasn't referring to His resurrection or even to the believer's death. This can mean nothing less than the Rapture of the church, when Christ will return for His own (1 Thess. 4:13-18). It is when we will be with Him (John 17:24) and remain with Him forever. No more separation, no more good-byes. We will be caught up to meet the Lord in the air, "and thus we shall always be with the Lord" (1 Thess. 4:18).

Piercing the calm

It was Thomas' poignant question that broke the air of promise and splendor. "Lord, we do not know where You are going, and how can we know the way?" (John 14:5). Thomas was utterly honest, frequently pessimistic and thoroughly uninhibited. He never suppressed his feelings but always voiced his opinion (cf. 11:16). Obviously, he reflected the despair and bewilderment of the other ten.

The answer to this doubter's question occasioned one of the most significant of Jesus' "I am" statements. This answer was not to supply information about where He was going, but to express that He was sufficient to provide a way for the disciples to get there too. Notice, Jesus didn't even answer the "where" question; He changed it to the "way" question. Not only is Jesus sufficient to provide a place for us, but He is also sufficient to be the Way to that place.

The "I AM" God said, "I am the way." The way to what, or to whom? What did Jesus mean? It is one of the most quoted verses in Scripture, but do we really know what the Master meant? There is hardly a Christian funeral that I attend and do not hear these verses. But what was Jesus really intending to say?

The way to what?

There can be no question that man has lost his way spiritually. Right from the Garden of Eden, we have been searching for something, for anything. Men and women have tried almost everything under the sun to find our way, but without success. But Jesus had the audacity to say, "I am the way."

Religions of all stripes have claimed to be the way, but the way to what? The Chinese Taoist philosopher Lao-tsu applied the phrase "the way" to the "supreme cause," by which he meant the passage to the highest perfection. But is moving to a higher state of consciousness the way, or are the Taoists just fooling themselves?

To what is Jesus the Way? Let your Bible provide the answer, and let's examine our own lives to see if Jesus is the Way for us. If Jesus is our sufficiency, He is sufficient to be the Way to all things good and glorious.

Jesus is the Way to God

Many people claim to have found the way to God. They go to church, they live in a moral manner, they are decent people who do good things. They claim to worship God as Creator and Father, but they know nothing of Jesus. They haven't read enough of their Bible to discover that, apart from the Savior, God is a consuming fire and is utterly unapproachable. Jesus is the Way to God.

God has always shrouded Himself to allow us to come near to Him. What He has shrouded Himself in has varied, but something was always necessary. Without such protection, He is unapproachable, inaccessible. So when Moses was called to go to the top of Mount Sinai and met God alone, the glory of the Lord rested on the mountain and God spoke to him out of the glory cloud. Even then Moses recorded, "The sight of the glory of the LORD was like a consuming fire" (Ex. 24:17). God had shrouded Himself in a cloud of glory to protect Moses from what would have certainly been disintegration by conflagration. Moses could not approach God except through the glory of God or he would have been burned alive.

And later, when Moses asked to see the glory of God, to come face to face with the Sovereign God of the universe, the unattainable God said, "No way, but I'll do something just as good. I'll put you in the cleft of the rock, cover you with My hand and when I pass by you shall see my back, but not my face" (a loose translation of Exodus 33:22-23). Being in the cleft of the rock was as good as it could get when it came to approaching God in the Old Testament.

But we have greater understanding of what God was doing with Moses than he did. It's not a coincidence that Jesus Christ is both the glory of God (Acts 7:55; Rom. 3:23) and the Spiritual Rock that Israel encountered in the wilderness (1 Cor. 10:4). The glory that Moses saw from the cleft of the rock is the glory that we see in Jesus. Jesus is the Rock, cleft for us. As the hymn writer pleads, "Rock of ages, cleft for me; let me hide myself in Thee."

The way cleared

Right from the start, as far back as the Garden of Eden, mankind has tried to find a way to God. But men and women, left to themselves, have always been unsuccessful. Why? They've been looking in the wrong places. They've looked in nature and the spirit world, and come up empty. They've tried being religious, and been unsatisfied. They've sought to do good things and stay out of serious trouble, but only found themselves in trouble with God. Men and women have consistently looked for a way back to God in places where it can't be found.

Adam and Eve sinned and the initial way was closed to God. But God opened a new way, in the right place, through the incarnation and sufferings of His Son. Thousands of years after our first parents were unsuccessful in bridging the gap between their sin and a holy God, that Holy God sent His Son to die for them, and for us, to pave the way back to Him. This was announced to our first parents when God pledged that the seed of the woman would bruise the serpent's head (Gen. 3:15).

Charles Simeon observed, "There were two obstacles to their [Adam and Eve's] re-admission to the divine favour; these were guilt and corruption. But both of these were to be removed by Jesus, the former by His blood, the latter by His Spirit. Thus is Christ our way also to the Father, making atonement for us by his meritorious death, and renewing us by his all-sufficient grace."[1]

It's abundantly clear. If you want to approach God, you have to use God's pathway. Jesus said, "I am the way" to come to God. Your search is over. Your struggles are finished. The way is open to you. The Way is Jesus Christ.

Jesus is the Way to heaven

You've heard that "all roads lead to Rome." When you're traveling the Italian countryside, it really seems as if they do. "Roma" signs appear on highways hundreds of miles from the Eternal City. But there's a similar belief that is definitely not true. It is not at all true that all roads lead to heaven. In fact, the opposite is true. All roads fall short of heaven, except one.

Can a Buddhist find the right road to heaven? Certainly, but not in Buddhism. Can a Hindu find the only way that leads to heaven? Absolutely, but not in Hinduism. The same is true for a Muslim. He can find the road to heaven, but not in the Koran. Different religions are not traveling different ways to heaven; they are simply following a circuitous route to hell. That's what the Bible says.

There is only one way to heaven. Jesus said, "I am the way . . . . No one comes to the Father except through me." If you want to go to God's heaven, you have to go in God's way. Jesus is the Way, the one Way.

There are not hoards of people making their way to God by their own ingenuity. Ingenuity is not the basis for eternal salvation. There are not many religions all leading to God. Religion is man's attempt to reconcile himself to God, but if we are to be reconciled, God has to do the reconciling.

Read Jesus' own words; they speak volumes by themselves: "Enter by the narrow gate, for wide is the gate and broad is the way that leads to destruction, and there are many who go in by it. Because narrow is the gate and difficult is the way which leads to life, and there are few who find it" (Matt. 7:13-14). The world is on the broad road to destruction. It is paved with good intentions, good deeds and manmade religions. The narrow way to God is paved with the blood of Jesus Christ.

175

Again Jesus' words: "No one has ascended to heaven but He who came down from heaven, that is, the Son of Man who is in heaven. And as Moses lifted up the serpent in the wilderness, even so must the Son of Man be lifted up, that whoever believes in Him should not perish but have eternal life" (John 3:13-15).

Jesus is not *a* way to heaven, one among many, but *the* Way to heaven. Remember what the Bible says: "There is no other name under heaven given among men by which we must be saved" (Acts 4:12). Jesus is the only name that God recognizes as the Way to heaven.

Heaven is God's home, and the only way to heaven is the only way to God. Jesus Christ said, "I am the way . . . . No one comes to the Father except through Me." Believe this, and start for heaven today. Look for another way, and you'll miss heaven completely. The "I AM" God said, "I am *the* way."

Jesus is the way to peace

This world is not a very peaceful place. A group of academicians and historians have estimated that since the year 3600 B.C., the world has known only 292 years of peace. During this period there have been 14,351 wars, large and small. If it's not a Latin American country, it's an Asian one. If it's not in the Middle East, it's an African nation teetering on the brink of genocide.

But the lack of peace in our world is eclipsed by an even greater problem—the lack of peace in our personal lives. This lack of peace drove six teenagers in Pearl, Mississippi, to band together in a satanic cult, which ended with the deaths of three people. This lack of personal peace contributes annually to the deaths of more than 4,000 teens in America between the ages of 15 and 24 by suicide. It's a need for peace in our lives that causes people to buy millions of dollars of tranquilizers, herbal remedies and self-improvement books annually. We are restless people and we don't know why.

Augustine (A.D. 354-430), one of the greatest of the Latin church fathers, nearly drove himself insane looking for peace. He tried everything he could think of, from philosophy to prostitution. Finally he went to Rome in search of meaning and there he encountered Ambrose, the Bishop of Milan. Ambrose led him to Jesus Christ, and Augustine found the way to peace. Of Jesus and his search for peace, Augustine said, "The heart is restless until it finds rest in Thee."

176

When we discover Jesus as the "I AM" God, we discover Him as the One who makes our peace between God and us (Rom. 5:1). We who had been at war with God now have laid down our arms, and through the cross (Col. 1:20) Jesus has become our peace treaty. Jesus didn't just negotiate our peace; He is our peace (Eph. 2:14). We enjoy peace as one of the fruits of the Spirit (Gal. 5:22), because now the peace of God rules in our hearts (Col. 3:15).

The way to peace is not the United Nations, not negotiations and not reparations. The way to peace is a person. Jesus said, "I am the way" to peace. He is the Prince of Peace (Isa. 9:6). When we trust Jesus and His death to be all that is necessary to reverse our rebellion against God, when we ask Jesus to bring peace to our lives, we discover true peace, inner peace, eternal peace, God's peace.

If your heart is restless like Augustine's was, find your rest in God. Job 22:21 says, "Now acquaint yourself with Him, and be at peace." Psalm 37:37 says, "Mark the blameless man, and observe the upright; for the future of that man is peace." And Isaiah 26:3 says of God, "You will keep him in perfect peace, whose mind is stayed on You."

When you give your life over to the Way, Jesus Christ, you will experience peace that you cannot conceive possible. With the psalmist David you will say, "I will both lie down in peace, and sleep; for You alone, O Lord; make me dwell in safety" (Ps. 4:8).

A friend visited an elderly woman who was badly crippled by arthritis. When he asked, "Do you suffer much?" the woman responded, "Yes, but there is no nail here" as she pointed to her hand. "He had the nails, I have the peace." Then she pointed to her head and said, "There are no thorns here. He had the thorns, I have the peace." She touched her side, "There is no spear here. He had the spear, I have the peace."

Jesus is our peace. He is not just the Way to heaven in the future. Jesus is the Way to peace right now. And there's more.

Jesus is the Way to joy

Do you know what it is to experience joy? If you won big in the lottery, would that bring you joy? If your team scored at the buzzer and beat its biggest rival, would that make you joyful? What gives you the greatest joy? Don't know? Can't decide? Maybe that's because you don't really know what joy is.

177

Let me ask the questions again and change one word. Do you know what it is to experience happiness? If you won big in the lottery, would that bring you happiness? If your team scored at the buzzer and beat its biggest rival, would that make you happy? What gives you the greatest happiness?

Did your perspective change when I changed the word? I thought it would. There is a difference between happiness and joy. Happiness can be experienced by just about anyone, but joy cannot. Happiness is a dog wagging its tail. Happiness is a Tin Roof sundae. Happiness is when you say "I do." Happiness is a brilliant sunset. Happiness is open to everyone, but not joy. Joy is an inner feeling of contentment, satisfaction and serenity.

Happiness arises out of things being right between you and your world. Joy arises out of things being right between you and your God. Happiness comes when good fortune comes. Joy comes when Jesus comes. Happiness is temporary and changeable. Joy is permanent and unchanging.

Joy is not a thermometer; it's more like a thermostat. Joy doesn't rise and fall with circumstances. Joy controls your spiritual temperature when you can't control what's taking place around you. Oswald Chambers understood this difference. He said, "Happiness depends on what happens; joy does not."

In the Old Testament when you wanted to express your joy, you shouted. The Hebrew word *rinnah* is used; it means a cry of praise or a shout for joy. Psalm 32:11 says, "Be glad in the LORD and rejoice, you righteous; and shout (*rinnah*) for joy, all you upright in heart!" And Psalm 35:27 says, "Let them shout (*rinnah*) for joy and be glad, who favor my righteous cause; and let them say continually, Let the LORD be magnified." In both cases those who have a right relationship with God, those living righteously, have a joy to shout about.

This expression of joy comes from a heart at peace with God. It comes from a righteous relationship with God that is permanent. The Hebrew word *simchah* means "gladness" or "inner joy." Psalm 16:11: "You will show me the path of life; in Your presence is fullness of joy (*simchah*); at Your right hand are pleasures forevermore." Psalm 21:1: "The king shall have joy (*simchah*) in Your strength, O LORD; and in Your salvation how greatly shall he rejoice!"

Anybody can be happy, but not everybody can have joy. Only those who have been shown the path of life have found full joy in the presence of God. To find joy, you must encounter the Way. Jesus is the Way.

Things aren't any different in the New Testament. The common Greek word for joy is *chara* and means "joy" or "gladness." It, too, implies a right relationship with God. Jesus said, "These things I have spoken to you, that My joy (*chara*) may remain in you, and that your joy (*chara*) may be full" (John 15:11). When the Word of God spread throughout Asia Minor, Acts 13:52 says, "And the disciples were filled with joy (*chara*) and with the Holy Spirit."

The apostle Paul understood this. Speaking of the need for believers to help others and not hinder their spiritual progress by personal actions, he said, "For the kingdom of God is not food and drink, but righteousness and peace and joy in the Holy Spirit" (Rom. 14:17). This kind of deep-down, heartfelt, relational joy is one of the fruits of the Spirit (Gal. 5:22).

Joy is very different from happiness. Everybody can be happy, but only those rightly related to God can have joy. And who is the Way to be rightly related to God? Who is the Way to true and permanent joy? Jesus said, "I am the way."

When you have Jesus living in you, joy never leaves. Happiness leaves every time you lose a ball game, blow an engine or have to cut the grass. Happiness fluctuates with your circumstances because happiness is related to your circumstances. True joy is not. True joy is related to God, and you are related to God through Jesus Christ.

There's a wonderful Swedish hymn set to a Swedish folk melody that speaks of this kind of joy. When translated into English the words don't always rhyme, but the message is too plain to miss.

> O let your soul now be filled with gladness,
> Your heart redeemed rejoice indeed!
> O may the thought banish all your sadness
> That in His blood you have been freed,
> That God's unfailing love is yours,
> That you the only Son were given,
> That by His death He has opened heaven,
> That you are ransomed as you are.
>
> — Peter Jonsson Aschan

Jesus is the Way—the Way to God, the Way to heaven, the Way to peace, the Way to joy and so much more. But you cannot enjoy the Way unless you are obedient to it. Once you discover the path that leads to God, you must stay on it. You must live in Him and not deviate to the right or left. You can not say, "I'll give Jesus a try for awhile and see if He works, and if He doesn't work for me, I'll try something else." That won't work because Jesus is the only game in town. Take very seriously what He said: "I am the way, the truth, and the life. No one comes to the Father except through Me."

J. C. Ryle commented, Christ is 'the way'—the way to heaven and peace with God. He is not only the guide, and teacher, and lawgiver, like Moses; He is Himself the door, the ladder, and the road, through whom we must draw near to God. He has opened the way to the tree of life, which was closed when Adam and Eve fell, by the satisfaction He made for us on the cross."[2]

Try as many ways as you wish, but they all lead to the same place. Only Jesus can save you from your sin. Only Jesus can lead you to God. Only Jesus can bring peace and joy to your heart. If you haven't trusted Him yet as Savior, remember: He is the only Way!

What does Jesus the Way mean to you?

Christianity, rightly understood, is the most exclusive religion in the world. For this it is criticized by all of man's religions. Pluralism is popular today. Saying there is only one way to God seems a bit restrictive. So be it. It's what the Bible says, and if the Bible is to be believed, Jesus as the only Way to God also must be believed.

So what does the Way mean to you? What have you discovered about Jesus the Way? What does it mean that Jesus is the only Way? Many things come to mind; let's think about three.

The Way means we are not eternally isolated from God

They've made a movie about it now, but I don't need the film version to remember. I was glued to my television when it happened. Houston gave the "good to go" and Apollo 13 blasted into space. It was April 11, 1970. Do you remember where you were? Every thing was fine until the third day, April 13th. Then, disaster struck. An explosion aboard the space craft damaged their oxygen source. For many hours it appeared as if the American space program was about to lose three more pioneers.

There was a real threat they might die of oxygen deprivation. Fortunately, they survived. But what if the explosion damaged their guidance system instead? They would have been able to breathe but not navigate. They might have drifted aimlessly into the cold darkness of space, cut off completely from all they had ever known.

None of us has any idea what such isolation would mean. Just imagine not being able to see your family again. Imagine not having a picnic in the park, a touch football game in the backyard, a round of golf. Imagine no one around, no people, no pets, nothing but silent emptiness. Imagine being fully aware that you had seen a human face for the last time. Imagine the isolation.

We aren't frequently cognizant of it, but the human race as a whole, and you and I as individuals, have experienced such isolation. When Adam and Eve sinned in the Garden of Eden severe consequences followed (Gen. 3:16-19). Severe consequences always follow sin. But the most severe of all must have been the isolation.

Genesis 3:23-24 records, "Therefore the LORD God sent him out of the garden of Eden to till the ground from which he was taken. So He drove out the man; and He placed cherubim at the east of the garden of Eden, and a flaming sword which turned every way, to guard the way to the tree of life." Man and woman were on the outside. They had lost everything. They were isolated from the tree of life, isolated from their home in paradise and most important, isolated from God.

When our first parents sinned, they burned the bridge back to God. There was no returning to the tree, no returning to paradise, no returning to God. Isolation was horrible; it was final; it was permanent. And then it happened. Man could not build a bridge back to God, but God could build a bridge to man. The loving Sovereign did just that one night in a little village called Bethlehem. Man couldn't go to God, so God came to man.

When Jesus said He was the Way, He meant that mankind was no longer eternally isolated from God. The Way had been made for us to return to communion with God, to return to a right relationship with Him. Jesus jettisoned the isolation and replaced it with access to God. It was the original space walk. God took the first step to come to our planet and remove the eternal isolation between us. Jesus is the Way.

The Way is personal, relational, understandable

Sometimes life can be complicated. If you don't believe that, try understanding a computer manual or the directions to program your VCR. Why do these things have to be so difficult?

Salvation isn't like that. It isn't difficult. God made it so simple that the smallest child could understand. God loves us. We sinned against Him and became isolated from Him. He sent His Son, Jesus Christ, to die and pay the penalty to have our sins forgiven and our guilt cleared. If we trust what Jesus did at Calvary as solely sufficient to cleanse us from our sin, we will be saved. There it is. The Gospel. Thousands of books have been written about it. Multivolume theological works have tried to explain it. But there it is! The simple Gospel.

What makes the Gospel so simple? The way God presented it to us. He didn't send a manual, a chart, a graph or an e-mail. He sent a baby. You can't get much simpler than that. He sent a person, not a proposal. He sent His Son, not a surrogate. He sent a Savior, not a commentator. God made salvation personal, relational, understandable.

I don't know who first said it, but it's absolutely correct. "If our greatest need had been information, God would have sent us an educator. If our greatest need had been technology, God would have sent us a scientist. If our greatest need had been money, God would have sent us an economist. But since our greatest need was forgiveness, God sent us a Savior."

Think of it. Not an idea, a reality. Not a machine, a baby. Not a warrior, a humble servant. Not a scholar, a man of the people. Not a directive, a person. It's the difference between getting voice mail or e-mail and receiving a visit from someone who loved you enough to die for you. Which would you rather have? God provided the Way. The "I AM" God came Himself to be the Way.

The Way must be followed to return to God

If you've ever been lost in the woods and couldn't find your way out, you know how terrifying it can be. But when you discovered the path that led to safety, did you follow it or did you decide to set out on your own and find another way?

Jesus is the Way. To return from isolation to a relationship with God you must discover the Way and follow Him. He is the path to God, the only path there is. When you find the path, stay on it.

A former teaching colleague of mine, Dr. Paul Fink, once told me about an incident in his family. His little daughter, Ann, and he went for a walk in the woods. Since there was poison ivy all around, plus briars and insects, Paul told his daughter toddling behind him to stay on the path. She said she would.

After a few minutes of walking, the father turned around to find little Ann over in the briars. "Ann, I told you. Stay on the path." "I will, Daddy." They resumed walking. A minute later and a quick check over his shoulder confirmed that Ann was in the poison ivy. A bit sterner this time Paul said, "Ann, you must stay on the path." "I will, Daddy." Satisfied, father and daughter continued their walk. It wasn't long before Paul heard the crunching of little feet on the sticks beneath the undergrowth of the woods. Sure enough, Ann had strayed from the path again. Dad was furious. This time very sternly Paul said, "Ann, you must stay on the path. If you don't stay on the path, I'm going to have to punish you. Do you understand?" The little girl nodded affirmatively.

Then the child taught her father a most valuable lesson. She asked, "Daddy, what's a path?"

Jesus is the path. Absolutely no one comes to the Father except by the way He provides. Once you have discovered the only way there is and you understand that He is the path, get to know the path and stay on it. For all who have found the way to God, the way to heaven, the way to peace and the way to joy, you have found Jesus the Way. Enjoy the journey, not just the destination.

"I am the Truth; let me persuade you."

CHAPTER 11

THE TRUTH

Jesus said to him, "I am the way, the truth, and the life. No one comes to the Father except through Me."
JOHN 14:6

There have been many classic one-on-one confrontations in history. Julius Caesar and Brutus ("*Et tu, Brute?*"). Mike Tyson and Evander Holyfield ("That's one small bite for man, . . . "). Charles V and Martin Luther ("Here I stand . . .). But the greatest confrontation had to be the one between Pontius Pilate and Jesus Christ. One was the governor of Judea, appointed by the Roman Empire. The other was the Son of God, sent from the Kingdom of Heaven. One was convinced he was in control of the interrogation. The other knew He was.

Pilate was the man with all the power, until he met Jesus. Pilate was the man with all the answers, until he met Jesus. Pilate was the man with all the confidence, until he met Jesus.

Isn't that the way it is with all of us? We think we have everything under control, until we meet the Sovereign Lord and our neat little plans fall apart. We think we have all the questions of life worked out, until we meet the Master who redefines life for us. We think we have the world by the tail, until Jesus takes us by the heart. Meeting Jesus has a way of changing everything.

In the classic encounter between Pilate and Jesus, the episode ends with a question. Jesus confirmed He was, indeed, King and then added, "For this cause I was born, and for this cause I have come into the world, that I should bear witness to the truth. Everyone who is of the truth hears My voice" (John 18:37). It was that mention of Jesus bearing witness to the truth that prompted Pilate's question, "What is truth?" (v. 38). As it is with so many people, the truth was standing in front of his eyes and he didn't even recognize it.

187

What is truth?

Pilate's question went unanswered in the confrontation with Jesus, but Jesus had already addressed this critical concern with His disciples, particularly with Thomas. John 14:6 tells us, "Jesus said to him, 'I am the way, the truth, and the life. No one comes to the Father except through Me.'"

When Pilate asked Jesus, "What is truth" (Gr. *aletheia*), he had in mind the abstract, intellectual meaning of truth. This was the truth that the Greeks discussed endlessly. In "the Greek conception of *aletheia* we find that its fundamental meaning is the real as against the unreal; that which is actually there as opposed to that which only seems to be there, the true as opposed to the false. In Plato the upper world of truth is opposed to the lower world of sense (*Rep.* vi. 508; *Phaedrus* 247). To reach this upper world of truth is the goal of all human striving."[1]

Socrates engaged those he met in profound philosophic discussions, believing that truth was discerned through self-knowledge. He tried to convince his fellow Athenians of the value of self-analysis. Plato, the disciple of Socrates, believed that the human mind could attain absolute truth. And Plato's disciple, Aristotle, sought truth in the theory of the Unmoved Mover. All of them died having never come close to the Truth.

Truth for the Greek philosophers was something to be thought or believed. Truth was something marinated in your mind. It is an actual state of affairs as contrasted with an assumed state of affairs or a rumor. Truth is truth. If what you believe squares with the laws of the intellect or corresponds to what is factual, then it is true. To the Greeks, truth was all in the mind.

Truth and trust

But in the Bible, truth is very different. Let's begin with the Hebrew concept of truth in the Old Testament.

For the Jews, "Truth (Heb. *emeth*) suggests notions of firmness, stability, reliability, faithfulness. The Lord is called a God of truth because he is one on whom his people can safely rely."[2] For the Hebrews, truth was not nearly so ethereal or cerebral as it was for the Greeks. Truth was what could be trusted, not what could be contemplated. The Hebrews couldn't adequately contemplate God, but they believed they could trust Him.

When Jesus said, "I am the truth," He was saying, "I am the way to God and you can trust Me. I am the faithful way to God. All other ways are false and will lead you nowhere. Don't trust them. Trust me and you will find God."

Let's think about how Jesus as the Truth enables us to trust the Father. Let's ask why Jesus alone is the faithful way to God. Let's not fail to understand what real truth is and why it is embodied in a person and not a theory. In what ways is Jesus the Truth?

Jesus is the Truth that reflects the character of God

What do we know about God? Can you define some elements of His character? Do you know some of His attributes? Let's see, there is holiness, omnipotence, goodness, righteousness, sovereignty and dozens more. But what about truth? Surely God must be truthful to be holy. He cannot be good and not be true. How could He be righteous if He were not truthful? Impossible.

God is Truth. His character demands it; His Word declares it. Exodus 34:6 describes God as "merciful and gracious, longsuffering, and abounding in goodness and truth." Deuteronomy 32:4 agrees, calling Jehovah "a God of truth and without injustice." David calls Him the "Lord God of truth" (Ps. 31:5). Again David says in Psalm 86:15, "But You, O Lord, are a God full of compassion, and gracious, longsuffering and abundant in mercy and truth." The prophet Isaiah also calls Him a "God of truth" (Isa. 65:16). Throughout the Old Testament, Jehovah is depicted as true or truthful, a God characterized by truth. Truth is one of the essential qualities of God's nature. Without truth, He couldn't be God.

It follows, then, that anyone or anything that represents God faithfully must likewise be reliable and true. A faithful God cannot allow Himself to be represented by unfaithful sources, and He won't. Thus, as God the Father is Truth, the two primary methods by which He reveals Himself to us—His Written Word (the Bible) and His Living Word (the Lord Jesus)—must be equally distinguished by the truth. If they are to reflect the divine character, they must demonstrate the same truthfulness.

The Written Word

The Bible claims truthfulness for itself. This alone does not prove it,

189

but you wouldn't expect a divine revelation of God not to make a claim of veracity. We know that His Law is truth (Ps. 119:142), all His commandments are truth (v. 151), and the judgments of the Lord are "true and righteous altogether" (Ps. 19:9). Daniel spoke of the "Scripture of Truth" (Dan. 10:21), and Jesus prayed to the Father for us, "Sanctify them by Your truth. Your word is truth" (John 17:17). Paul said the Ephesians received Jesus as Savior when "in Him you also trusted, after you heard the word of truth, the gospel of your salvation" (Eph. 1:13). And the apostle encouraged Timothy to be diligent in "rightly dividing the word of truth" (2 Tim. 2:15).

The Bible defines and reflects the character of God truthfully. If you want to know about God, don't ask your neighbor. Don't ask your university professor. Don't ask the philosopher in your local McDonalds. The truth about God is revealed in the Word of God. God's Word reflects God's character. The Written Word is God's Truth.

The Living Word

But the Living Word is also God's Truth. The Son of God reveals as much about the character of God as the Written Word does. Jesus could say He was the Truth because He reflected the truth of God's character. Jesus Christ is the "brightness of His glory and the express image of His person" (Heb. 1:3). "In Him dwells all the fullness of the Godhead bodily" (Col. 2:9). If you want a written disclosure of the truthful character of God, look at your Bible. If you want living disclosure of the truthful character of God, look at your Savior, Jesus.

Read again the words of John as he begins his gospel. "And the Word became flesh and dwelt among us, and we beheld His glory, the glory as of the only begotten of the Father, full of grace and truth. . . . For the law was given through Moses, but grace and truth came through Jesus Christ. No one has seen God at any time. The only begotten Son, who is in the bosom of the Father, He has declared Him" (John 1:14, 17-18). John believed that the truth of God came through Jesus Christ, who absolutely reflected the true character of God.

Our freedom from the penalty of sin comes only when we trust Jesus Christ as Savior. "And you shall know the truth, and the truth shall make you free" (John 8:32). Jesus is the Truth because Jesus is the only person who ever completely and accurately reflected the character of God.

190

Do you long to know God better? You can. God has already provided the Way for you to know Him. He's God's Truth. Look to God the Son in order to understand the character of God the Father. He reflects the true character of God. And there's another way. Read God's Word if you want to understand the character of God the Father. It reflects the true character of God as well. Look to someone else or read something else, and who knows what you'll see reflected.

The "I AM" God said, "I am the Truth." In what ways is Jesus the Truth? How does Jesus depict Himself as God's Truth? If you're asking Pilate's question, "What is truth?" how does the Son of God help you with an answer? Let's investigate.

Jesus is the Truth that dispels the shadow of the past

Have you ever seen a two-year-old trying to step on his shadow? It's great fun, especially if you capture it on video. The little tike will goose-step right, then left in order to step on that black image on the pavement that mysteriously keeps following him around. Shadows are hard for two-year-olds to understand.

As we get a bit older, shadows can actually be frightening. The mystery of the shadow can easily turn to terror. The words you heard when you were eight are still ringing in your ears: "Fraidy cat, fraidy cat. He's scared of his own shadow." How embarrassing. And yet we adults are sometimes afraid of the shadows in our lives, too, especially the emotional ones. "Yea, though I walk through the valley of the shadow of death, I will fear no evil; for You are with me" (Ps. 23:4).

Shadows represent many things in the Bible. They often refer to the brevity or frailty of our life (1 Chron. 29:15; Job 8:9). They can speak of relief from the heat of the sun (Isa. 4:6; 25:4). Sometimes shadows even relate to our need for God. When we are facing the pressures of life and things are going crazy, that's when we need "the shadow of a great rock in a weary land" (Isa. 32:2). When Satan is menacing us with temptations too difficult to resist, that's when we need to "abide under the shadow of the Almighty" (Ps. 91:1).

But often shadows are windows into the world of the potential. Shadows, while they are genuine, are not real. They tell us something real is nearby, but the shadow is just a figure of what is real. When you see a shadow of a tree, it's the tree that's the real article, not the shadow. The shadow is just an outline of it. Often when you are taking off or land-ing at an airport you can see the shadow of your airplane on the ground beneath you. It's enjoyable to watch, but don't try to fly on that shadow. It's not the real thing; the airplane is the real thing.

Symbols of things to come

The same is true in the Bible. Shadows are called types, figures or ex-amples. A type is a "symbol of something to come, as an event in the Old Testament foreshadows another in the New Testament. Types gen-erally find their fulfillment in the person and ministry of Christ."[3]

Some more clearly defined examples of types in the Bible include Melchizedek, the king-priest of Salem (Gen. 14:18-20), who is a type of Christ; the brazen serpent in the wilderness (Num. 21:4-9) was a type of Jesus' crucifixion (John 3:14-15); and the tabernacle in the Old Testa-ment foreshadowed the Person and work of Jesus Christ in the New Tes-tament (Heb. 9-10).

When Paul is contrasting Adam, the first man, with Jesus Christ, the last Adam, he said, "Death reigned from Adam to Moses, even over those who had not sinned according to the likeness of the transgression of Adam, who is a type of Him who was to come" (Rom. 5:14). The Greek word for type is *tupos*, which means a shadow of things to come. Adam was the shadow; Jesus is the real thing.

The writer of Hebrews speaks of Jesus as our great High Priest and likens Him to the high priest in the Old Testament. Our High Priest is seated at the right hand of the Majesty's throne in the heavens; the Jew-ish high priest is on earth and serves as "the copy and shadow of the heavenly things" (Heb. 8:1-5). Jesus the High Priest is the real thing; the high priests of Israel were just a shadow of the real thing.

So often Jesus as the Truth dispels the shadows of the past by present-ing Himself as the real thing. The manna that came down from heaven was the past shadow; Jesus is the true bread (John 6:32). Israel needed water to drink and God provided a rock in the wilderness to quench their thirst. But that was just a past shadow; Jesus is the real rock (1 Cor. 10:4). When Abraham was about to slay his son as a sacrifice, God pro-vided a ram in the thicket, which Abraham sacrificed instead. The sub-stitute ram was just a past shadow; Jesus is the true substitute. Only what is real can atone for our sins. That's why Jesus could legitimately say, "I am the truth," because all that was a shadow of God's work on earth is now seen in the substance of the Truth.

Jesus is no proposal, no scheme, no pattern, no type. He is the real thing. Jesus is the Truth that dispels the shadow of the past.

Jesus is the Truth that reveals falsehood

Have you ever had anyone lie to you? Sure you have. But how did you know he was lying? Lucky Louie the used car salesman (my apologies to all honest used car salesmen) says to you, "This thing is a cherry. It runs like a top. Been maintained regularly. Hardly ever driven more than 35 miles per hour. In fact, it was owned by a little old lady from Pasadena. You'll get years of good service out of this car." Is Louie telling the truth? Buy the car, and the day after the 30-day warrantee runs out you'll know.

What is the best way to identify a fake? Put it next to the real thing. The best way to reveal what is false is to look at what is true. I've read that when the U.S. Treasury wants their employees to be able to spot phony bills, they make them study the real bills. The better they know the true item, the easier it is to identify the false.

Once a young Chinese boy wanted to learn about jade, so he went to study with a talented old teacher. The elderly gentleman put a piece of jade into the boy's hand and told him to hold it tightly. Then the master began to talk about philosophy, men and women, life in general, the weather, the sun and just about everything under it. After an hour he took back the jade and sent the boy home. This happened week after week until the boy became frustrated. When was he going to learn about jade? But he was too polite to interrupt his venerable teacher. One day, the old man put a stone into his hand, and the boy cried out instantly, "That's not jade!"

When Jesus said, "I am the truth," He was giving us the best tool to spot the phonies in this world. How better to identify falsehood than to become better acquainted with the "I AM" God, the real thing, the true Truth. Here's how it works.

We are very familiar with standards in our society. We judge everything and everyone else by appropriate standards. On February 2, 1997, Jeremy Sonnenfield, a sophomore at the University of Nebraska at Lincoln, showed the world just how difficult it is to meet the standard in bowling. He bowled three consecutive 300 games, a perfect 900 series. In golf, par is the standard. You determine whether or not you have had a good game depending on how far under, or more likely, how far over par you are. Industries set standards for quality and productivity. Universities set standards for academic performance.

In every area of life we learn to operate with standards—every area, that is, except spirituality. Somehow we think there should be no standards there. If we talk about standards of righteousness, we're afraid we'll offend someone. If we talk about standards of behavior, everybody thinks we just fell off the turnip truck. If we talk about standards of moderate dress, people think we are fashion failures. But God has a standard for ethical, moral, spiritual, righteous, acceptable behavior. That standard is His character reflected perfectly in the "I AM" God, Jesus Christ.

The standard of character

So, if you expect the Truth to reveal falsehood, you must get to know the Truth. You must see His life, His teaching and His demeanor as the standard.

"Character is a description or manifestation of a person's nature," writes Floyd Barackman. "Some inner qualities of Jesus' humanity are His meekness and humility (Mt. 11:29), compassion (Mt. 9:36), obedience (Jn. 8:29), love (Jn. 13:1), industry (Jn. 9:4; 17:4), patience (Jn. 14:1-9), grace (2 Cor. 8:9), forgiveness (Lk. 23:34), tenderness (Jn. 8:3-10), firmness and courage (Lk. 9:51), and holiness (Mk. 1:24)."[4]

Our character is reflected in what we say and do. Almost everything Jesus said or did astounded His audiences. When He healed the paralytic and said, "Your sins are forgiven you. . . . the multitudes saw it, they marveled and glorified God, who had given such power to men" (Matt. 9:2, 8). And when the chief priests and scribes tried to trick Jesus by asking, "Is it lawful for us to pay taxes to Caesar or not?" Luke 20:26 records, "But they could not catch Him in His words in the presence of the people. And they marveled at His answer and kept silent."

Jesus gave sight to the blind, enabled the lame to walk, cast out demons from tortured bodies and raised the dead. Those are pretty amazing things, and Jesus understood the importance of what He did. "I have a greater witness than John's; for the works which the Father has given Me to finish—the very works that I do—bear witness of Me, that

194

the Father has sent Me" (John 5:36). Once Jesus boldly claimed, "If I do not do the works of My Father, do not believe Me; but if I do, though you do not believe Me, believe the works, that you may know and believe that the Father is in Me, and I in Him" (10:37-38).

God's standard

Jesus' character, His words, His works—everything about Him—reflected God's standard of holiness, righteousness and goodness. Jesus was the Father's perfect standard. Everything true and false is judged against Him.

That's why it's important that we abandon the foolish notion that God will judge our good works against our bad works to determine whether or not we get into heaven. The Bible teaches no such thing. What the Bible declares is that both our good works and our bad works are judged against God's perfect standard of righteousness—Jesus Christ—and when placed next to the "I AM" God, everything we have, everything we are, is found wanting.

This couldn't be made any clearer to us than it is in Romans 3:23: "For all have sinned and fall short of the glory of God." Jesus is the glory of God (Acts 7:55; John 1:1-2, 14). It is against the Truth that our falsehood is judged. God places us next to His perfect standard of righteousness and we don't measure up.

Jesus said, "I am the Truth," and as such He reveals everything that is false, unworthy, inadequate, unacceptable to God. Every pseudo-messiah, every new doctrine, every screwy idea, every lofty philosophy must be judged against God's standard of truth—Jesus Christ. Look around you. There is much falsehood in our world today that needs to be exposed by the Truth. It's always been that way.

Finding the phonies

To the prophet Jeremiah the Lord lamented that "prophets prophesy lies in My name. I have not sent them, commanded them, nor spoken to them" (Jer. 14:14). The prophet Isaiah blasted those false prophets who made lies their refuge and under falsehood hid themselves (Isa. 28:15). Jesus spoke about false prophets circulating in sheep's clothing (Matt. 7:15). He said the day would come when "false christs and false prophets will arise and show great signs and wonders, so as to deceive, if possible, even the elect" (24:24). The apostle Paul was constantly plagued with "false apostles" (2 Cor. 11:13) and "false brethren" (Gal. 2:4).

It is evident that Satan is working overtime to spread falsehood not only in the world, but also in Christ's church. The words *prophets, apostles* and *brethren* imply wolves among the sheep, not just threatening them from the outside. All who are false take their marching orders from one person—Satan. Every liar learns his trade from the master liar—Satan. Every oddball cultist takes his cue from the oddest of all—Satan.

Jesus knew this. That's why He said to the religious leaders of His day, "If God were your Father, you would love Me, for I proceeded forth and came from God. . . . You are of your father the devil, and the desires of your father you want to do. He was a murderer from the beginning, and does not stand in the truth, because there is no truth in him. When he speaks a lie, he speaks from his own resources, for he is a liar and the father of it. But because I tell the truth, you do not believe Me" (John 8:42-45).

So our choices are clear and simple. Believe every lie we hear on television or radio. Trust every dynamic leader who can sway a huge audience with his words or even with signs and wonders. Or place everything we see and hear against the standard of God's righteousness and let the chips fall where they may. How does what we hear square with the One who said, "I am the truth"? Does what we see meet the criteria of the "I AM" God?

That's what the apostle John told us to do. He said, "Beloved, do not believe every spirit, but test the spirits, whether they are of God; because many false prophets have gone out into the world. By this you know the Spirit of God: Every spirit that confesses that Jesus Christ has come in the flesh is of God, and every spirit that does not confess that Jesus Christ has come in the flesh is not of God" (1 John 4:1-3).

The test of truth

The litmus test to expose falsehood is to place it next to the Truth. What does the new church say about Jesus? What does the new Bible study leader believe about the infallibility of the Bible? What does the old cult teach about the deity of Christ? What does the old denomination say about the blood of Jesus? Those are the questions. It's not how loving and caring they seem to be, or how high their moral standards are. All of these things fall short of the glory of God. The standard is

Jesus. Who is He? Is He really the only Way, the only Truth, and the only Life?

When someone comes to my door and says he is a Bible student and wants to talk with me, I immediately ask, "Tell me this in a simple yes or no answer. Do you believe that Jesus Christ is God?" If he hesitates half a second, we have nothing to talk about. He has failed the test of truth. When truth is present he will quickly reply with the kind of answer Peter did when asked who Jesus is: "You are the Christ, the Son of the living God" (Matt. 16:16). No ifs, ands or buts. No hesitation. No question.

The One who said "I am the truth" is forever the standard against which we measure and expose falsehood. Jesus is the "I AM" God, eternal truth, always truth, nothing but the truth. If you're looking for someone to trust, trust the Truth.

But Jesus as the standard of Truth is not a sanitized, sterilized, untouchable, uncaring, sacrosanct monument of holiness. Though He is sinless and holy, God's standard is loving, intimate, tender and affectionate. "We do not have a High Priest who cannot sympathize with our weaknesses, but was in all points tempted as we are, yet without sin" (Heb. 4:15). God's standard is high and holy, but He is also sympathetic and caring. In a word, He is perfect.

Verifying the Truth

Are you looking for something to verify that Jesus is the Truth? Pick up your Bible. Read about Him. Think about what you read. Ask God to help you discover the Truth.

The bishop of Durham Cathedral in England and great Bible scholar Brooke Foss Westcott wrote, "The witness to Christ . . . extends over the whole range of possible attestation of divine things. In due succession there is, (1) the witness of the Father; (2) the witness of Christ Himself; (3) the witness of works; (4) the witness of Scripture; (5) the witness of the Forerunner; (6) the witness of disciples; and that which illuminates and quickens all, (7) the witness of the Spirit."[5] There is enough testimony to the sufficiency of Christ to be the Truth of God that any unbiased seeker will surely come to this truth, if he looks for it in Jesus Christ.

Perhaps you're confused about what is truth. You've heard your university professor say one thing. Your friends tell you something else.

You're tired of people telling you to obey the truth that's deep within you. You know yourself better than they do and you don't want to listen to that "truth." If you're looking for someone who is sufficient to tell you the truth, someone sufficient to show you the truth, someone sufficient to be the Truth, then you want Jesus Christ. He is God's Way, God's Truth and God's Life. He is sufficient for all you need.

What does Jesus the Truth mean to you?

The "I AM" God is the Truth. Of what importance is that combination? In Him there is equivalency. God does not simply tell the truth. He does not merely verify the truth. The "I AM" isn't just about the truth. Jesus is an absolute. The "I AM" God is *the* Truth. Here's what that means.

When you believe Jesus is the Truth, you are no longer left guessing what's right or what's wrong

With Jesus as the Truth, You no longer have to ask, "Should I do this?" "Should I go there?" "Should I watch that?" If you believe the One who said, "I am the truth," all you have to do is ask, "What would Jesus do?" (I suggest you read Charles Sheldon's delightful little book *In His Steps,* where the members of a small-town church are changed by covenanting together not to do anything for a year without first asking, "What would Jesus do?") If you ask yourself what Jesus would do in your situation, you have the answer to what is right.

When you believe Jesus is the Truth, you no longer have to wonder whether or not what you hear is a lie

Have you noticed that some people can't bring themselves to tell a lie? Others can't ever seem to tell the truth. But most people simply can't tell the difference. When you believe that Jesus is the Truth, you'll be able to tell the difference. You can judge everything you hear by what you know of the "I AM" God. Does what you hear square with what you know? I suppose that depends on what you know, and that's why it's so important that you and I spend some time each day in God's Word so that we know what the truth really is.

> We search the world for truth. We cull
> The good, the pure, the beautiful,
> From graven stone and written scroll,
> From all old flower-fields of the soul;

And, weary seekers of the best,
We come back laden from the quest,
To find that all the sage said,
Is in the Book our mothers read.
— John Greenleaf Whittier

When you believe Jesus is the Truth, you can no longer
be silent toward those who are trapped by Satan's lies

If we know the truth, we must speak the truth. Someone has said that truth is often violated by falsehood, but it can equally be outraged by silence. Jesus words "You shall know the truth, and the truth shall make you free" (John 8:32) apply to freedom of all types. But the greatest need of mankind is not freedom from want or freedom from drugs, or even freedom from tyranny. The greatest freedom of all is freedom from eternal hell.

To know Jesus is the Truth and not to share that Truth with those who will be condemned forever is unconscionable. It's like having an antidote to a deadly poison and, for fear of embarrassment or rejection, refusing to give the antidote to a dying friend.

Do you believe Jesus is the Truth, and only He is the Truth? Then truth demands action. Truth is not something you hear and hold and have. It is something you obey and share and do. Phillips Brooks said, "Christianity knows no truth which is not the child of love and the parent of duty." Obey the Truth. Share the Truth. Do the work of the Truth among your friends and family.

When you believe Jesus is the Truth, you have found
sufficiency of God's eternal truth

It is true: "All truth is God's truth." But not all truth is equally important. Two plus two equals four; that's truth. But don't major on the minor. You can fail to believe that truth and it won't change your eternal destiny. But if you fail to believe the truth of Jesus' words "He who hears My word and believes in Him who sent Me has everlasting life, and shall not come into judgment, but has passed from death into life" (John 5:24), you will miss heaven by a mile.

Trust the "I AM" God, the One who said, "I am the truth." He's your only hope of discovering irrefutable truth. He is the only One sufficient to lead you to God.

"*I am the Life; let Me give meaning to your life.*"

CHAPTER 12

I Am

THE LIFE

Jesus said to him, "I am the way, the truth, and the life. No one comes to the Father except through Me."
JOHN 14:6

Isn't it interesting the many ways we use the word *life*. There's a biological use of the word: life is an organismic state capable of metabolism, growth, reproduction and reaction to stimuli. Then there's the biographical use of the word: the period between birth and death. And there's also the spiritual use of the word: a spiritual existence that transcends death.

We speak positively of life as "just a bowl of cherries" or, negatively, that "life is no bed of roses." We talk about a gifted leader "breathing new life" into an old organization or institution. Prisoners are convicted and sentenced to "life," while others are given a "new lease on life" and set free. Are you old enough to remember the old television show "The Life of Riley"? Warrantees have a life, as do contracts and batteries.

There's life in the forest, in the country and in the inner city. There's life in the air, in the ground and under the sea. Politicians who are behind in the polls work hard, as if their life depended on it, to generate some life in their campaign. Americans are interested in "life, liberty and the pursuit of happiness." For some, that interest apparently doesn't extend to the life of the unborn, but for all we allow to live, we want them to grow up and enjoy the "good life." Life is so good for most of us that we even have a magazine by that name, *Life*.

But life is much more than existence, and it's a great deal more than a bowl of cherries. Life is the most precious commodity we have because our eternal destiny depends on a relationship developed during that period between birth and death, the brief period we call "life."

When the "I AM" God said, "I am the life," what could He possibly have meant? He has just said, "I am the way" and "I am the truth," and those were difficult enough to understand. But in what sense of the word can Jesus say He is the Life? When I need answers to eternal questions like this, I go to the eternal source. I go back to the Bible. Let's go back to the beginning, the first chapter in the Bible, Genesis 1. This sets the stage for all of the 1,188 chapters that follow.

Christ is the generator of natural life

Where did the world come from? How did our earth come into being? The usual answer today has something to do with spontaneous generation, a horrific bang in another universe or some other equally foolish and equally unverifiable speculation. Men and women devise the most fanciful schemes to deny the obvious. The most succinct, most plausible, most unambiguous statement of creation is found in God's Word. Frankly, it takes no more faith to believe the account of Genesis than it does in the big bang theory, and many people think it takes far less.

Here's God simple, yet profound explanation of how it all began: "In the beginning God created the heavens and the earth" (Gen. 1:1). For people of faith, further explanation is intriguing, elucidating and fascinating, but not necessary.

According to the Bible, the work of creation was the joint work of the Trinity. God the Father is the origin of all things good (1 Cor. 8:6) and thus the origin of creation (Rev. 4:11). God the Spirit is the means by whom the Trinity works (Job 26:13), and thus the Holy Spirit was the medium of creation (Gen. 1:2). But God the Son is the Person of the Trinity who affects our world most directly, and Jesus Christ was the active agent of creation. Thus, when Genesis 1:1 says that God created the heavens and the earth, it means that the Trinity was involved, but God the Son was the actual Creator of all that we know and enjoy (Col. 1:16).

How do we know that? How can we be sure that they aren't correct who say that some primordial protoplasm gave rise to all life as we know it today? It's a matter of faith. You can trust the guesswork of scientists who project their theories back billions of years and must amend them frequently when some theory deemed more plausible is advanced, or you can trust the Book that has withstood the attacks of the centuries and is itself changeless while it still changes lives today. The choice is yours.

The real witnesses

Here's what the first chapter of John's Gospel says about the Creator: "In the beginning was the Word, and the Word was with God, and the Word was God. He was in the beginning with God. All things were made through Him, and without Him nothing was made that was made" (John 1:1-3).

I won't take the time to rehearse the arguments that the Word in these verses is, in fact, Jesus Christ. John 1:14 makes that abundantly clear. And I don't want to take the time to refute the Jehovah's Witnesses' claim that this verse says the Word was "a" God because there is no definite article before the noun. They are right; there is no definite article. But they are dead wrong in what that means.

This verse says that all the essence of being God—all that it takes to make God—is part and parcel of both God the Father and the Word, God the Son. The bottom line is unchanged—Jesus is God and He is the God who created all things. Nothing was made that was not made by Him. That's what John 1:1-3 says, and that's exactly what it means.

But the Levitical law required that everything be established in the mouth of more than one witness if it were to be believed. "By the mouth of two or three witnesses the matter shall be established" (Deut. 19:15). So in addition to the testimony of the apostle John that the "I AM" God generates all natural life, we also note the testimony of the apostle Paul. Speaking of Jesus the apostle said, "For by Him all things were created that are in heaven and that are on earth, visible and invisible, whether thrones or dominions or principalities or powers. All things were created through Him and for Him. And He is before all things, and in Him all things consist" (Col. 1:16-17).

That evidence for Christ the Creator is so direct, so complete, so definite that more is hardly needed. But since two or three witnesses establish a matter, let's go to the max. Here's a third writer, the author of Hebrews, who says what John and Paul have said, and he agrees completely: "God, who at various times and in different ways spoke in time past to the fathers by the prophets, has in these last days spoken to us by His Son, whom He has appointed heir of all things, through whom also He made the worlds" (Heb. 1:1-2). Time and space were the creation of the "I AM" God, who is above both. In this passage the third witness testifies. Jesus Christ is the One who actually created the world. God the Father "made the worlds" through God the Son. Nothing could be plainer.

Forever settled

If you choose to trust whatever the current theory about origins is, be ready to adapt. Theories come and theories go. Since creation happened a long time ago, any investigation of how it occurred belongs in the realm of history, not science. True science is objective, applying the scientific method to present reality, to learn all it can from what it can test and analyze. False science takes what it knows to be true today and tries to extrapolate what it thinks happened in the deep recesses of history, and that cannot be done with any degree of certainty.

On the other hand, "Forever, O LORD, Your word is settled in heaven" (Ps. 119:89). The Bible remains our best source for reliable information about origins and ends. And that unimpeachable source says, "In the beginning, God created the heavens and the earth." Jesus Christ is the generator of all natural life as we know it today, and it continues by the same power that generated it—the power of the Son of God. Natural life comes from God, the "I AM" God, the God who said, "I am the life."

Christ is the Giver of new life

But there's so much more to life than breathing and metabolizing. It's a shame to see how so many people have no higher concept of life than working hard, playing hard and making money. Life is especially tragic for those who have plenty to live on but nothing to live for. Jesus Christ gives us much more to live for than just to face a coffin with our hands clutched tightly to our credit cards.

In *Macbeth* we remember Shakespeare's piercing words: "Life . . . is a tale told by an idiot, full of sound and fury, signifying nothing." It must seem that way to so many, but not those who have discovered the real meaning of Jesus' words "I am the life." God the Son is much more than the generator of natural life. He is also the giver of new life, a completely new kind of life.

Jesus Christ gives meaning to our natural life by giving us spiritual life to go with it. When you receive this new life in Christ, suddenly many of the things that were incomprehensible before begin to make sense. Life has new meaning, new purpose, a new goal beyond the daily grind, the checkbook and the pointless relationships you've formed and thrown away.

Made and marred

We begin with natural life, physical life, the living and breathing kind of life. The kind we all have between our first cry as a baby and our last groan as an adult. When we are born physically, we are born alive. But the physical realm is only one dimension of our existence. We are spiritual beings as well as physical beings. We were created with a relationship to God, not just to the world around us.

Here's what the Bible says: "So God created man in His own image; in the image of God He created him; male and female He created them" (Gen. 1:27).

What is the image of God? Not a physical form, certainly, because God doesn't have a physical form. He is a spirit (John 4:24). But being created in God's image means that human beings share, although imperfectly and finitely, in God's nature. That includes sharing in qualities such as life, truth, love, holiness, justice and personality. We have been created with a capacity for spiritual fellowship with our Creator. That's the good news.

Here's the bad news. We muffed it. We rebuffed our Creator, rebelled against Him and refused to enjoy that spiritual fellowship with God. Genesis 3 records the sad story. Adam and Eve sinned in the Garden of Eden. Their intimacy with God was shattered. Instead of enjoying His company, they "hid themselves from the presence of the LORD God among the trees of the garden" (Gen. 3:8). Rebellion always brings consequences, and the consequence of Adam's sin was death. God said, "For dust you are and to dust you shall return" (v. 19). Instead of living forever, Adam would one day die physically. It happened, just as God said. "So all the days that Adam lived were nine hundred and thirty years; and he died" (5:5).

But there was also an immediate result to sin. Physical death was in the future; spiritual death was immediate. Adam and Eve's fellowship with God was severed instantly. So everyone born of Adam and Eve enter this world awaiting a day of physical death, but already are spiritually dead. In a word, you and I were spiritually stillborn. Spiritually speaking, we were born dead in our trespasses and sins. And it's only when we are made alive by the Spirit of God and trust in the Son of God as our Savior that we are made spiritually alive (Eph. 2:1-2).

Famed British pastor and Bible expositor from the last century Alexander Maclaren said it this way: "Dead men cannot walk a road. It is of no use to make a path if it starts from a cemetery. Christ taught that men apart from Him are dead, and that the only life that they can have by which they can be knit to God is the divine life which was in Himself, and of which He is the source and the principle for the whole world."[1]

From death to life

It is this spiritual life that is God's gift to us when we are saved. Our sin brought us death; Jesus' death brought us life. "For the wages of sin is death, but the gift of God is eternal life in Christ Jesus our Lord" (Rom. 6:23). The Giver of spiritual life is the same One who generated natural life. He is the Life-giver in every respect. Little wonder Jesus said, "I am the life." He alone is our spiritual Life-giver.

When the "I AM" God said, "I am the life," He did not mean natural life. He wasn't talking about your breath or spirit (Gr. *pneuma*), that which animates your body. He was not talking about your soul (Gr. *psyche*), or even the days of your life (Gr. *bios*). He was talking about life as opposed to death (Gr. *zoa*). Spiritually, you were born dead, without any capacity for a relationship with your Creator. But Jesus is the Life. He is thoroughly sufficient to restore your severed relationship with God. In fact, not only is He sufficient, He alone is sufficient. No one can do it but Him. He is not just suitably sufficient; He is solely sufficient. He said, "I am *the* life." He's the only one.

Because He has the life of God and eternity within Him, Jesus is the source of new life for us. He is the Giver of new life. How often that theme is stressed, even in the Gospel of John (for example, 3:16; 6:33; 10:28; 11:26). Just as death spells separation from God, life means communion with Him, a restored relationship with Him.

A second birth

How does this happen? That's what Nicodemus, a Jewish aristocrat, wanted to know. When he asked Jesus, the Life said, "I say to you, unless one is born again, he cannot see the kingdom of God" (3:3). The idea of being born again implies two things: 1) we were born once physically, but that is insufficient in itself to bring about a relationship with God; and 2) a second birth, this time spiritual, is essential to restore that right relationship with God that was lost in the Garden of Eden.

But the whole concept of being born a second time was understandably foreign to Nicodemus. In fact, he asked, "How can a man be born when he is old? Can he enter a second time into his mother's womb and be born?" (v. 4). Ridiculous. No grown man can return to the warmth of the womb and repeat the process of birth.

But even if we could, we'd be physically born a sinner the second time, because no clean person can be born of unclean parents (Job 14:4). Even if we could return to our mother's womb and be born, we'd be in the same sorry state we are now—spiritually dead, stillborn in our relationship with God.

But that's not what Jesus was saying. The "I AM" God explained, "Unless one is born of water and the Spirit, he cannot enter the kingdom of God. That which is born of the flesh is flesh, and that which is born of the Spirit is spirit. Do not marvel that I said to you, 'You must be born again'" (John 3:5-7).

Many good people differ on the meaning of the word *water* in what Jesus said. Some believe it refers to the Word of God (Eph. 5:26); others, to a symbol of the Holy Spirit (John 7:37-39); still others, to baptism as an essential part of regeneration. This last suggestion cannot be the case since this interpretation contradicts the clear teaching of God's Word that salvation is by faith alone (John 3:16, 36; Eph. 2:8-10; Titus 3:5).

Good Bible students always permit the context to determine the meaning. When we do that, especially with the added help of John 3:6, the meaning becomes clear. There is a physical birth and a spiritual birth. The physical is characterized by the flesh; the spiritual comes by means of the Spirit of God. One birth (the physical) comes with the breaking of the water. The second birth (the spiritual) comes by the means of the Spirit's drawing us to salvation. Physically and spiritually—those are the two ways we must be born if we are to see God.

Nicodemus would not have to return to his mother's womb to be reborn because the "I AM" God was not talking about physical birth. He was talking about spiritual birth. Like Nicodemus, you and I have been born physically, naturally. But that one birth is insufficient to get us to the kingdom of God because it cannot produce the relationship with God that was severed by rebellion in the Garden of Eden. That relationship is essential to a future with God in heaven. It is only as we are reborn spiritually that this relationship is restored. It is only when we are born by the Spirit of God that we become spiritually viable. Unless that occurs, we are spiritually dead.

Key to life

The One who said, "I am the life," is the key to life. Jesus is the key. The spiritual life that we must have if we are to be rightly related to God is found in Him. Jesus said, "He who hears My word and believes in Him who sent Me has everlasting life, and shall not come into judgment, but has passed from death into life" (John 5:24). Often Jesus promised us that if we would repent of our sin and trust what He did for us at Calvary, we would receive new life, spiritual life, everlasting life. Who else could make such a claim? No one else is sufficient to do so.

That the "I AM" God is the Giver of new life, everlasting life, is surely the theme of the Gospel of John. It occurs too frequently not to be. In the following verses, notice the frequent mention of everlasting or eternal life and how each time it is exclusively connected to belief in the work of Jesus at Calvary's cross.

John 3:15-16: "Whoever believes in Him should not perish but have eternal life. For God so loved the world that He gave His only begotten Son, that whoever believes in Him should not perish but have everlasting life."

John 3:36: "He who believes in the Son has everlasting life; and he who does not believe the Son shall not see life, but the wrath of God abides on Him."

John 4:14: "Whoever drinks of the water that I shall give him will never thirst. But the water that I shall give him will become in him a fountain of water springing up into everlasting life."

John 6:27: "Do not labor for the food which perishes, but for the food which endures to everlasting life, which the Son of Man will give you, because God the Father has set His seal on Him."

John 6:40: "And this is the will of Him who sent Me, that everyone who sees the Son and believes in Him may have everlasting life."

John 6:47: "He who believes in Me has everlasting life."

When some of Jesus' disciples were turning away from Him because the heat was turned up on them, Jesus asked His Twelve if they, too, wanted to desert Him. Peter responded, "Lord, to whom shall we go? You have the words of eternal life" (John 6:68).

Have you believed?

Thus the question is not, "Can the "I AM" God give you everlasting life?" for the answer plainly is yes He can. The real question is, "Have you believed in Him as your Savior to receive this free gift of eternal life?" If you do, He gives you the right to be a child of God (John 1:12). Here's what the Bible says: "He came to His own, and His own did not receive Him. But as many as received Him, to them He gave the right to become children of God, even to those who believe in His name: who were born, not of blood, nor of the will of the flesh, nor of the will of man, but of God" (John 1:11-13). If you believe in the "I AM" God and trust Him to save you from the penalty of your sin, you become a member of His family, and it's a great place to belong.

If you are to enjoy eternal life in a restored relationship with God, you must trust Jesus Christ as your Savior. Nothing more, nothing less. The One who said, "I am the life," can provide everlasting spiritual life for you, not just physical or natural life. Do you remember Paul's answer to the Philippian jailer's question, "What must I do to be saved?" It's the answer for you today. "Believe on the Lord Jesus Christ, and you will be saved, you and your household" (Acts. 16:31). Unlike scientific theories, God's Word never changes to adapt to the truth. It is the truth!

But there's much more to life than birth. Imagine how horrible life would be if you were still a baby. Sure, you've be fed and cared for every moment of the day (and night too). You'd hear adults saying those childish and meaningless things we all say to babies. You'd have it made.

But is that what you really want? Do you want strained peas to eat forever? Do you want to sit in dirty diapers? Do you want to be confined to a small "cage" because you can't walk by yourself? Is that what you really want? I don't think so. We all want to grow to adulthood and we all need to grow. Jesus the Life not only gives us life, but He gives us growth.

Christ is the grower of spiritual life

Because we are spiritually reborn, born from above, born again by the Spirit of God, we begin a long journey. It's called the Christian life. It has many twists and turns, many pitfalls, many sand traps and not a little danger. But as we grow and mature we learn how to negotiate those twists and turns, avoid those pitfalls, chip out of those sand traps and stay out of danger. It all comes with spiritual growth.

Just as physical growth is important and necessary to our natural lives, so spiritual growth is important and necessary to our spiritual lives. But the secret to growth is the same as the secret to birth—it's the life we find in the "I AM" God.

Jesus gives us physical life; He is our Creator. He gives us spiritual life; He is our Savior. He gives us growing life; He is our Sustainer. We are born babes in Christ, but we have no right to remain babes. We should have no desire to either. But, unfortunately, many people seem to have little motivation to grow in their new life in Christ. It's not that they lack opportunity; they lack the initiative, commitment and conviction.

The Corinthian church had that problem. It was filled with spiritual infants, people who had become babes in Christ but who had never grown in their new life. Quite sharply Paul said, "And I, brethren, could not speak to you as to spiritual people but as to carnal, as to babes in Christ. I fed you with milk and not with solid food; for until now you were not able to receive it, and even now you are still not able" (1 Cor. 3:1-2). Nothing is more disappointing to a parent, nor more devastating to a child, than a baby who remains a baby all her life. Some Christians are like that.

On the road

How long have you enjoyed new life in Christ? How long have you been a Christian? Has it been a year? Ten years? Forty years? It doesn't really matter, because it has little or no bearing on how mature you are in Christ. I once heard Vance Havner say, "How long you've been a Christian only tells how long you've been on the road. It doesn't tell how far you've come."

In the years you've been on the road, how far have you come in your faith? Are you still eating mashed bananas, or are you thriving on a strong spiritual diet of meat and vegetables and potatoes? What did you have for lunch today? Was it a spiritual snack or a solid meal in God's Word? Are you opting for the spiritual equivalent of junk food or for a balanced diet in the Old and New Testament? What is the nutritional benefit of your spiritual food? You need green beans, but are you constantly nibbling on gummi bears?

Are you politically correct in what you eat? Is your diet low fat, low cholesterol and low calorie? How about your spiritual diet? Is it low value, low energy, low nutrient, lite fare? If you've gobbled your gummi bears from television or radio but neglected to sit down to a meal of green beans from God's Word, it's little wonder you're stymied in your spiritual growth. You're not getting the spiritual vitamins you need. Maybe instead of reading so many Christian fictions, romance novels, how-to books, finance manuals and marriage-enrichment books, you ought to set them aside for awhile and to get back to *the* Book. Get back to the Bible. Jesus provides the potential for spiritual growth in your Christian life, but not if you continue to opt for anemic meals.

Famine check

There are two prophets of the Old Testament whose words ought to haunt the church today. One of those prophets is Hosea. He could have been sitting in many of our thriving, growing churches today when he recorded God's comment, "My people are destroyed for lack of knowledge" (Hos. 4:6).

How central is the Word of God in your church? Does your pastor teach from the Bible, or only occasionally refer to it? If you left your Bible at home, could you make it through the service? How much spiritual meat do you take home from your pastor's message? Or do you just get nuggets of truth? Little wonder God's people are being destroyed. If we lack a significant knowledge of God and His Word, those pastors who are anemic Bible teachers cannot escape their share of the blame.

The other prophet that seems to have his finger on the pulse of our day is Amos. He wrote, "'Behold, the days are coming,' says the Lord GOD, 'that I will send a famine on the land, not a famine of bread, nor a thirst for water, but of hearing the words of the LORD'" (Amos 8:11). That famine isn't coming; it's arrived!

Want to take a famine check? Turn on your Christian radio station and listen for God's Word. Listen to the music and write down all you can of the lyrics. Give them the "gummi bear" check. Walk into your Christian bookstore and look for books that offer you real spiritual meat.

In the case of Christian radio, you often have to wait through hours of endless talk and musical entertainment before Amos' concern is addressed. In the latter case you'll have to wade through racks or shelves of trinkets and T-shirts before you come to anything that contains genuine spiritual food. It's not just Amos' prophecy anymore; it's today's reality.

Thankfully, God always has His remnant. There are pastors who are committed to preaching the Word, not just using their Bible as a springboard to some spiritual lesson. There are radio stations and programmers who are committed to using the airwaves for something that touches eternity, rather than simply capturing a greater market share. And there are still bookstores that actually have Christian books, even books composed of more than a few biblical principles strung together with anecdotes and stories. That's what it takes to grow spiritually in your new life. It takes spending significant time at the table of God's Word and getting a little help from mature believers.

The Grower

The Grower in our spiritual life is the One who said, "I am the life." He's the One who said, "You search the Scriptures, for in them you think you have eternal life; and these are they which testify of Me" (John 5:39). Jesus knew what would get the growing job done. The Scriptures are essential. A daily dose of God's Word will do more for you than an unlimited budget to purchase endless spiritual resources that are light on the Word and heavy on entertainment.

The Grower in our spiritual life is the One of whom it was said, "But grow in the grace and knowledge of our Lord and Savior Jesus Christ" (2 Pet. 3:18). Growing in grace and knowledge together will require a concentration on the Grower. We become like Him when we become knowledgeable of Him. He is our Life. We can't hope to grow without Him.

The Grower in our spiritual life gives us the capacity for fellowship with others who are growing too. This is one of the great joys of growing in God's grace and knowledge. We grow with others; we grow together. Speaking of Christians as a building, Paul says it "being joined together, grows into a holy temple in the Lord, in whom you also are

214

being built together for a habitation of God in the Spirit" (Eph. 2:21-22). To the Colossians the apostle likens God's Church to a body and says, "knit together by joints and ligaments, [the Church] grows with the increase which is from God" (Col. 2:19). The Grower gives us each other so we may help each other grow in our spiritual lives. We should be great encouragers of each other, accountability partners, teachers and learners together.

The Grower in our spiritual life has a purpose for us to achieve strong bones and spiritual muscles. "Whoever of you does not forsake all that he has cannot be My disciple" (Luke 14:33). Only the soldier fed on the meat of the Word and spiritual veggies will be adequate for the fight against Satan. Jesus doesn't want an army of spiritual sissies. He consistently uses the less advantaged, less gifted, less attractive of His soldiers to win great battles for Him. Often those with greater advantages, gifts and beauty have been munching on gummi bears so long they don't know their own weakness.

What does the Life mean to you?

Henry Wadsworth Longfellow said, "Life is real! Life is earnest! And the grave is not its goal."

Jesus gives us resurrection life on the other side of the grave; He gives us abundant life on this side. He is the Life. In the midst of His "I am the Good Shepherd" teaching, Jesus said, "The thief does not come except to steal, and to kill, and to destroy. I have come that they may have life and that they may have it more abundantly" (John 10:10). Here's what having the Life in your life means.

The good things of salvation are not just future

Abundant life begins the day spiritual life begins. Before being born again, we were dead. After we were born again, we have abundant life. It's not a future promise. It's not a post-grave abundance. It's right now, right here. Abundant life in Christ is a now thing.

The word translated *abundantly* in John 10:10 is the same as found in Mark 6:51. When Jesus came to His disciples walking on the water, Mark recorded, "They were greatly amazed in themselves beyond measure, and marveled." They were so shocked to see Jesus walking on the Sea of Galilee, you couldn't measure their marvel. They were astonished, flabbergasted, taken aback in immeasurable fashion. That's what abundantly means—in immeasurable fashion.

The word is also used in Ephesians 3:20, where Paul prays to "Him who is able to do exceedingly abundantly above all that we ask or think." Clearly the intent is that Jesus gives us much more than we can dream.

Jesus Christ, who said, "I am the life," gives us a life so immeasurably filled with good things, so astonishingly beyond anything we deserve, we can't find words to describe it. If you aren't experiencing that kind of life today, may I suggest two things.

First, check to see if you really have the new life that the Life-giver provides to all who ask Him. Make sure your are saved. Was there a time and a place when you felt so burdened by your sin that you repented of it and asked Jesus Christ to save you from it? If not, then do so right now. That's the only hope you have to experience the kind of abundant life Jesus talked about.

Second, if you are saved, maybe there's something standing between you and the joy of the Christian life. It could be a spat with a brother in Christ or an argument with your spouse. Don't allow these faulty relationship to sour your Christian life. They're easy to fix, if you're willing. Simply go to that person, admit every unkind thought you've had or unjust thing you've said, and ask them to forgive you. Maybe they'll have to do the same. You can't control what they do, but you can control what you do.

God has good things in mind for you right now, not just in heaven. Are you enjoying those good things? Or are you robbing yourself of them?

You aren't making this journey without a guide

The One who gives life, the One who gives the ability to grow in your spiritual life, doesn't just give you a book of instructions and say, "Good luck. You're on your own!" Jesus the Life is also Jesus the Guide.

"In Hellenistic religion there was a widespread conception of what is called 'the journey of the soul'. The souls of men have descended from heaven originally, and by their incorporation in human bodies have lost their divine qualities. To reach again their real home, they must after death make a long and weary journey through the spheres of the planets, becoming purified so that they may be fit to enter into the Kingdom of light. There is also a belief in some divine leader who gives help to the soul in its wandering flight. The theme pervades many Gnostic writings."[2]

What a pathetic prospect—not just beyond death, but waiting for death and that ultimate journey. Contrast this with the "I AM" God's promises. "I will fear no evil; for You are with me; Your rod and Your staff, they comfort me" (Ps. 23:4). "Go therefore and make disciples of all the nations . . . and lo, I am with you always, even to the end of the age" (Matt. 28:19-20). "He Himself has said, 'I will never leave you nor forsake you'" (Heb. 13:5).

It's true that Jesus sends us out to make disciples of all nations. But He does more. He guides us out. When Jesus said, "Go," He also said, "I am with you." The Giver of Life sends us out as sheep amid the wolves (Matt. 10:16). Now I have to tell you, the prospect of being sent into the world as a sheep isn't so bad, but being sent as a sheep amid the wolves is terrifying. Have you seen what wolves can do to sheep? If you haven't actually seen it, be thankful. But imagine it anyway.

The only comfort that I receive from knowing that I, as a sheep, am being sent out among the wolves of this world is also knowing that my Good Shepherd goes with me. That makes my journey bearable. It makes it possible. It even makes it exciting. Jesus not only is the Giver of my life, He is the Guide in my life.

You have something to live for in the present that touches eternity in the future

While others search for the meaning of life, the Christian searches for ways to share the abundance of life. It is only in the abundant life given to us by Jesus Christ that there is any meaning at all. All that we do now must have some impact on eternity or it is a colossal waste of time. So with new life in Christ comes new responsibility, new opportunity, new meaning, new challenges, new titles.

Because I have the Giver of Life in my life, I am an heir of God and a joint-heir with Jesus Christ (Rom. 8:17). All that belongs to the "I AM" God belongs equally to me. I don't know what that means entirely, but I don't question it either. God's Word says it's so. I am fabulously wealthy because of who my Father is.

What's more, I am an ambassador for the King of Kings. You talk about giving meaning to your life. Ask someone what they do and they proudly say, "I am a teacher " or, "I am a homemaker" or, "I am a doc-tor." You ask Christians what they do and they say, "I am a royal am-bassador for the King of all Kings and Lord of all Lords. I serve the Kingdom of Heaven." Somehow that makes me feel a bit more fulfilled than other occupations in life.

I am a son. I am a servant. I am soldier. I am a slave. I am a new cre-ation in Christ. I have new life in Christ. I am different from the way I used to be. "Old things have passed away; behold, all things have be-come new" (2 Cor. 5:17). I have a new reason to live. I have new goals, new assignments, new meaning, a new master. I'm living with eternal at-titudes now. I see the world differently. I see my possessions differently. I see my gifts and abilities in light of eternity. In fact, I begin every day at eternity and work backward. That way I know if the time I spend today and the things I do today have any eternal meaning. I do an "eter-nity check" at the beginning and end of every day.

> He liveth long who liveth well
> All other life is short and vain;
> He liveth longest who can tell
> Of living most for heavenly gain.
>
> — Horatius Bonar

John 14:6 is one of the greatest verses in the Bible. In it we gain three perspectives on the sufficiency of Jesus Christ. Jesus alone is sufficient to be the Way to God. Jesus alone is sufficient to be the Truth of God. Jesus alone is sufficient to be the Life we have in God. Thomas asked the timely question; Jesus gave the eternal answer.

Merrill Tenney writes, "Jesus' reply is the ultimate foundation for a satisfactory philosophy of life. First, it is personal. He did not claim merely to know the way, the truth, and the life as a formula he could im-part to the ignorant; but he actually claimed to be the answer to human problems. That is, Jesus' solution to perplexity is not a recipe; it is a re-lationship with him."[3]

Jesus is all you need. If you're lost, He is the Way. If you're confused, He is the Truth. If you're afraid of facing death, He is the Life. Jesus is sufficient to be whatever you need Him to be. Let Him do more than give you eternal life. Let Him be your Life.

"I am whatever you need; let Me satisfy you."

CHAPTER 13

I Am

WHATEVER YOU NEED

And we have such trust through Christ toward God. Not that we are sufficient of ourselves . . . but our sufficiency is from God.
2 CORINTHIANS 3:4-5

Taking exams seems to get harder over the years. In seminary and graduate school many of my exams were oral. No bluffing there. If they weren't oral, I had to use one of those little blue exam books and fill it with knowledge. I remember sitting six hours one Friday afternoon in Speer Library at Princeton taking a single exam, filling three such notebooks.

But high school exams were much easier, as I remember. The exams were more tests of your powers to recall rather than your powers to reason. Many high school exams asked for true or false answers, matching or "you're guess is as good as mine." My favorite high school exams, however, were the fill-in-the-blank kind. I was pretty good at those. There were not infinite possibilities for the answer, but there was some flexibility.

In many respects, that's the way the "I AM" God is too. When we find our sufficiency in Jesus Christ, we find every sufficiency in Him. Jesus is all I need. He is my "fill in the blank." Each of the "I am" statements focuses on a particular need filled by the Savior. If we need someone to lead us, Jesus said, "I am the Good Shepherd." If we need someone to feed us, Jesus said, "I am the Bread of Life." Jesus is whatever I need, all I need. In every essential way, Jesus is my "fill in the blank."

Fill in the blank. It's a wonderful concept. Jesus is our *carte blanche*. Anything that we really need, anything legitimate, anything helpful, Jesus is that for us. Jesus is our everything. The "I AM" God says, "I am whatever you need. I AM _____. You name it, from A to Z. I'm there for you. I am sufficient to be whatever you need." That's quite a promise!

Let's see some of the needs you and I have that Jesus can fill. He has already told us, "I am the Alpha and the Omega, the First and the Last" (Rev. 1:11). Not only is He the first and last, but the "I AM" God is also everything in between. He is the first letter of the alphabet—A; He is the last letter of the alphabet—Z. He is also every letter in between. Jesus is all you need.

A You need ACCESS to God. You can't live if you are shut out from Him. The "I AM" God says, "I am the *access* you need."

Imagine being denied to talk with someone who loves you and can do a world of good for you. That's like being in prison without visitation privileges. But that's exactly what sin has done to us. It has shut us out from the presence of God. Ever since our first parents, Adam and Eve, were driven from the Garden of Eden because of their sin, we have had only a distant, impersonal relationship with God.

But all of this changed at a place called Calvary. There Jesus died for us and paid the debt for our sin. There the broken lines of communication with God were forever repaired. There Jesus once again gave us access to the Father. "Therefore, having been justified by faith, we have peace with God through our Lord Jesus Christ, through whom also we have *access* by faith" (Rom. 5:1-2, emphasis mine). To the Ephesian believers Paul said of Jesus Christ, "For through Him we both have access by one Spirit to the Father" (Eph. 2:18; see also 3:12). Without Him, we are shut out from the Father. We have no access to Him. But with Jesus Christ as our Savior, we can go directly to the Father through the Son.

The "I AM" Son gave us access to the "I AM" Father. We're no longer cut off from God. We have an engraved invitation to enjoy His presence anytime we like, an invitation written in the blood of Jesus Christ. Jesus is all you need.

B You need a BROTHER to look out for you. Life would be far less threatening if you had a big brother protecting you. The "I AM" God says, "I am the *brother* you need."

When my son, Tim (who is now a pastor), was about five or six, he came to me with a question. Dad knows all the answers, or so he thought, and it was obvious that Tim had been pondering this issue in his mind. He said, "Dad, Jesus is the Son of God, right?" I affirmed that. "And, Dad, we are the sons of God too, right?" Again, no argument. Then Tim's early powers of deduction began to show. "Well, if Jesus is God's Son, and I am God's son, then that means that Jesus and I are brothers."

Immediately my mind reasoned that there had to be something theologically awry here, but after I thought a minute I assured my son that he was absolutely right. Jesus is our brother. The writer of Hebrews thought this fraternal relationship was very important in righting our relationship with God. He said, "But we see Jesus, who was made a little lower than the angels . . . that He, by the grace of God, might taste death for everyone. . . for which reason He is not ashamed to call them brethren . . . . Therefore, in all things He had to be made like His brethren, that He might be a merciful and faithful High Priest" (Heb. 2:9, 11, 17).

If you're pint-sized and often picked on, you can appreciate the need of a big brother coming to your aid. In comparison to the devil, we are all pint-sized and picked on. But when we are tempted, when we are in trouble, when we are most vulnerable to the attacks of Satan, that's the time we need to call for help from our merciful and faithful High Priest, our Brother—Jesus Christ. He is our advocate to the Father. He is our defense against Satan. To make right what's wrong, Jesus is all you need.

C You need COURAGE to face life's most difficult days. You need to know that your courage is real and not just in your head. The "I AM" God says, "I am the *courage* you need."

All who were glued to their television will never forget 18-year-old Kerri Strug making one last run at the vault in the 1996 Summer Olympic Games. Her pain from an injured ankle was obvious, but her 9.712 score insured the first U.S. team gymnastics gold medal ever. It was a display of raw courage. As Winston Churchill said, "Success is never final; failure is seldom fatal. It is courage that counts."

But the courage you and I need is different. We need daily courage. Think of all the threats and difficulties of life for which you need more than your own courage. There's the threat of being held bondage by sin. There's the difficulty of caring for aging parents. There's the threat of a deadly disease ending your life prematurely. There's the difficulty of getting along with a cantankerous neighbor. Life is filled with threats and difficulties.

That's why God spent so much time encouraging people in the Bible; that's why He spends so much time encouraging us. Take Joshua, for example. One of Moses' last acts as leader of Israel was to call an assembly and, in the presence of all Israel, publicly encourage Joshua. "Be strong and of good courage" (Deut. 31:6-7). And when Moses died and was no long around to encourage his young friend, God did it for him. "Be strong and of good courage; do not be afraid, nor be dismayed, for the LORD your God is with you wherever you go" (Josh. 1:9; see also 1:6-7, 18).

God does the same for you and me today through His Son. Jesus is our courage. He's the One who promised to anchor us (Heb. 6:19), to strengthen us (Phil. 4:13) and never to leave us or abandon us (Heb. 13:5). He makes our position in Him secure; He makes our performance for Him strong; He makes our presence with Him continual. What better way to give us courage. Jesus is all you need.

D You need a DELIVERER from Satan's subtle traps. You're no match for the devil all by yourself. The "I AM" God says, "I am the *deliverer* you need."

When Jesus instructed His disciples in the way to pray (what we have called the Lord's Prayer), He included this often underappreciated phrase: "and do not lead us into temptation, but deliver us from the evil one" (Matt. 6:13).

David, the shepherd psalmist, often wrote of God as his deliverer. "The LORD is my rock and my fortress and my deliverer; my God, my strength, in whom I will trust" (Ps. 18:2; see also 40:17; 70:5; 144:2). But it is David's Great Descendant, the Lord Jesus Christ, in whose strong name deliverance comes to you and me. He delivered us from the curse of the Law (Gal. 3:13). He delivered us from the sting of death (1 Cor. 15:55-56). He delivered us from the certainty of hell (Matt. 25:41). And every day, He delivers us from the potential failure of succumbing to Satan's temptation (1 Cor. 10:13).

Trying to outwit Satan is a losing proposition. His temptation is too sweet, too subtle, too irresistible. It's like putting honey on the hand of a two-year-old and a feather in the other. The outcome is certain. But not when you have Jesus as your deliverer. It is possible for you to walk away from the devil's devices in the strength of Jesus' name. But it's only possible when He delivers us. Fortunately, we can not only count on His strength, we can draw on it too. He will deliver you from the evil one. Jesus is all you need.

E You need an EXAMPLE, someone who has traveled the road before you, someone to show you where the potholes are. The "I AM" God says, "I am the *example* you need."

After Jesus washed the disciples' feet, He instructed them about servanthood by saying, "For I have given you an example, that you should do as I have done to you" (John 13:15). There is no greater example than the kind that says, "Here, watch me do this, and then you do it the same way." My father taught me to drive nails with a hammer that way; my mother taught me to vacuum the carpet that same way. Jesus taught me to serve others that very same way.

The apostle Peter said, "When you do good and suffer for it, if you take it patiently, this is commendable before God. For to this you were called, because Christ also suffered for us, leaving us an example, that you should follow His steps" (1 Pet. 2:20-21). The word Peter chose for "example" is *hupogrammos*. It speaks of a writing book or a pad that includes all the letters of the alphabet and is given to beginners to help them learn to draw the letters.

Do you remember those cards above the chalkboard in preschool or kindergarten? There was capital W and small w; a capital K and small k, and so forth. They were there to help young learners to write. There was nothing ethereal about the process. You just looked at the cards and copied what you saw. You didn't have to think about it. The teacher wouldn't allow you to try to improve on it. You just did it.

That's the way it is with Jesus. He is our example. We simply listen to what He said and say the same. We just watch what He did and do the same. It's not hard if you have the desire. Jesus will be your example in every area of life, if you will just pattern yourself after Him. Jesus is all you need.

F You need a FRIEND. We all have enough so-called friends; what we really need is someone who will be there for us all the time. The "I AM" God says, "I am the *friend* you need."

What is a friend? An English publication offered a prize for the best definition. Thousands entered the context. Some of the better entries were, "One who multiplies joys and divides grief"; "One who understands our silence." But the winning entry was, "One who comes in when the whole world has gone out."

Friends are there when we need them. They share our sorrows and our joys. The show up at the hospital soon after our surgery. They sit silently with us when a daughter runs away from home. They invest themselves in our lives. Where do we get such friends? We invest in them. Ralph Waldo Emerson said, "The only way to have a friend is to be one." He got that line from the Proverbs: "A man who has friends must himself be friendly" (Prov. 18:24). But that verse continues, "But there is a friend who sticks closer than a brother." That friend is the "I AM" God.

We all need friends. The Sequoia trees of California tower as much as 300 feet above the ground. Strangely, these giants have unusually shallow root systems that reach out in all directions to capture water. That's why they grow in clusters. Seldom do you see a redwood standing alone because high winds would uproot it. Their intertwining roots provide support for one another against the storms.

The greatest support you get is from the greatest friends you have. "What a Friend we have in Jesus, all our sins and griefs to bear!" He is that friend who sticks closer to you than does your own brother. Whatever you face today, you don't face it alone. You have the strength of your friends, particularly your best friend. Jesus is all you need.

G You need a GUARANTEE. Some people think there are no guarantees in life, but they are wrong. The "I AM" God says, "I am the *guarantee* you need."

A guarantee is the assurance for the fulfillment of a condition. Guarantees come in many forms. You've heard them. "You'll enjoy this pre-owned, classic automobile. It comes with a 30-day guarantee." "We'll win the football game; I guarantee it." The problem, of course, is that sometimes those who make guarantees are not in a position to fulfill them. Used cars fail. Football teams lose.

We can all live with that, but can we live with no guarantee of our future? No one does, of course, because we are all guaranteed a future: "He who believes in Him [Jesus] is not condemned; but he who does not believe is condemned already, because he has not believed in the name of the only begotten Son of God" (John 3:18).

What makes a guarantee useful are the conditions of the guarantee and the integrity of the one making it. Here are the conditions of Jesus' guarantee. If we recognize that our personal sin brings us God's condemnation, and we recognize that Jesus died at Calvary to pay the penalty for that condemnation, and if we have faith to believe that He will save us if we ask Him, when we ask, we will be saved from condemnation and hell. That's Jesus' guarantee. And how do we know it's any good? Because He died to make it good. He gave His life as our guarantee.

Do you need to know what your future holds? Read your Bible. Do you need to know where you will spend eternity? Trust Jesus Christ as your Savior. Do you need to know what guarantee you have of eternal life in heaven? Jesus is all you need.

H You need a HELPER. Life is filled with too many hazardous hairpin turns. You need someone to help you negotiate those dangerous curves. The "I AM" God says, "I am the *helper* you need."

David cried out to God, "LORD, be my helper!" (Ps. 30:10). He knew God was: "Behold, God is my helper" (54:4). We can know the same. Listen to what the writer of Hebrews says about Jesus as our helper. "For in that He Himself has suffered, being tempted, He is able to aid those who are tempted" (2:18). "Let us therefore come boldly to the throne of grace, that we may obtain mercy and find grace to help in time of need" (4:16). "For He Himself has said, 'I will never leave you nor forsake you.' So we may boldly say: 'The LORD is my helper; I will not fear. What can man do to me?'" (13:5-6).

Several years ago nine physically handicapped people conquered Mount Rainier. One of the mountain climbers had an artificial leg. Another was an epileptic. Two were deaf and five were blind. They successfully negotiated the 14,000-foot climb because, as one blind man put it, "We had a lot of help from each other."

Need help getting along with the person next door? Jesus is your helper. Ask Him to give you an opportunity to show genuine love to your neighbor. Need help understanding why God does what He does? Ask Jesus to help you understand correctly God's Word as you consistently read it. Need help discerning God's will? Come boldly to the throne of grace. Ask for clear leading. Pray for mercy and grace to help in time of need. When you need a helper, you know where to look. Jesus is all you need.

227

I You need an INTERCESSOR. Sometimes you just can't come boldly to the throne of God yourself. That's when you need someone to do it for you. The "I AM" God says, "I am the *intercessor* you need."

Intercession is when someone else prays for you, or you pray for someone else. When you are too sick, too discouraged, too ashamed, you need someone to pray for you. Fortunately, you have Someone who will do that.

On the night He was betrayed, Jesus prayed in the Garden of Gethsemane. He said, "Father, if it is Your will, remove this cup from Me; nevertheless not My will, but Yours, be done" (Luke 22:42). He was praying for Himself. But He also prayed for His disciples. "I do not pray that You should take them out of the world, but that You should keep them from the evil one. They are not of the world, just as I am not of the world. Sanctify them by Your truth. Your word is truth" (John 17:15-17).

Jesus was skilled in the art of intercession. He still is. Paul said that Jesus is now "at the right hand of God, who also makes intercession for us" (Rom. 8:34). "He is also able to save to the uttermost those who come to God through Him, since He ever lives to make intercession for them" (Heb. 7:25). Some people live to golf. Others live to eat. Jesus lives to make intercession for you and me.

When you need someone to pray for you, someone to pray with you, someone to pray in place of you, you want to make sure it's someone who is good at getting through to God. Jesus is all you need.

J You need a JUSTIFIER, someone who can not only understand your sin, but who can do something about it. The "I AM" God says, "I am the *justifier* you need."

Do you know what it means to be justified? The great patriarch Abraham did. To be justified means that God declares you to be righteous and treats you as if you were.

Genesis 15:6 records, "And he believed in the LORD, and He accounted it to him for righteousness." When Abraham put his full faith and confidence in God, God credited that faith to Abraham's account as if it were righteousness. Abraham was justified by the divine justifier. Was Abraham righteous? Did he never sin again? Read on. Twice after this he lied about Sarah being his sister instead of his wife. He had other problems too. No, being justified does not mean we are sinless; it just means we are forgiven and treated by God as if we were sinless.

Jesus is the way we are justified in the eyes of God. We are "justified freely by His grace through the redemption that is in Christ Jesus" (Rom. 3:24). We are "justified by His blood" (Rom. 5:9). You need a justifier. Without one, you stand guilty before God and the consequences of sin and guilt are eternal death (Rom. 6:23). But to be justified you must have a redemptive sacrifice that's acceptable to God. What can wash away your sins? Nothing but the blood of Jesus. There is only one justifier. Jesus is all you need.

K You need a KINSMAN. A kinsman is more than kin; he is kin who purchases your freedom. The "I AM" God says, "I am the *kinsman* you need."

We hear a lot these days about friends and family. We need both. But neither your friends nor your family have what it takes to be your redeemer. You need a kinsman for that.

Since an Israelite could sell himself, his family or his land (Lev. 25:39-43) in cases of poverty, the kinsman-redeemer (v. 25) was provided to protect the clan. The kinsman had the first option by law to buy any land being sold, allowing it to be kept in the family (vv. 23-28). The story of Ruth is an excellent example of the kinsman-redeemer. Boaz was a near kinsman of Naomi, Ruth's mother-in-law. He purchased the widow Ruth and thus restored all the rights of her husband's family to his clan.

But there's an even better example. Jesus Christ is our kinsman-redeemer. He "gave Himself for us, that He might redeem us," but the price He paid was not money or precious metals. The price was His own life sacrificed at Calvary's cross. "You were not redeemed with corruptible things, like silver or gold . . . but with the precious blood of Christ, as of a lamb without blemish and without spot" (1 Pet. 1:18-19). Jesus, our brother, became our Savior when He redeemed us with His blood.

Without a kinsman, you would still be carrying the horrible weight of your own sin, which ultimately would crush you and condemn you. But you have a kinsman-redeemer. Jesus is all you need.

L You need a LIGHTHOUSE. Life is a bit more challenging than the peaceful picture of red sails in the sunset. When shipwreck is a danger, you need a lighthouse. The "I AM" God says, "I am the *lighthouse* you need."

Recently I visited the Old Portland lighthouse, one of the most photographed lighthouses in the world. As I surveyed the impressive structure, I was reminded that lighthouses aren't just photogenic wonders; they are real warnings of danger.

There's an old story about a sea captain who was negotiating his ship through very treacherous waters. The fog was incredibly thick; visibility was almost zero. In the distance through the fog he saw a light and recognized immediately that he was on a collision course. He sent a message by signal saying, "Adjust your course ten degrees to the north." The response came back, "Adjust your course ten degrees to the south." Undaunted but angered the captain repeated, "Adjust your course ten degrees to the north. I am a freighter." Word came back, "Adjust your course ten degrees to the south. I am the lighthouse."

Lighthouses are designed to warn sailors that there is danger in the waters ahead of them. But they are of little value if they are not heeded. Jesus is the lighthouse in your life. He knows what's ahead and can warn you in plenty of time for you to make adjustments in your life. But you must always alter the course of your life to that of the lighthouse. If you insist on the other way around, the result is disaster.

We all need a lighthouse to guide us through the treacherous waters. We especially need a lighthouse when the fog is thick and we can't see too clearly what lies ahead. Jesus is all you need.

M You need MOTIVATION. When there are lots of choices and many reasons to do nothing, we all need something or someone to motivate us to do what is right. The "I AM" God says, "I am the *motivation* you need."

The loaded station wagon pulled into the only remaining campsite. Four youngsters leaped from the car and began feverishly unloading gear and setting up the tent. The boys then rushed to gather firewood; the girls set up the camp stove and cooking utensils. The camper next door marveled at the remarkable display of teamwork. The father replied, "I have a system. No one goes to the bathroom until the camp is set up."

Motivation is a wonderful thing. Some Christians find themselves in need of motivation often. There are so many plans to be made, so much television to watch, so many social events on their calendar. Often Jesus has to call us back to what's really important. People need the Lord.

The best motivation I know to help keep our eyes focused on eternity is not just to remember what Jesus did for us on the cross, although that is strong motivation. The best motivation I know is the love of Christ that took Him to Calvary and kept Him there. "For the love of Christ constrains us" (2 Cor. 5:14). That's what motivated the apostle Paul. It's what motivates us as well.

The next time you need a little motivation, think about the love of Christ for a world who spit in His face while He was dying for them. Do you need motivation to service? Jesus is all you need.

N You need a NAVIGATOR. The issues are too complex. The questions are too difficult. Through the sea of moral turbulence, you need a navigator. The "I AM" God says, "I am the *navigator* you need."

Think about it. Remember when the big ethical issues were smoking, drinking and dancing? Those are still issues, but they pale in significance to the moral and ethical questions we face today. A generation ago we didn't have to wrestle with partial-birth abortion, doctor-assisted suicide, cloning, organ harvesting, genetic engineering, computer privacy and a whole lot more. Life has become so complicated, the issues so complex. Much of the world is at sea about absolutes. Where can we turn for answers?

Turn to the navigator. Find in Jesus Christ and the Bible the answers to your questions. If the direct answer isn't there, find the biblical principle upon which answers can be founded. The alternative is the moral malaise the world seems to be drowning in.

God promised David, "I will instruct you and teach you in the way you should go; I will guide you with My eye" (Ps. 32:8). God sent the Dayspring (Jesus) "to give light to those who sit in darkness . . . to guide our feet into the way of peace" (Luke 1:79). When the waters are murky and it's not clear what you should believe, you need a navigator, someone who will teach you and guide you rightly. Jesus is all you need.

O You need an OASIS. The world is a desert—a desert of ideas, a desert of goals, a desert of destiny. In such a desert, the Christian needs a quiet and refreshing oasis. The "I AM" God says, "I am the *oasis* you need."

Once in the jungle of Ecuador I made the rookie mistake of asking an Indian how many inches of rain that part of the world received every year. He laughed and said, "We get 26 feet."

But your life may not be like that, at least spiritually. You live in a household where you are the only committed Christian. You work in an office where swearing, flirting and gossiping are the norm. It's a spiritual desert. You'd dry up, too, if you didn't have an oasis to visit in the middle of your desert. Jehovah issued this call: "Ho! Everyone who thirsts, come to the waters" (Isa. 55:1). Jesus said, "If anyone thirsts, let him come to Me and drink. He who believes in Me, as the Scripture has said, out of his heart will flow rivers of living water" (John 7:37-38).

Are you spiritually dry today? Are the desert sands around you constantly creeping into your life and choking you spiritually? Take some time each morning, or during your break, or at lunch or whenever, to get away for a cool drink from Jesus and the water of the Word. When you are dry, come to God's oasis and be refreshed. Jesus is all you need.

P You need PEACE. Peace is not the absence of conflict, but the presence of Jesus. We all need peace—peace with God and peace in our lives. The "I AM" God says, "I am the *peace* you need."

Peace and war are mutually exclusive. There can be no peace where there is war, and we are naturally at war with God. "Whoever therefore wants to be a friend of the world makes himself an enemy of God" (James 4:4). Whether we consciously know it or not, we have been at war with God since the Garden of Eden. Rebellion against God led to a long war with Him. That battle continues in the hearts of men and women today.

But it doesn't have to. Jesus Christ died to end the war. Paul told the Ephesian believers, "For He Himself is our peace . . . and He came and preached peace to you" (Eph. 2:14, 17). Again, to the Romans the apostle said, "Therefore, having been justified by faith, we have peace with God through our Lord Jesus Christ" (Rom. 5:1). Martin Lloyd-Jones wrote, "When a person has peace with God, the person's mind is at rest about his relationship to God."[1] You and I no longer have to be at war with God. Jesus offers Himself as our peace treaty.

And once we lay down our arms against God and accept what Jesus did at Calvary as our peace treaty, the peace that God gives floods our lives. "And the peace of God, which surpasses all understanding, will guard your hearts and minds through Christ Jesus" (Phil. 4:7). So whether it's wartime peace or lifetime peace, Jesus is our peace. Jesus is all you need.

Q You need a QUARTERBACK. Imagine how fragmented and ineffective a football team would be without a quarterback. The same is true for our life. The "I AM" God says, "I am the *quarterback* you need."

If you are a sports fan at all, you recognize their names: Johnny Unitas, Bart Starr, Terry Bradshaw, Dan Marino, Troy Aikman. They are (or were) quarterbacks. They run the offense for professional football teams. Usually, they are either heroes or heels, depending on whether or not the team is winning. It's a tough job calling the plays, reading the defense, making changes at the line of scrimmage and performing under the intense scrutiny of coaches, fans and critics.

Jesus is our quarterback. He calls the plays, hands off the ball to us, pats us on the back when we gain ground, picks us up, dusts us off and encourages us when we do not. When the entire team performs as it is supposed to, we win. When one member of the team doesn't perform adequately, the whole team suffers, but the pain is most evident on the face of the quarterback.

Are you still trying to call the plays in your life? Are you running the way you want, even when your blockers are running the other way? Is life for you just a game, one in which you pay no attention to the playbook or the quarterback? Run to win. Memorize God's playbook, the Bible, and let His quarterback, Jesus Christ, help you find the holes, follow your blockers and make big gains. To chew up big yardage in Satan's territory, you need the right quarterback. Jesus is all you need.

R You need a RAISON D'ÊTRE. That's what the French call it: a reason to be. We all need to know why we are alive, what we want to get out of life. The "I AM" God says, "I am the *raison d'être* you need."

You've heard them. They echo on the street, in the office, on television. The reasons people give for being alive are pretty standard and pretty bad: "I want to live to a good old age"; "I want to become a movie star"; "I want to make a lot of money and retire."

If you're a Christian, why are you alive today? What's the purpose of your life? Have you taken the time to answer that question satisfactorily? After all, if heaven is so wonderful (and it is), and if we go there when we die (and we do), why doesn't God just take us home as soon as we become a Christian? Wouldn't that be a better plan? Why does He leave us here?

The answer is found in Ephesians 2:8-10: "For by grace you have been saved through faith, and that not of yourselves; it is the gift of God, not of works, lest anyone should boast. For we are His workmanship, created in Christ Jesus for good works, which God prepared beforehand that we should walk in them." There you have it—our *raison d'être*. We are saved to serve the Savior. Living for Jesus is the reason we live. That's God's plan for your life.

If you aren't working that plan, begin focusing all you do on the Lord Jesus Christ. He is the reason you live; He is your reason to be. Get that fixed in your mind, and you'll have little trouble working out the rest of life's details. Discover what God wants for you in life. Jesus is all you need.

S You need STRENGTH. In a world filled with health clubs, vitamin supplements and fitness gurus, we seem to know very little about spiritual strength. The "I AM" God says, "I am the *strength* you need."

Strength is determined largely by what is on the inside, not what is on the outside. In 1994 a six-tier parking garage was built next to the old office of Back to the Bible in downtown Lincoln, Nebraska. This gave our staff an intriguing opportunity to view firsthand a major construction project. When it was finished, the building looked like it was just made of concrete. But those of us who watched it being built knew better. We saw the thousands of feet of metal rods and wire that went inside that concrete to make the building strong.

That's true in our spiritual life as well. Jesus promises to be our strength and consequently to strengthen us in every thing we do. We don't have to be great physical specimens to be strong in the Lord. Jesus said, "My grace is sufficient for you, for My strength is made perfect in weakness" (2 Cor. 12:9). When we have Jesus on the inside, we have strength, even in a weakened body. And He gives us the strength to live in a way that pleases Him. "I can do all things through Christ who strengthens me" (Phil. 4:13).

As Chuck Swindoll said, "The Lord doesn't promise to give us something to take so we can handle our weary moments. He promises us himself. That is all. And that is enough." The "I AM" God is your strength. Jesus is all you need.

T You need a TREASURE. Every Christian wants to hear "Well done," but God gives more than that. The "I AM" God says, "I am the *treasure* you need."

The March 17, 1987, edition of the *Atlanta Journal Constitution* carried a story about a rock hound named Rob Cutshaw. It seems Rob found a rock he described as "purdy and big." He guessed the blue chunk could bring as much as $500. Was he ever wrong. That blue rock is today known as "The Star of David." This nearly one pound sapphire could easily sell for nearly $3 million. What a treasure!

Imagine finding such a treasure. Better yet, what if you were obedient to God and discovered that your reward for obedience was a fantastic treasure? After the great battles of history, each of the fighting men received a portion of the spoils of war. That's how they lived—on the booty from battle. They fought, they won, and they received a portion of what was captured.

Imagine, after the battle was over, to discover that your portion was God Himself. David said, "You are my portion, O LORD" (Ps. 119:57; see also Ps. 16:5; 73:26; 142:5). The great treasure that comes from obedience to God is God Himself. "I am your shield, your exceedingly great reward" (Gen. 15:1).

Jesus counseled us, "Seek first the kingdom of God and His righteousness" (Matt. 6:33), and the spoils of war will be greater treasure than you can imagine. Your portion is Jesus Himself. There will be more, of course, but there will be none greater. Jesus is all you need.

U You need an UPGRADE. Life is too short and eternity too long to live like a spiritual beggar. The "I AM" God says, "I am the *upgrade* you need."

I am a member of the frequent flier programs of four airlines. Most of my flying, however, is with United Airlines. In this program I am a Premier Executive, a flying status that brings with it a great number of privileges and amenities. Often United will send me complimentary upgrade certificates. At Back to the Bible we don't fly first class, but we do enjoy those free upgrades.

In life, Jesus is my upgrade. He's the difference between flying first class and flying coach. Many Christians are satisfied with "peanuts and a snack" method of flying, but not me. I want the meat of the Word, not just milk. I desire to live in the fullness of the Holy Spirit, not just to get along the best I can. I want that "abundant" life Jesus promised, not merely an average life. I want to be intimate with God, not simply acquainted with Him. I want to live the "upgrade" life, not the ordinary life.

Jesus is sufficient to provide for upgrade living. Upgrades are gifts from the airlines. The upgrade life is Jesus' gift to us as well. There's a lot more to flying than coach, I've discovered, and there's a lot more to the Christian life than living. Jesus makes the difference. Jesus is all you need.

V You need a VICTORY. If it seems like your life is headed for a perfect 0-10 season, you need a victory. The "I AM" God says, "I am the *victory* you need."

Here's what the Word of God says about victory: "For whatever is born of God overcomes the world. And this is the victory that has overcome the world—our faith. Who is he who overcomes the world, but he who believes that Jesus is the Son of God?" (1 John 5:4-5). Victory over the world is always related to Jesus; we have victory in Jesus.

In his book *Forever Triumphant,* F. J. Huegel tells the story of Gen. Jonathan Wainwright, who was captured during World War II and held by the Japanese in a Manchurian concentration camp. Wainwright was cruelly treated by his captors until the day the Japanese surrendered. A United States army colonel arrived at the camp to tell the general personally that the war was over. After Wainwright heard the news, he returned to his quarters and was confronted by his guards, who began to mistreat him again. "No!" shouted the general, "I am in command here!" And from that moment on, General Wainwright was in complete control of the concentration camp.[2]

That's what it means for you and me that Jesus has given us victory. He has conquered temptation, He has conquered sin, He has conquered death. "In all these things we are more than conquerors through Him who loved us" (Rom. 8:37).

Don't let sin and temptation defeat you. Jesus has already beaten them. Assert that He is in command now. You can live above all that. Jesus is all you need.

W You need a WELLSPRING. To make it to the end, we need enough to keep us going strong. We need a source that will not dry up. We need a wellspring. The "I AM" God says, "I am the *wellspring* you need."

Cars run out of gas. Computer disks run out of storage space. Reservoirs run out of water. Batteries run out of charge. What we need is something akin to the Energizer Bunny—something that will keep us going and going. We need a wellspring.

The dictionary defines a wellspring as "a source of continual supply." Nobody thinks about supply until there is no more. Wells run dry. Then we worry. Our computer notifies us that our disk is full. Then we scramble. Supply lines are cut. Then we go hungry. What if we had a continual source of supply? One that never runs out, one that never gets severed, one that never goes away? We do. We have the "I AM" God. Jesus Christ is sufficient for all our needs. "And my God shall supply all your need according to His riches in glory by Christ Jesus" (Phil. 4:19).

The amazing thing about this promise is that little preposition *according*. The promise is not that God will supply your need "out of" His riches. If He did that, they would eventually become depleted. It may take millions of years, but "out of" means eventual depletion. But God supplies "according to" His riches. How great are His riches? Greater than any of your needs. The key is that they come to you by Christ Jesus. For a never-ending source of God's supply, Jesus is all you need.

X You need a XENOPHILE. When you are on the outside looking in, you need someone on the inside looking out at you in love. The "I AM" God says, "I am the *xenophile* you need."

You say you never heard of a xenophile? You wonder where I came up with that word? Consider my other "X" options. It's a good word, made up of two Greek words: *xenos*, which means "stranger," and *phile*, which means "lover of." Often our best English words are composed of two or more Greek or Latin words. Xenophobia is a fear of strangers (*xenos* and *phobia*), but a xenophile is just the opposite.

Because we were all strangers to God and His grace, we desperately needed someone to love us. Loving strangers is not easy; you do not know them. But when you do know them and they are nasty and obnoxious, strangers are even harder to love. Yet Scripture says, "For when we were still without strength, in due time Christ died for the ungodly. For scarcely for a righteous man will one die; yet perhaps for a good man someone would even dare to die. But God demonstrates His own love toward us, in that while we were still sinners, Christ died for us" (Rom. 5:6-8).

We were strangers to God, rebels without a cause. Yet still the Father loved us enough to send His Son to die for us, and the Son loved us enough to go to Calvary's cross for us. That's loving a stranger to death.

The whole world needs God's sacrificial love. You need someone to love you, Stranger. Jesus is all you need.

Y You need a YARDSTICK. Whether we're making great progress or little, life is still a series of measurements. The "I AM" God says, "I am the *yardstick* you need.

On an upstairs wall at my parents' home is a series of pencil etches. They rise vertically from a foot and a half to about six feet. They chart the growth of my mother's grandchildren. She started doing this more than three decades ago. Now, many of her grandchildren have their own children. Is it time to wash those pencil marks off the wall? Not unless you want your fingers broken. They are the concrete proof of progress.

Life is a journey, and the only way to know for sure we are being successful on that journey is to stop every now and then and measure our progress. That's what my mother's wall does. That's also what Jesus does in the spiritual realm. He is our yardstick.

Before our new life in Christ began we stood next to the perfect Son of God and didn't measure up. "For all have sinned and fall short of the glory of God" (Rom. 3:23). Even now we don't measure up, but we ought to be getting taller each time we stand next to the yardstick. Jesus not only died to give us new life, but He died to help move us on from spiritual infancy to spiritual maturity. Jesus "gave Himself for us, that He might redeem us from every lawless deed and purify for Himself His own special people" (Titus 2:14).

Take a poll. Compare your stats. Ask around. But if you really want to know how you're doing in your Christian life, stand next to the yardstick. Jesus is all you need.

Z You need a ZION. Life is hard. The disappointments are huge. We need some aspirations that help us rise above it all. We need a mountain. We need a Zion. The "I AM" God says, "I am the *Zion* you need."

Zion is the name of a citadel in Palestine that was the nucleus of Jerusalem. It was a mountain, part of the later settlement of Jerusalem, that embodied all that was strong and safe about the Holy City. Later still the name was given to the Jewish homeland. Zion was symbolic of Judaism or the Jewish national aspiration. At the word *Zion*, Jews all over the world perked up their ears, raised their weary heads and quickened their step. Zion is everything to the Jewish people.

Jesus is our Zion, whether we are a Jew or a Gentile. He is the center of our aspirations. We live for Him; we would die for Him. He is our zeal, our burning desire that lifts us up out of the mundane and gives us something to press on for. He is our banner, our battle cry, our battalion leader. Jesus is what stirs us in the morning, sustains us through the day and sends us to bed each night exhausted but eager to get up the next day and do it all again.

Jesus is Zion, your citadel of strength and safety. Jesus is Zion, giving meaning to life. Jesus is Zion, raising your aspirations from the ordinary to the exceptional, from the inconsequential to the inconceivable, from the everyday to the eternal. To rise to the citadel of Zion, Jesus is all you need.

The Whatever God

So what do you need the "I AM" God to be for you? Whatever it is, He is sufficient. "And God is able to make all grace abound toward you, that you, always having all sufficiency in all things, have an abundance for every good work" (2 Cor. 9:8).

Did that verse grab you the way it did me? What incredible power. If that verse is true, and God's Word is always true, then we have every reason to expect to succeed. We have every reason to believe we can do whatever God asks us to do. We have "all sufficiency in all things." We have "an abundance for every good work."

When we see Jesus Christ as our greatest resource, we see Him in all His fullness, all His empowerment, all His sufficiency. He will be to you whatever you need Him to be. He is sufficient for any task, from A to Z.

"Not that we are sufficient of ourselves to think of anything as being from ourselves, but our sufficiency is from God" (2 Cor. 3:5). Jesus is the great "I AM." He is sufficient to supply all your needs, because He is the Father's gift to you for _____ (fill in the blank).

Jesus is all you need!

CONCLUSION

Names are much more than a way to identify people. They tell something of their essence.

Generations ago names were given in faith. They reflected the hopes of the parents for their children. When you asked, "What's your name?" you were really asking, "What's your character?" That's certainly why Joseph and Mary were not given the privilege of naming the Christ child. The angel said to Joseph, "You shall call His name JESUS, for He will save His people from their sins" (Matt. 1:21). Jesus was not just His name; salvation is what He is all about.

Proverbs 30 records the reflections of a man named Agur. Comparing the insufficiency of man with the sufficiency of God, Agur asked, "Who has ascended into heaven? . . . Who has established all the ends of the earth? What is His name, and what is His Son's name?" (v. 4). We would expect Agur to ask, "What is His name?" But, "What is His Son's name?" Did Agur, thousands of years ago, believe God had a Son? And did he believe God's Son's name was significant? Apparently so.

The name of the Father is "I AM." The name of the Son is "I AM." Like Father, like Son. Everything the Father provides for us, the Son provides for us. All the sufficiency of the Father is the sufficiency of the Son.

The bottom line of sufficiency is this. Jesus Christ is the "I AM" God. Each of His "I am" expressions illustrate that He is sufficient to meet whatever need you have.

If you need God in your life, Jesus has sufficient credentials. He is fully God and fully man, the unique God-man. As man, He knows all about your struggles. As God, He is able to do something about them. Jesus is all the God you need.

If you need a king, Jesus is sufficient to be King of Kings. One day He will rule the world with a rod of iron. But His reign will be one of peace and righteousness, where the lion and lamb will lie together. Jesus is all the king you need.

If you need life, Jesus is sufficient to give you life. The life He gives is not just adequate or equal to your present life; it is much more. The Bible calls the life Jesus gives "abundant" life. Abundant life now will one day burst forth as eternal life. Jesus is all the life you need.

If you need resurrection, Jesus is sufficient to be your resurrection. When you die, that's not the end. Because Jesus lives, He promises to raise you from the dead. His resurrection is the guarantee of your own. Jesus is all the resurrection you need.

If you need the truth, Jesus is sufficient to reveal all truth to you. In Him all the wisdom of God is contained. There is no purer repository of truth, truth for life. When you're looking for the truth, look no further than the Savior. Jesus is all the truth you need.

If you need to find the way, Jesus is sufficient to be the way for you. We have all lost our way, but when people are lost they try many ways to get back to God. But there is only one way. Jesus is all the way you need.

If you need bread, Jesus is sufficient to satisfy all your spiritual hunger. Bread is the basic need of life. Jesus as the Bread of Life can meet all the needs of your spiritual life. Jesus is all the bread you need.

If you need a door, Jesus is sufficient to be your door to all the good things God has in store for you. Jesus is the door to God, the door to good, the door to blessing, the door to heaven. Jesus is all the door you need.

If you need a light, Jesus is sufficient to light your world. It's a pretty dark world. Sin has a way of making the darkness even darker. But Jesus shines the light of truth, the light of love, the light of the Gospel into this dark world. Jesus is all the light you need.

If you need a shepherd, Jesus is sufficient to shepherd you to God. Sheep are never driven; they are led. To find the way to God, we must be led to Him, not driven to Him. Jesus lovingly, tenderly, graciously led the way to God through the cross of Calvary. Jesus is all the shepherd you need.

If you need the Son of God, Jesus alone is sufficient to be God's Son. To be God's Son is to show identity with God, equality with God, oneness with God. The way to the Father is through the Son. Jesus is all the Son you need.

If you need a vine, Jesus is sufficient to sustain you throughout your life. Vines bring nutrients from the soil and feed the branches. Vines support the branches; they give life to the branches. Let Jesus sustain you. Jesus is all the vine you need.

Years ago, there was a very wealthy man who, with his devoted young son, shared a passion for art collecting. Priceless works by Picasso, Van Gogh, Monet and many others adorned the walls of the family estate. The widowed, elder man looked on with satisfaction as his only child became an experienced art collector, just like his father.

As winter approached, war engulfed the nation, and the young man left to serve his country. After only a few weeks, his father received a telegram. The young man had died while rushing a fellow soldier to a medic. Distraught and lonely, the old man faced the upcoming Christmas holidays with anguish and sadness. The joy of the season would visit his house no longer.

On Christmas morning, a knock on the door awakened the depressed old man. As he opened the door, a soldier greeted him with a large package under his arm. "I was a friend of your son," the soldier said. "In fact, I was the one he was rescuing when he died. I have something for you." The old man invited him in and the soldier continued, "I'm an artist and I want you to have this."

As the old man unwrapped the package, the paper gave way to reveal a portrait of his son. Though the world would never consider it the work of a genius, the painting featured the young man's face in striking detail. Overcome with emotion, the man thanked the soldier and promised to hang the picture above the fireplace.

True to his word, the painting was placed above the fireplace, pushing aside priceless paintings. The man sat in his chair and spent Christmas gazing at his special gift.

During the weeks that followed, the man came to realize that his son would live on in his memory through this painting. Soon it became his prized possession, eclipsing his interest in the pieces for which museums around the world clamored.

The following spring, the old man became very ill and passed away. According to the old man's will, all his paintings were to be sold at auction, including the one of his son.

The day soon arrived and art collectors from around the world gathered to bid on some of the world's most spectacular paintings. The auction began with the painting of the man's son. The auctioneer asked for an opening bid. His call was met with deafening silence. "Who will open the bidding with $100?" he asked. Time stood still. No one spoke. From the back of the room one art critic voiced, "Who cares about that painting? It's just a picture of his son. Get on with it." More voices echoed in agreement. But the auctioneer replied, "No, we have to sell this one first. Who will bid?"

Finally, a friend of the old man spoke. "Will you take ten dollars for the painting? That's all I have. I loved the father and his son, and I'd like to have it."

The auctioneer bellowed, "I have ten dollars. Will anyone go higher?" After more silence, he said, "Going once. Going twice. Gone." The gavel fell.

Cheers filled the room and someone exclaimed, "Now we can get on to the real treasures."

But the auctioneer announced that the auction was over. Stunned disbelief quieted the room. Someone asked, "What do you mean it's over? What about all those masterpieces? They're worth millions."

The auctioneer replied, "According to the man's will, whoever takes the son . . . gets it all."

That's the message of the Bible. Whoever takes the Son . . . gets it all. Jesus is the "I AM" God. Only Jesus is sufficient to meet all your needs. Thomas à Kempis, in his classic book The Imitation of Christ, said of the sufficiency of Jesus Christ: "The Savior said, 'Follow thou me, I am the way and the truth and the life.' Without the way, there is no going; without the truth there is no knowing; without the life there is no living. I am the way which thou must follow: the truth which thou must believe; the life for which thou must hope."

Said another way: Jesus is the "I AM" God. Find your sufficiency in Him. Rethink His "I am" statements in light of Him being the greatest treasure in your life. Get to know the "I AM" God intimately. Treasure Him. Enjoy Him. Jesus is all you need, because whoever gets the Son, gets it all!

NOTES

INTRODUCTION
[1]J. B. Phillips, *Ring of Truth* (London: Hodder & Stoughton, 1967), pp. 47-48.

CHAPTER 1: THE "I AM" GOD
[1]Richard Lee and Ed Hindson, *No Greater Savior* (Eugene, Oreg.: Harvest House, 1995), p. 74.

[2]C. S. Lewis, *Mere Christianity* (New York: Macmillan, 1943), p. 56.

CHAPTER 2: I AM THE LIGHT OF THE WORLD
[1]Anthony Hoekema, *Four Major Cults*, (Grand Rapids, Mich.: Eerdmans, 1963).

[2]J. Gordon Melton, *Encyclopedic Handbook of Cults in America* (New York: Garland Publishers, 1992).

[3]J. Gordon Melton, *Encyclopedia of American Religions*, 2nd ed (Detroit: Gale, 1987).

[4]William Barclay, *The Gospel of John*, Vol. 2 (Philadelphia: Westminster Press, 1975), p. 13.

[5]Amy Nevitt, *Fetal Alcohol Syndrome* (New York: The Rosen Publishing Group, 1996), p. 13.

CHAPTER 3: I AM THE BREAD OF LIFE
[1]Alexander Maclaren, "St. John," *Expositions of the Holy Scripture* (Chicago: W. P. Blessing Company, n.d.), p. 298.

CHAPTER 4: I AM THE GOOD SHEPHERD
[1]"Jeremiah," *Nelson's Illustrated Bible Dictionary*, ed. Herbert Lockyer, Sr. (Nashville: Thomas Nelson, 1986), p. 544.

[2]Doug Erlandson, "What's in It for Me?" *Moody* (March/April 1997), pp. 8-13.

[3]Alexander Maclaren, "St. John," *Expositions of the Holy Scripture* (Chicago: W. P. Blessing Company, n.d.), p. 38.

CHAPTER 5: I AM THE DOOR
[1]Wlliam Barclay, *The Gospel of John*, Vol. 2, rev. ed. (Philadelphia, Pa.: The Westminster Press, 1975), p. 58.

CHAPTER 6: I AM THE SON OF GOD
[1]William Hendricksen, *Exposition of the Gospel According to John*, Vol. 2 (Grand Rapids, Mich.: Baker), p. 126.

[2]Edwin A. Blum, "John" in *The Bible Knowledge Commentary*, Vol. 2, eds. John F. Walvoord and Roy B. Zuck (Wheaton, Ill.: Victor Books, 1983), p. 311.

CHAPTER 7: I AM THE TRUE VINE
[1]Leon Morris, *The Gospel According to John* (Grand Rapids, Mich.: Eerdmans, 1971), p. 668.

[2]Howard Ferrin, *Unto All* (Grand Rapids, Mich.: Zondervan, 1939), p. 87.

[3]J. C. Ryle, *Expository Thoughts on the Gospels*, Vol. 2 (New York: Fleming H. Revell, 1873), p. 94.

CHAPTER 8: I AM THE RESURRECTION AND THE LIFE
[1]C. H. Dodd, *The Interpretation of the Fourth Gospel* (Cambridge: University Press, 1963), p. 365.

[2]William Barclay, *The Gospel of John*, Vol. 2 (Philadelphia: The Westminster Press, 1975), p. 95.

CHAPTER 9: I AM THE KING
[1]Merrill C. Tenney, "John" in *Zondervan NIV Bible Commentary*, eds. Kenneth L. Barker & John Kohlenberger III (Grand Rapids, Mich.: Zondervan, 1994), pp. 364-365.

[2]Charles R. Erdman, *The Gospel of John* (Philadelphia: The Westminster Press, 1944), p. 161.

CHAPTER 10: I AM THE WAY
[1]Charles Simeon, *Expository Outlines on the Whole Bible,* Vol. 14 (Grand Rapids, Mich.: Zondervan, 1955), p. 26.

[2]J. C. Ryle, *Expository Thoughts on the Gospels: St. John*, Vol. 3 (New York: Fleming H. Revell, 1873), p. 59.

CHAPTER 11: I AM THE TRUTH

[1]R. H. Strachan, *The Fourth Gospel: Its Significance and Environment* (London: Student Christian Movement Press, 1941), p. 141.

[2]Clark H. Pinnock, "Truth," *Baker's Dictionary of Christian Ethics,* ed. Carl F. H. Henry (Grand Rapids: Baker, 1973), p. 679.

[3]*Nelson's Illustrated Bible Dictionary,* ed. Herbert Lockyer Sr. (Nashville: Thomas Nelson, 1986), p. 1,077.

[4]Floyd H. Barackman, *Practical Christian Theology* (Old Tappan, N.J.: Fleming H. Revell, 1984), p. 118.

[5]B. F. Westcott, *The Gospel According to St. John* (Grand Rapids, Mich.: Eerdmans, 1964), p. xiv.

CHAPTER 12: I AM THE LIFE

[1]Alexander Maclaren, *Expositions of Holy Scripture: St. John* (Chicago: W. P. Blessing Company, n.d) p. 287.

[2]E. Bevan, *Stoics and Skeptics,* quoted in R. H. Strachan, *The Fourth Gospel: Its Significance and Environment* (London: Student Christian Movement Press, 1941), p. 281.

[3]Merrill C. Tenney in *Zondervan NIV Bible Commentary,* Vol. 2, eds. Kenneth L. Barker and John Kohlenberger III (Grand Rapids, Mich.: Zondervan, 1994), p. 345.

CHAPTER 13: I AM WHATEVER YOU NEED

[1]H. Norman Wright and Rex Johnson, *Characteristics of a Caring Home* (Santa Anna, Calif.: Vision House, 1978), p. 10.

[2]Frederick J. Huegel, *Forever Triumphant* (Grand Rapids, Mich.: Zondervan, 1955), p. 52.

CONCLUSION

[1]Thomas à Kempis, *Imitation of Christ* (New York: Grosset & Dunlap, 1972), p. 230.